TRAINING IN BUSINESS AND INDUSTRY

TRAINING IN BUSINESS AND INDUSTRY

WILLIAM MCGEHEE, Ph.D.
Director, Personnel Research and Training
Fieldcrest Mills, Inc.

PAUL W. THAYER, Ph.D.
Vice President, Research
Life Insurance Agency
Management Association

John Wiley & Sons, Inc., New York · London · Sydney

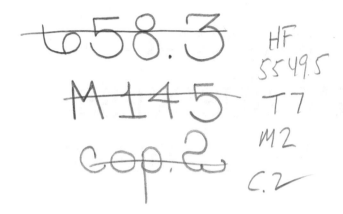

Library of Congress Catalog Card Number: 61-15403
Printed in the United States of America
FIRST CORRECTED PRINTING, SEPTEMBER, 1967

TO HORTENSE AND BJORG

PREFACE

Managers of industrial and business organizations have in common the responsibility for directing and coordinating the activities of others. This, of course, is not their sole responsibility, but it is one that requires considerable time, skill, and patience. Part of this activity is the instruction of others in how to accomplish specific objectives or to perform certain tasks. This instruction ranges from relatively informal episodes to highly formal, carefully planned programs. In many industries and businesses, responsibility for planning, coordinating, and, frequently, for instructing, has become a staff function centered in a training department.

We hope that this book will have as its audience not only those persons who have staff responsibilities for training, but also those who manage training as part of their day-to-day line responsibilities. Those who manage such training have as much concern with industrial training as training directors because of the contribution of efficient training to the goals of an enterprise. So although we believe that this book will prove to be of assistance directly to training directors, we hope that it also will help them indirectly by stimulating managers to think about and help to solve the current day-to-day problems of training in business and industry.

This book is not an attempt to present panaceas for problems in industrial training. In fact, there will be a minimum of "how to do it" information here. We will present a point of view concerning industrial training. One of our points is that there has been entirely too much written and spoken about how to carry on training and too little about the basic problems underlying training and basic approaches to their solution. We hope to present many of these problems and suggest approaches for solving them, but suggest few, if any, solutions. The present state of knowledge concerning training in industry justifies only the presentation of problems and suggested techniques for solutions.

In order to stimulate problem-solving in industrial training, we feel that we should make explicit certain of our assumptions concerning training. We assume, for example, that training, properly done, can contribute substantially to the achievement of the overall goals of an industrial organization. This may come through increased production and lower unit costs, higher quality, reduction of waste, or through indirect channels, such as improved morale and provision for adequate continuity of succession in management. On the other hand, we must admit that this assumption is as yet only partially tested. Too little systematic research has been done in industrial training to test fully this assumption. Neither can we develop a set of principles for training that are not open to easy assault. The few things that are known about industrial training we hope to present, and at the same time point to those "facts" and "principles" which rest on questionable grounds. We are, indeed, trying to present our particular viewpoint of training. Our point of view can be summarized by two basic statements:

1. Training is a management tool, not an entity or a field in itself.

2. Much must be done in implementing training before it can become a well-established, valuable management tool.

Training has been taken on faith (as has much of general education), and little or no demands have been made to evaluate it in a rigorous fashion. Until training is submitted to systematic and carefully controlled research and evaluation, management will continue to use (or discard) a tool of unknown worth or, worse yet, jump from bandwagon to bandwagon as training fads skip from the case method, to role playing, to brainstorming, and back again. These techniques *may* have merit. We do not know, and the research which will tell us remains to be done. The evidence submitted thus far raises more questions than it answers.

We are not presenting an exhaustive review of the literature in the field of industrial training. We have ignored particularly the "cookbook" literature. With only one major exception, we have drawn our materials primarily from studies of industrial and military training problems. In discussing learning as a basic training process, however, we have dipped into the numerous laboratory studies conducted in this area. In writing, we may have confused our ideas with the points of view and statements of others; we have tried, however, to acknowledge by footnotes and bibliographical references our indebtedness to others.

Basically, this book expresses our viewpoint, which emphasizes the role of training as a tool of management along with selection techniques, engineering, cost accounting, time study, and the numerous other techniques which management has found necessary to use in order to achieve organizational goals. We have insisted that full utilization of training requires thorough-going research and evaluation, if sound principles for its use are to evolve. If we can stimulate one more member of management to demand rigorous research in industrial training, we will have accomplished at least one purpose of this book.

WILLIAM MCGEHEE
PAUL W. THAYER

June, 1961

ACKNOWLEDGMENT

It is extremely difficult for anyone to indicate fully his indebtedness to others when he writes a book. A chance conversation with a stranger, a remark by someone unidentified during a conference, or simply the cumulative experience of association with many individuals in his field may shape and mold what he has to say in a significant way. We first, therefore, acknowledge our indebtedness to the numerous unknown people who unknowingly helped fashion this book. Of those known to us, we particularly thank Dr. S. Rains Wallace who read the entire manuscript and made many valuable suggestions. We have incorporated the majority of them. Perhaps it would have been a better book if we had incorporated all of his suggestions but then the book would probably have never been written. Mr. Raleigh Biggerstaff corrected many of the grammatical faults in the manuscript. We appreciate this and absolve him from any responsibility for inherent faults in style which are entirely the work of the authors. Our appreciation of authors and publishers who have given us permission to quote from their publications is expressed here and is acknowledged in the citations throughout the book.

W. McG.
P. W. T.

CONTENTS

1 TRAINING IN BUSINESS AND INDUSTRY TODAY

THE ROLE OF TRAINING

In the United States there are more than 65 million people in the work force. These people operate machines, package goods, write letters, tell other people what to do, buy and sell raw materials, and perform innumerable other acts involved in producing goods and providing services for a population of 180 millions. Not one of these individuals was born possessing the skills, knowledge, and attitudes required to perform the acts which produce these goods and services.

Annually, a million and a half newcomers join the ranks of this work force. These newcomers have been to public schools; many of them have completed courses at colleges and universities; others have received varying amounts of technical and professional training. From this group the individual who can perform effectively even the simplest task in business or industry without further training is the exception rather than the rule.

Complete and adequate statistics on the number of individuals who change from one job to another in American industry and business in any year are not available. Certainly, the number runs into the millions. The individual who changes jobs, as a rule, must learn something if he is to perform his job efficiently even if it is just how to get along with his new boss.

No data are available as to the number of employees who must each year acquire new ways of performing their tasks because of changes in job content. With the constant introduction of labor-saving devices, trends toward automation, changes in practices in financing, buying, selling, and administrative procedures, job content can be assumed to show considerable variation from year to year. Each change in job content requires the worker to modify in some way what he does, if he is to perform his job in a satisfactory way.

The skills, the knowledge, and the attitudes required to perform the acts of working must be learned by each individual in the work force; certainly, many employees have acquired these through experience in industry. Yet others have learned outside the factory, or office, ways of responding to job demands on which improved skills and additional knowledge can be built. It is fairly well accepted, however, that the skill required to run a bulldozer, or the knowledge necessary to buy raw materials for processing into sheets, blankets, or bedspreads, must be acquired in some way.

We have used repeatedly the term "learning" in the preceding paragraphs. Much will be said about this concept in subsequent chapters. It is sufficient to indicate here that we are referring to the process or processes which take place when an individual acquires a skill, knowledge, or an attitude. Industrial training, therefore, refers to the efforts made to facilitate the processes we call learning and which result in on-the-job behavior required of a member or members of an industrial organization.

Training Defined

Training, at one time, had the restricted meaning of "education in a narrow sense" or "to drill." In modern industry, the term has become much broader than merely indicating efforts to develop sensory-motor proficiency. It now encompasses activities ranging from the acquisition of a simple motor skill up to the development of a complex technical knowledge, inculcation of elaborate administrative skills, and the development of attitudes toward intricate and controversial social issues. In spite of the fact that in some quarters the term "training" still has the emotional connotation of the earlier, narrow meaning, we have been able to find no adequate substitute. It will be used, therefore, in the broader sense.

As previously indicated, those activities which are designed to develop or modify the behavior of employees are a part of training. We do not imply, however, that what employees do on their jobs is a result solely of company sponsored training programs. Actually, the behavior of an employee can be, and frequently is, modified by experiences which are not in any sense the results of a training program. He reacts to his superiors, his peers, his subordinates, his psychological environment of tools, equipment, materials, and machinery whether or not a formal effort is made to channel these reactions along specific paths. An employee learns much without and, sometimes, in spite of, a formal training program. In fact, learning of this sort may result in behavioral changes which negate efforts at training. We propose to limit discussion of training to those formal programs and procedures which an organization uses to bring about the development or modification of appropriate job-related skills, knowledge, and attitudes.

Training in industry has a specific purpose. It should provide experiences which develop or modify the behavior of employees in such a way that what the employee does at work is effective in the attainment of the goals and objectives of the organization. Although square dancing and other plant-directed recreational activities may some day be shown to have an effect on the productive ability of employees, we prefer to exclude such activities from our definition of training until a more concrete link between them and on-the-job behavior can be demonstrated.

Training in industry, therefore, is the formal procedures which a company uses to facilitate employees' learning so that their resultant behavior contributes to the attainment of the company's goals and objectives.

TRAINING—A MANAGEMENT TOOL

Proper utilization of training in modern industry and business requires that it be put in its proper context. It is not an end in itself, but a means to an end. The function of an industrial organization is to produce goods and services which have social utility, not to train members of society. Furthermore, the goods or services produced must be competitively priced, yet at a level that allows the enterprise to derive a profit so that it can continue its existence.

The complexity of modern business and industry has given rise to utilization of many tools which are not directly related to the production of goods and services at a profit. Among these are cost accounting procedures, engineering services, research activities, and numerous others. Although each of these tools is utilized as means to the achievement of the goals of the enterprise, none of them produces directly any product or service for the ultimate consumer.

One such set of tools widely used by management is comprised of a group of activities concerned with the effective utilization of the human resources of an enterprise. These personnel procedures constitute an effort to fulfill in a systematic fashion the functions which formerly were served by a face-to-face interaction between employer-owner and employee. They include such activities as the selection and training of employees, establishing and maintaining rates of pay, and building employee loyalty and *esprit de corps*. The growth of these personnel procedures as a special function in modern business and industry is indicated by studies conducted by the National Industrial Conference Board (Seybold, 1954) and by the annual studies of Yoder (1957).

We must point out here that personnel procedures differ in one important respect from such management tools as cost accounting, engineering services, and research. The individuals in an industrial enterprise who directly supervise production do not have to be cost accountants or perform engineering services. These activities can be left to specialists. This is not true of personnel procedures. The manager, whether he is a first line foreman or the chairman of the board, must perform personnel functions even though a group of personnel specialists are available to assist him. The responsibility for personnel is an integral part of a line assignment and cannot be delegated. The implications of this for line personnel and training specialists will be brought out subsequently.

The Interaction of Personnel Procedures

The effectiveness of training in an organization is related closely to a number of factors, and particularly to the effectiveness of other personnel procedures. This is especially true of its relationship to the effectiveness of the employee selection and placement procedures utilized by the organization. Individual differences in aptitudes and temperament and their relationship to learning specific skills and acquiring specific knowledge will be discussed in a later chapter. Figure 1.1, however, illustrates the differences in speed of learning of power sewing machine operators all trained by the same method. A careful selection of

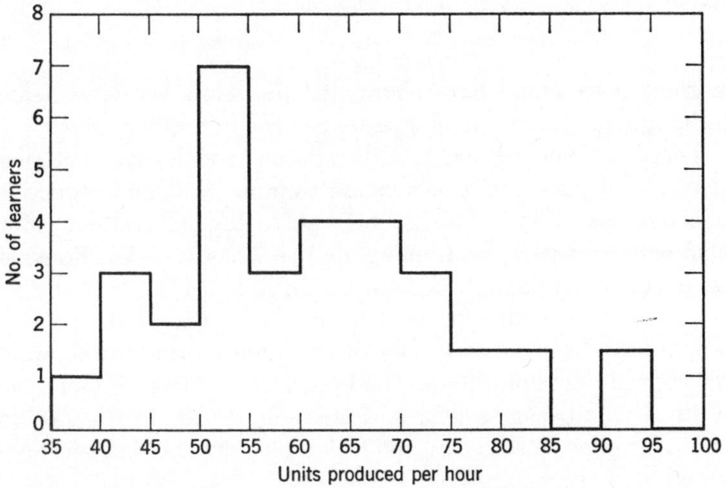

FIGURE 1.1 Individual differences in learning on power sewing machines. Median production during 13 weeks of training for 30 learners. Range 38–92 (unpublished data).

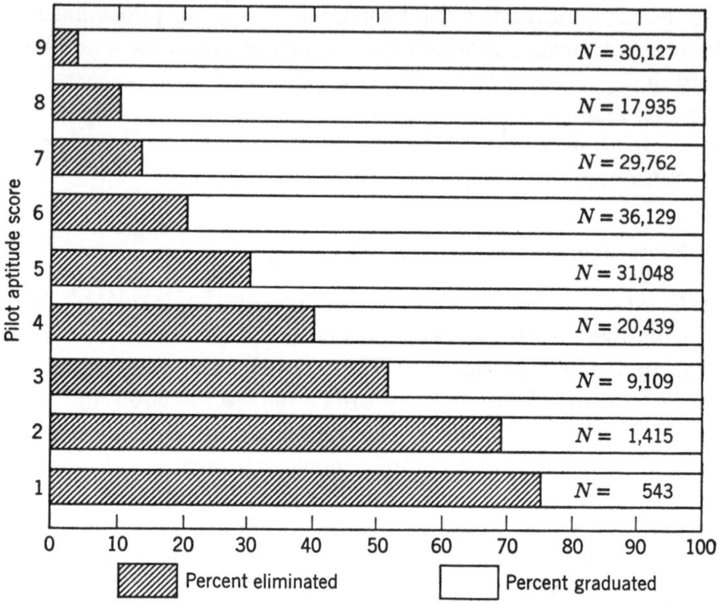

FIGURE 1.2 Elimination of cadets from elementary flight training in relation to pilot aptitude score (after Philip DuBois).

learners here would have eliminated the "slow learners" before training and brought much greater returns to training efforts.

There is some evidence, although not conclusive, that poor selection of personnel can increase training costs and reduce its effectiveness. Figure 1.2 shows the percentage of aviation cadets eliminated from flight training in the American Air Force at each level of a pilot aptitude score (DuBois, 1947). It is obvious from the data in this figure that not only money but also time would have been saved if only those cadets scoring in the upper half of the pilot aptitude test had received training. The impact of these data becomes even greater when one recalls that the demand for pilots, instructors, and training equipment was great and all were in short supply.

A further example from industry also points to the relationship between selection of trainees and the outcome of training efforts (Figure 1.3). Cook (1947) estimates the cost to the company employing and training the girls who did not pass the dexterity test as approximately $10,000. From the standpoint of training, it is apparent that inadequate selection of these trainees reduced the effectiveness of the training procedures and their possible contribution to company goals. It is entirely possible that the failure of well-planned training programs in industry may be attributed, at least in part, to poor selection and placement of personnel.

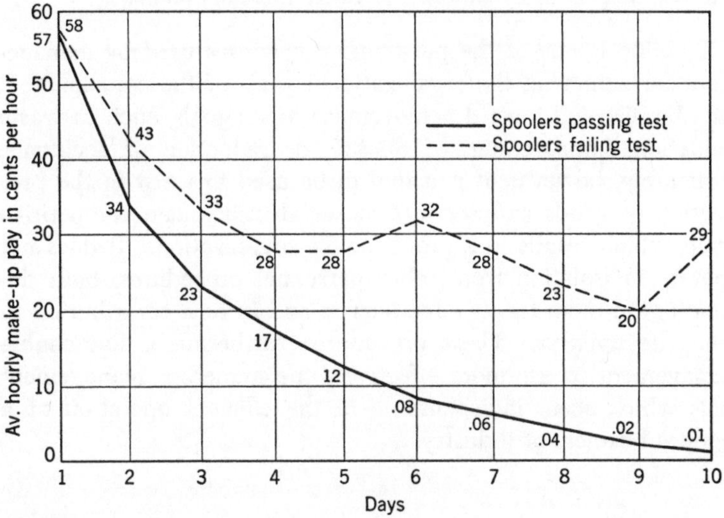

FIGURE 1.3 Difference in average hourly make-up pay in cents per hour between spoolers passing and spoolers failing finger dexterity test (after D. Cook).

The effectiveness of any training program is related to other personnel procedures and conditions existing in the organization. In the insurance industry, for example, training of new agents is frequently done in the many agencies. The quality and amount of training varies widely from agency to agency. This suggests that agents with the same potential for success do not receive equivalent training. It is quite possible, therefore, that the tests and other techniques used for selection are less capable of predicting success, because potentially able men do not receive the requisite training. Standardization of training programs might make it possible to improve the effectiveness of selection procedures. On the other hand, conditions in the organization can have marked effects on a training program. Social pressures from experienced employees can affect the rate of performance of new employees. The general managerial climate of a company can materially affect the outcomes of a supervisory training program (Fleishman, 1951).

The Achievement of Organizational Goals Through Training

Training is one of the personnel procedures used by management for achieving the organizational goals of the company. It may be directed toward achievement of subgoals, such as waste reduction, improvement of quality, or reduction of accidents. Ultimately, however, it is a tool to be used to assist in the production of goods and services of social utility at a competitive price, which results in a profit for the organization. It does not operate in isolation from other personnel procedures, both depending on them for its effectiveness and in turn contributing to their effectiveness. These procedures, furthermore, may enable management to use more effectively the numerous management tools which seem indispensable in the efficient operation of a modern business or industry.

THE STAKE OF BUSINESS AND INDUSTRY IN TRAINING

As we have seen, training is a tool of management, but to what extent, where, and how can management utilize training in achieving organizational goals?

As indicated earlier, each new employee must learn something, if only the location of the washroom. The problem of getting each new employee to the point where his efforts contribute to the company goal of profitable operations is an imperative one. As long as John Doe is receiving $1.85 per hour for productive activity and is producing less than this for his organization, he is a liability. He does not start becoming an asset until he regularly produces goods and services which can be sold for considerably more than he is paid. There are many costs of maintaining John other than his salary: costs of fringe benefits, differences in overhead costs between keeping John as opposed to a more productive employee, the impact of John Doe on the productivity of other employees, the waste produced by John in the course of his work, as well as many others.

The cost of John Doe's failure to meet the requirement of producing goods or services which can be sold in excess of the amount of money paid him frequently is masked. This is especially true if only one or two substandard producers are in a given department or section of a business. However, the cost of substandard production can become quite dramatic when a large number of novices are brought into an operation at the same time. One organization had to expand its work force approximately one-third in a very short period of time. During this period, the differential between actual earnings and minimum wage increased 165%, and defective goods increased 110% over the period prior to expansion of the work force. The excess cost of producing the commodity was attributable almost entirely to the lack of skill and knowledge of the new employees who were being trained.

Training Cost and Profitability

It is quite clear, therefore, that substandard production can result in expensive costs. Training is designed, at a minimum, to raise productivity to the point where all costs of the end product are low enough to permit a profit. One cost is that of training. One objective of any training program is to increase productivity to the point where the end product costs less with training than it does without. Simply put, one should not focus on the fact that a given training program costs $10,000 in personnel, equipment, and overhead. One must determine whether the benefits exceed $10,000. Whether or not a given training program is profitable cannot be determined in terms of the cost of the end product unless a comparison can be made of end-product costs with and without training.

Estimates are usually made as to the actual dollar costs of training employees for various jobs without regard to profitability. These estimates are of the costs of training using methods and procedures current in American business and industry regardless of the efficiency of these training methods. Actually, no estimates exist as to the actual profitability where inefficient rather than efficient training methods and procedures were used. Certain isolated studies do suggest that improved training methods and procedures can increase considerably the profitability of training production employees (Lawshe, 1944; Lindahl, 1945; Greenly, 1941).

It must be emphasized that training is not concerned only with new employees. Each change of method in producing products and each new product introduced usually require some sort of training effort. Each time an employee is transferred or promoted to a new assignment, he must undergo at least a minimum of training. In a company employing approximately 6000 workers, 13.5% of the employees were transferred to jobs requiring some training, and 9.5% were promoted to jobs requiring, in some instances, extensive training. This was not an abnormal year for this company. Although the company may not be typical of industry at large, these figures do give some indication of the training required, resulting from transfer and promotion in a medium-sized company.

Business and industry may use training procedures for purposes other than developing job skills and knowledge in new employees or in present employees who are transferred or promoted to new assignments. Present methods of performing jobs frequently can be improved to increase organizational efficiency. Usually, some form of training is involved in these activities. Greenly (1941) reports that operators were trained in a new method of replacing knives on flying shears which reduced the operation by 11 minutes. This resulted in a savings of $20,880 per year. McGehee and Livingstone (1954) show that training operators in ways to reduce waste resulted in a reduction of 61.6% in a 29-week period. The results of this training had persisted for a period of two years at the time of the last report.

One approach toward improving organizational efficiency is automation. The exact effect of automation on the work force is not known. It is thought, however, that automation may result in any one of three effects on employees and the training of employees. First, for some employees there will be job enlargement and the necessity of acquiring additional skills and knowledge. Second, other employees may find the scope of their jobs reduced with a consequent narrowing of the skills and knowledge required. Finally, certain employees will find their jobs disappearing, requiring that they learn new skills and acquire knowledge in a different occupation if they are to remain gainfully employed (Bright, 1958). In addition, automation will bring with it the major problem of attitude toward the changes in work, work organization, and social interactions of employees affected by it. One aspect of automation is obvious to any thoughtful observer. The effectiveness of a change from a conventional plant to an automated one will depend on how well individual employees develop the skills, knowledge, and attitudes basic to working efficiently in an automated plant. To develop these desired skills, knowledge, and attitudes will require careful planning of training and its execution by those who direct the operations in an automated plant. It may revise, also, our thinking about methods and techniques of training.

The importance of the correct planning and execution of training for automation is documented by an investigation of Mann and Hoffman (1960). They studied work, work organization, supervision, and employee attitudes both in an automated and in a conventional power plant. The employees in the automated plant were generally dissatisfied with the training they had received for work in the automated plant. Although there existed no criteria of the effectiveness of the training, Mann and Hoffman thought that the planning and execution of training were not adequate. Their summary of this situation should be required reading both for executives and for training directors who are confronted with a change to automation in their organization. They conclude, in part:

> In situations like the present one, where a company transfers employees from jobs in older parts of the company to jobs in the automated section, training the men for their new jobs is a major problem. The successful functioning of a new automated system will depend in a large part on the adequacy of the training given to the men, and this training must take into account the fact that the workers need to acquire new skills and knowledge as well as adapt to new types of jobs (Mann and Hoffman, 1960, p. 205).
>
> . . . A man who is placed in an entirely new situation without sufficient preparation may find it too demanding an experience, and the anxiety and insecurity resulting from such an experience may

render him incapable of, or at least hinder him in, performing his functions effectively. The "sink or swim" method or even "book learning" alone provides obviously inefficient and inadequate preparation for the people responsible for the operation of new and expensive automated equipment (Mann and Hoffman, 1960, p. 207).

The research of Mann and Hoffman, as well as other evidence, indicates clearly that the effectiveness of automation in achieving organizational goals will depend, in a significant way, on the nature and efficiency of the training employees receive for assignments in automated production units.

Training, therefore, must be used in bringing new employees to a level of skill and knowledge so that performance of their assignments is profitable for their company. Employees already on the payroll may require training to improve their present job skills or to perform their tasks in a more effective way. A progressive organization also must make provisions for developing individuals who can assume responsibilities greater than they now have. This includes upgrading in mechanical or manual skills, preparation for the assumption of technical positions, and developing individuals who can move into supervisory and managerial assignments.

We can only speculate as to the effect of improved training of supervisory, technical, sales, and managerial personnel upon the achievement of organizational goals. Even *inadequate* research data on this subject are so rare that we can draw inferences only from our knowledge of how a business operates. The investment in a new employee at this level ranges between $2000 and $15,000 until he is trained. A 5% turnover in a staff of 300 employees at this level would cost a company between $75,000 and $225,000. At the lower figure, a company would have to sell $1,500,000 worth of products to recover this investment, provided it could realize 5% on the sales dollar after taxes. This clearly indicates how expensive is the training of managerial personnel.

Supervisors have a direct responsibility for training employees. Frequently, a supervisor who is inadequately trained in developing employees contributes materially to excess manufacturing costs through losses in productive efficiency of individual employees, excessive waste of materials, and production of defective goods. Another supervisor, improperly trained in personnel relations, might create personnel problems in his work group which lead to excessive costs from turnover, absenteeism, grievance handling, and low morale.

Management at the middle and upper level of a company can, by a wrong decision, cost a company more in a few minutes than any loss growing out of ineffective training of personnel at lower levels. Training, of course, is no panacea for poor decision making. But it is entirely possible that a considerable number of faulty decisions come from executives who are trained inadequately for the performance of their duties. When it is realized that many executives learn their jobs in the same hit-or-miss fashion as lower level employees, it can be assumed that inefficiencies at the executive level can be attributed, at least in part, to faulty training. In a free enterprise system the company which survives must produce its goods or services at a cost which will result in a profit to its owners.

The Contributions of Efficient Training

Efficient training procedures should contribute to the achievement of this organizational goal in the following ways:

1. Reduction of overhead and labor costs by reducing the amount of time required to perform the operations involved in producing goods or services and by reducing the time required to bring the inexperienced employee to an acceptable level of job proficiency.
2. Reducing the costs of materials and supplies by reducing losses due to excess waste and to the production of defective products.
3. Reducing the costs of managing personnel activities as reflected in turnover, absenteeism, accidents, grievances, and complaints.
4. Reducing the costs of efficiently servicing customers by improving the flow of goods or services from the industry to the consumer.
5. Reducing the general overall costs of administration for conducting a business by creating a psychological climate which orients the activities of each employee toward achieving the major goals of the organization.

Certain of these contributions of training can be documented by reports of the results of improved training procedures, that is, decreased time required to learn a task, reduced waste of materials, decrease in accidents, absenteeism, and labor turnover (Tiffin, 1952). Although rigorous experimental controls were not used in the investigations producing these data, there is enough evidence to indicate that organized training is superior to letting the operator learn the best way he can.

The Impact of Employee Attitudes

We have hinted but have not touched directly upon the problem of attitude development in an industrial or business organization. Certainly, the attitudes an employee has toward his company are acquired through many experiences other than those provided by a training program. Nevertheless, these attitudes can and often do negate the effective use of skills and knowledge laboriously inculcated by company-sponsored training. Some industrial and business organizations have seen this and try through orientation programs to develop attitudes in new employees which are favorable toward the achievement of organizational goals. Other companies have tried to mold the attitudes and opinions of all employees concerning broader issues, such as the free enterprise system, through training in economics and similar subjects. We suspect, however, that modification of employee attitudes toward problems which are directly related to achieving organizational goals must be an integral part of knowledge and skill training rather than something apart. We suspect, also, that unless formal training designed for this purpose is consonant with the overall organizational climate it is doomed to failure. In spite of the problems inherent in this area of developing or modifying attitudes through training, this is perhaps one of the most important uses which can be made of the tool of management we have called training.

THE EMPLOYEE'S STAKE IN TRAINING

Training is a management tool. What then is the stake of the individual employee in the training activities of his company? Training programs can be of relatively little value if careful consideration is not given to the individual or individuals for whom these programs are designed. We also are well aware that the individual employee must receive some personal benefit from his training experiences if he is to participate in them in an effective manner. Furthermore, many personnel activities including training, which ignore the basic worth of the employee and are thinly disguised attempts at manipulation, are doomed to eventual failure. So although training is a management tool, we must insist that training will be effective only insofar as it is geared to both immediate and long-range needs of individual employees. Let us now examine the individual employee's stake in training.

The Interrelatedness of Employee and Company Objectives

From a long-range standpoint, an employee's stake in training is the same as the stake of the management or the owners of the company. If, over a period of time, an organization fails consistently to achieve its goals and objectives, the organization ultimately disappears. Insofar as training assists a company in producing goods and services of social value with adequate return to the stockholders, training assists the individual employee by providing a continuous opportunity for employment. Although not subscribing, in the narrow sense, to the statement that "what is good for General Motors is good for the country," we do believe that continuous successful operation of a company is "good" for its employees. To such extent that training contributes to successful company operation, it contributes also to the welfare of the employees of the company.

Immediate Benefits to the Trainee

There are, however, certain immediate and obvious advantages for workers in a company with an effective training program. The first of these is that the employee is given an adequate opportunity to learn the duties and responsibilities of his job. He is not left to learn what he is expected to do in a haphazard, time-consuming manner. If he has the required capacity and temperament, he will not experience the frustrating failure which might come when he is not trained properly to carry out his duties. The number of discharges or resignations arising from inadequate training is not known. We suspect that the number is considerably greater than zero. Adequate training gives the employee a fair chance to experience success and avoid the frustrating experience of failure in performing the duties for which he is being paid.

It may be that a well-planned, well-executed training program will impress employees with the feeling that a company has a real interest in his welfare. He senses that an effort has been made to help him quickly adjust to the demands of the work environment and the expectations of superiors, co-workers, and subordinates. Such a program probably helps to reduce the feeling of strangeness and aloneness usually generated by being in an alien or novel situation.

The production worker in American industry is frequently paid on some system of piece work. Even when day rate is the method of pay, there exist different levels of pay for different degrees of skill. An employee who is trained properly can reach a higher level of piece rate or day rate pay more quickly than can the poorly trained employee. There is also some suggestive evidence that fatigue is reduced when the individual can perform a task in a skilled and habitual manner. Finally, there is some evidence that accidents occur with less frequency to employees who are well trained. If all these things are true the production worker clearly has a stake in company training from the point of pay, reduction of fatigue, and safety.

The white-collar worker derives the same benefits from training as the blue-collar employee. These benefits may not be quite as obvious and may differ somewhat in kind, but they are as real. Whether the employee is a secretary, a laboratory technician, a foreman, or a vice president his chances of finding economic, personal, and social values in his work are higher if he is well-trained for his job than if he were poorly trained or not trained at all.

In addition to satisfactory performance on the job, an employee may secure from an adequate training program opportunity to learn additional skills and acquire knowledge. The additional skills and knowledge can pave the way for promotion to jobs of greater responsibility. The employee, thus, not only improves his economic status but also secures improvement in social and personal areas.

Training cannot solve all problems of the employees' well-being. It is, however, one of the tools of management which, if properly used, furthers not only the attainment of goals in terms of goods and services produced, but also assists in terms of effective development of a climate in which employees can work with minimum frustrations and maximum satisfaction. An adequately trained employee, in our opinion, has a better opportunity to derive the maximum satisfaction out of his daily life both inside and outside the mill, factory, store, or office.

The stake of an employee in training is not just the general achievement of organizational effectiveness, but also a highly personal and intimate matter.

DETERRENTS TO EFFECTIVE TRAINING

Individuals concerned with achieving the major goals of an organization are concerned with training only as one of the many means they can use for obtaining the desired outcome of organizational activities. Training is one of the many tools competing for their attention. It also is a tool whose direct relationship to achievement of organizational goals is difficult to establish. The cost of inefficient training procedures is rarely separated from the multitude of other costs in producing goods or services. On the other hand, a faulty machine, a defective product, or a sour advertising campaign is immediately focused in the attention of company planners by the profit and loss statement. As a result, the upper levels of management rarely are aware of the dollars and cents implications of training outcomes. Since these costs are hidden, the upper level of management puts little or no pressure on other members of management and supervision to see that efficient training procedures are followed. In contrast, there is constant pressure to reduce labor costs and to improve material and supply usage. It is almost axiomatic that subordinates attempt to escape pressure from superiors. Since little or no pressure is placed on efficient training from above, subordinates make little effort to see that training is handled in such a way as to escape nonexistent pressure. Consequently, training is probably the least effectively used management tool in industry and business.

Even when management accepts training as a necessary evil, the responsibility is shifted to someone else, usually a staff department. The growth of training departments in American business and industry has been considerable in the past decade. Usually, the function of this department has not been clearly defined nor has its place in the industrial hierarchy been made clear to managers and supervisors. In part, this is the fault of persons who have assumed training responsibilities. But the fault has originated largely with managers who believe they have fulfilled their training obligations to their company by appointing a training director and forgetting him. As we shall try to show later, one of the responsibilities of any individual who supervises the work of another is that of instructing him or seeing that he is properly instructed. If the superior is not concerned with how well a subordinate learns his job duties, the subordinate, himself, will not be overly concerned. Too frequently in business and industry, the presence of a training department on the organizational chart is an indication of ducking the responsibility for efficient training procedures.

The reason for slighting training responsibilities by management and supervisors is not difficult to understand. Very few, if any, members of management are skilled teachers or have extensive information about or insight into how people learn. They usually are experts in some phases of business administration or industrial technology. Few, if any, have had substantial training in how to teach, how to organize a program for teaching, or how to evaluate the outcomes of teaching. They are in foreign territory when they have to deal with the specifics of learning and teaching. Furthermore, they are under constant pressure to do what they best know how to do—to make a decision concerning a financial matter or to investigate a technological malfunctioning in a department. They do what they can do best and comfortably, and avoid behavior which requires skill or knowledge which they possess to a minimum degree. The foreman who complained he was so busy answering employees' questions that he could not train them is by no means atypical of persons at many levels of management.

Learning is an everyday occurrence. It is as common as eating and sleeping. On the other hand, organic chemistry, nuclear physics, and matrix algebra are phenomena which are not in the common experience of mankind. Anyone who is expected to deal with problems in these areas usually is willing to undergo rigorous training in the subject matter of these fields. Since learning is such a common everyday phenomenon, few people believe they need any special instruction in how to order learning experiences for others. Few people outside of specialists in the field of learning know that there exists an organized body of knowledge concerning learning; few realize that instruction of others requires any special skills. Yet those who would not venture to attempt to solve a problem in nuclear physics for which they have no training, blithely will attempt to organize, direct, and carry out training of subordinates. Frequently, they rely on the folklore which has grown up around training such as "practice makes perfect" and "if the learner has not learned the teacher has not taught." Experimental evidence has shown that practice of a habit can eliminate the habit, and data on the effect of the learner's perception of his task raise serious questions about the JIT shibboleth concerning the teacher. Slogans are nice supports, if one is not particularly concerned with whether or not he falls. This is particularly true concerning many verbalized statements of folklore regarding training.

Efficient use of training by management has been blocked by: (1) training being regarded as an end rather than a means to an end, (2) failure of management to accept responsibility for training, (3) lack of knowledge and skill on the part of management in directing and executing training, and (4) lack of information concerning the nature of the learning process. Even when these causes of inefficient training are absent, the general climate of an organization may render training efforts ineffective. If fellow employees can see no reason for learning job duties in an efficient manner, real pressure can be brought on a trainee to slow his rate of mastering his assignment. If no provision is made for job advancement, there is little incentive to learn the jobs ahead.

FADS AND FASHIONS IN MODERN TRAINING

As indicated in an earlier section, business and industrial enterprises have been increasingly aware of the necessity of organizing their training activities to secure the benefits which are assumed to come from adequate training of employees. This has led many of them to centralize the training function in a department, usually as a part of the general personnel division. Once this is done, general management has expected minor miracles in improved employee performance from simply having a training department. Little or no attention has been paid to basic philosophy of training or to the relationship of training activities to organizational goals. Furthermore, often the person who receives the assignment as training director has had little or no real educational background or experience essential to performing the duties of his position. Consequently, both he and his superiors start looking for quick results and short cuts to effective training. This has given rise to a prevalent condition in industrial training of "one approach" solutions to all training problems. These approaches have concentrated invariably on techniques of training and have neglected important factors in the training situation such as the learner, course content, organizational climate, and goals.

Certain examples can be cited to highlight this situation. In supervisory training, the lecture techniques became outmoded and supplanted by the conference method of instruction. Training directors accordingly became more concerned with proper arrangements of the conference room than with what actually took place in the conference. Conferences were held on a wide gamut of subjects such as labor relations, how free enterprise works, and safety. The question was never raised as to the outcomes desired or whether or not the conferences were necessary to secure organizational goals. Similar situations exist in the use of the case method, the incident technique, and role playing. Training directors and line management often become so intrigued with techniques that they lose sight entirely of the purpose training should serve in their organization. Then, when the particular training fad fails to produce its miracle it is dropped and supplanted by a newer fad. Training directors, who know better, are pressured into using techniques because a vice president hears the vice president of another company singing their praises. Keeping up with the Joneses is not an exclusive foible of suburbia. Communication racks may become a necessity in a company just because General Motors has used this medium of employee training and has widely publicized it.

We do not mean to imply that conference techniques, role playing, the case method, and communication racks are necessarily ineffective procedures for training employees. The point we are trying to make is that the effectiveness of these techniques depends upon their actual utility in developing employees in such a way that the behavior of the employee contributes more effectively to the attainment of organizational goals. Their effectiveness depends, also, upon the climate of the organization in which they are used. Finally, techniques are only means to an end and not the end they appear to be when they are swept up in a current training fad.

Even where a company has established a systematic long range training program devoid of fads, these programs can be ineffective if based on the wrong premises. Many companies have instituted and carried on carefully designed training programs in the area of human relations for supervisors. These programs have grown out of the obvious need in the organization for more effective direction of employees' efforts by first and second line supervisors. The basic assumption underlying these courses is that by formal training in a classroom, skills, knowledge, and attitudes can be acquired which will improve the way in which the supervisor will supervise his subordinates. Rothlisberger (1951), among others, has questioned the assumption that the usual classroom training in human relations is the type of experience which actually modifies behavior in this area. More recently, Argyris (1956) has criticized cogently basic assumptions as to how a supervisor must behave to perform effectively in the area of human relations. If these and other critics of current procedures in human relations training are correct, human relations training, however carefully planned, will be less than effective since the planning is based on wrong premises.

This implies, not only in the field of human relations training, but also in many other kinds of training necessary in industry, that a careful examination be made of the basic premises on which a training program is predicated.

THE RESEARCH APPROACH TO TRAINING

Training, if it is to become an effective tool of management, must be a systematic, orderly procedure constructively applied to solutions of organizational problems and attainment of organizational goals. It must consist of more than casual instruction of learners and haphazard utilization of techniques. It further requires that basic premises underlying training activities must have foundation in fact.

Training, to be effective, must be backed up by careful and continuous research. The research may be a relatively simple collection of existing data, collating it in an orderly manner, and deriving meaningful conclusions. It may be highly complex and technical experimentation concerning the investigation of the learning process itself in multidimensional situations in the production of goods and services.

Training will not come of age until it abandons intuitive approaches to the solution of training problems. The training director of the future must have more than a bag of techniques and a facility with flannel board presentations. He must be able to investigate pertinent problems in his own organization which bear on the effective utilization of training. He must be able to understand and utilize information concerning learning stemming from research specialists. He must have a relatively high degree of sophistication in research and utilization of research techniques. Above all, he must be skilled in communicating the results of investigations in training to line management.

Specifically, an adequate training program depends upon securing *reliable* data as a basis for answering the following persistent questions:

Who is to be trained?
In what are they to be trained?
By whom are they to be trained?

How are they to be trained?
How are the results of training to be evaluated?

The implications of these questions for effective training have been briefly reviewed by McGehee (1949). In order to approach the securing of answers to these questions, we must effectively utilize research techniques and methods of investigation. We cannot rely on the opinions of experts, the enthusiasm of our trainees, the acceptance of top management, and logic alone to answer these questions. Empirical research—decades of research—is necessary. The remaining pages of this volume are directed toward suggested approaches to securing answers to these persistent problems in industrial training.

2 ORGANIZATION ANALYSIS

THE GENERAL PROBLEM OF TRAINING NEEDS

Training in industry is not an end but a means to an end; it exists only to help achieve organizational goals and objectives. To be effective, this management tool must be used when and where it is needed and not as window dressing to impress visiting firemen with the alleged "personnel mindedness" of an organization. We suspect that the effectiveness of a training program may be an inverse function of the elaborateness of the lithography, and the multiplicity of forms and manuals which are shown visitors.

The use of training to achieve organizational goals requires careful assessment of the training needs within a company: a determination of the goals which can be served by training, the people who require training and for what purposes, and the content of training. These are initial steps and those with which we are concerned in this section. Subsequent sections deal with how training should take place, who should carry on the training, and the ever present problems of measuring the outcomes of training.

The determination of training needs requires something more than armchair cerebration. It requires careful digging for facts, frequently with inadequate tools. It is a grimy business, frustrating, and often carried on under increasing pressure to get something, just anything, going.[1] Consequently, many training efforts are begun without any reason, continued with no purpose, and end with no results—at least in terms of the only legitimate reason for training in industry.

Organization, Operations and Man Analysis

There are probably as many rationales for approaching the problem of determining training needs as there are persons who are concerned with planning and directing training. The approach which we present is no easy side-step of the basic investigations which are necessary in determining training needs. We hold no particular brief for it except that it has and does assist in our ordering of the problems in this complex area. It is a three-fold but closely interrelated approach to thinking about the training requirements of an organization or a component of an organization. It consists of the following:

1. Organization analysis—determining where within the organization training emphasis can and should be placed.
2. Operations analysis—determining what should be the contents of training in terms of what an employee must do to perform a task, job, or assignment in an effective way.
3. Man analysis—determining what skills, knowledge, or attitudes an individual employee must develop if he is to perform the tasks which constitute his job in the organization.

In order to understand our use of these three terms, let us point to certain essential differences in them. Organization analysis places an emphasis on a study of the entire organization, its objectives, its resources, and the allocation of those resources as

[1] Evidence that industry had done little in a systematic way to determine training needs is found in Mahler and Monroe (1952). The authors state that about one company in ten surveyed reported the use of a systematic approach for determining training needs.

they relate to the organizational objectives. To a certain extent, we are focusing upon employees in an impersonal way. Although we are concerned with discovering individuals who are in need of training, we are not as yet concerned with the specific training needs they have. Operations analysis and man analysis are concerned with the specific training needs of individuals.

Operations analysis focuses on the task or job regardless of the employee performing that job. It includes a determination of what an employee must do, the specific behavior required, if the job is to be performed effectively. Again, the focus is on the task, not the man. Man analysis does focus on the man. It involves two things: (1) determining the knowledge, attitudes, and skills of the incumbent in a position, and (2) the knowledge, attitudes, and skills which *he* must develop if *he* is to fulfill the job requirements. Here, the focus is clearly on the individual in his present position and in possible future positions. The techniques to achieve these objectives are not yet fully developed. Considerable methodological research must be done before we can reach these goals with any precision.

The three phases of determining training needs are closely related and are not performed in isolation of each other.

Evidence of training needs, in terms of the entire organization, may arise because of the structure of jobs in an organization, or because of the people who perform the jobs. The job of determining training needs is a continuous matter. It must receive the attention of both professional training personnel and of those persons responsible for managing the organization. The staff work of securing and presenting the facts about training needs may be done by professionals, but understanding the implications of the facts and acting upon them is a managerial responsibility. Although we present the various phases of determining training needs as it might be performed by professionals, we must emphasize the necessity of managerial personnel participating actively in determining training needs and taking decisive action to meet the needs.

The remaining sections of this chapter are concerned with organization analysis whereas the next two chapters present descriptions of operations analysis and man analysis.

ORGANIZATION ANALYSIS

Organization analysis serves as a basis for determining where the training emphasis can and should be placed. We can assume that a certain amount of training will take place at all times in any organization, whether formally sanctioned or not. Yet this training effort may be so directed that it does little or nothing to contribute to the attainment of organizational objectives.

Several years ago, one of the authors observed in a large retail establishment an elaborate program for the education of the employees in the basic economic principles of free enterprise. While this program was in progress, this company was losing thousands of dollars and considerable customer goodwill because of errors in shipping and billing merchandise. So far as could be determined, no real effort had been made or was being made to teach employees proper procedures in the vital function of delivering and collecting for mechandise.

Careful and continuous organization analysis sometimes leads to prosaic training efforts. Though lacking glitter, these efforts can contribute substantially to organizational efficiency. On the other hand, training efforts in technicolor and cinemascope, unless oriented toward organizational needs, are a waste of the resources of the company.

THE INDUSTRIAL ENTERPRISE AS A SOCIAL ORGANIZATION—IMPLICATIONS FOR TRAINING

The preceding paragraphs have stressed the necessity for careful analysis of training needs if training is to contribute maximally to organizational efficiency. Before we can be specific about organization analysis, the nature of an industrial enterprise requires some delineation; otherwise our concept of the role of training and the determination of training needs in the achievement of organizational goals will not be clear.

An industrial enterprise is more than its buildings, physical equipment, material, and people; it is a social organization. A social organization is a special kind of social group "in which the members are differentiated as to responsibilities for the task of achieving a common goal" (Stodgill, 1950, p. 3). Among the characteristics of a social organization is the awareness by the members of their belonging to an identified group, the perception of the group as a group by nonmembers, and the dynamic interaction between members of the group (Smith, 1945). Furthermore, there exists the assignment of and the acceptance of certain responsibilities by the members of the group (Kretch and Crutchfield, 1948). Finally, in addition to personal aims, there appears to be an organizational objective or objectives (Simon, 1958).

As Simon (1958) has pointed out, "the organization objective is, indirectly, a personal objective of *all* the participants. It is the means whereby their organizational activity is bound together to achieve a satisfaction of their own diverse personal motives" (p. 17). At the risk of oversimplification, we could then say that The Chrysler Corporation has as its objective the manufacture and sale of automobiles. In turn, the achievement of this objective is necessary to the realization of the more personal aims of the owners, the managers, and the employees of The Chrysler Corporation. In this way, the objective of a company becomes the objective of its human components as a means of realizing their own personal objectives. As long as personal objectives are satisfied in at least a minimum way, the individuals in a business will accept, to some extent as their own, the general organizational objective.

Personal vs. Organizational Objectives

Certainly, conflict between personal and organizational objectives is one source of inadequate and inefficient functioning of an industrial or business enterprise (Argyris, 1957; Stagner, 1956). It represents one of the most serious problems of our modern industrial civilization. To the extent that this conflict is the result of inadequate skills, insufficient knowledge, and inappropriate attitudes, it falls into the province of training within the industrial framework. To the extent that the conflict is a function of our modern system of the production and distribution of goods and services, the role of training, particularly training *in situ,* is made less clear. It is our firm belief that training used as a means for the manipulation of employees will backfire on the manipulators. On the other hand, except through the influence of training on managers and the consequent modification of their attitudes toward the nature of an effective organizational framework and procedures for achieving organizational objectives, training within the factory or office can accomplish very little to eliminate the conditions which lead to conflict between the individual and the industrial system of which he is a part. This perhaps is a function of social change and is entirely too ambitious an assignment for the average training director or for the activities which we are discussing under the rubric of industrial training.

Training and the Enterprise as a Social Organization

From the standpoint of training, two points are apparent, if the concept of an industrial enterprise as a social organization is accepted. First, even though it is necessary to analyze the organization on a global basis in order to direct training efforts properly, we must ultimately focus on what the individuals in the organization actually are doing. One organization analysis may show that the productivity of department X is low in comparison to other similar departments in the company or in rival companies. If the analysis further reveals that low productivity is not a function of machinery, equipment, materials, or other physical factors, attention will have to be concentrated on the human components of the department—the employees. Their level of skill, degree of knowledge, and their attitudes as related to their responsibilities become the focus of analysis. Resulting training activities must then be directed not toward increasing the productivity of department X *but toward modifying the behavior of the employees* in department X so that their individual productivity changes. Training then becomes a personal matter and not a program. Only an individual can modify his behavior. Training functions only create situations which facilitate these behavior changes of the individual or individuals. Organization analysis is the initial step for diagnosis of individual behavior. It is essential, however, if this diagnosis is to be other than a hit-and-miss affair.

A second point in accepting the social organization concept of a business enterprise centers around organizational objectives and the responsibility for achieving these objectives. Drucker (1954) has presented a strong argument against the classical economic concept of the business enterprise with the sole objective of maximizing profits. In fact, he has stated eloquently the fallacy of trying to operate an industrial organization in terms of one "right" objective; rather "objectives are needed in every area where performance and results directly affect the survival and prosperity of the business" (p. 63). Those areas in which he believes objectives should be set are "market standing; innovation; productivity; physical and financial resources; profitability; manager performances and development; worker performance and attitudes; public responsibility" (p. 63). Drucker does not minimize either the difficulty of setting objectives in these various areas or measuring the degree of attainment once the objectives are set. Whether or not the objectives are achieved is a function of many factors both within and without the organization.

The implications of Drucker's thesis, however, are clear when we consider their bearing on organization analysis, both in terms of training needs and in terms of general overall direction of a company's activities. If an organization does not have definite objectives, it has little or no means for determining whether it is still alive, dead, or near the point of death. Because of the way economic events occur (especially in an expanding economy) funeral rites for a company frequently take place a considerable period of time after its demise. Furthermore, if a company does not have fairly accurate methods of measuring the degree to which objectives are reached, the objectives themselves are of little or no value in planning and directing the activities of the company. One of the most important functions of modern management is developing realistic objectives and determining the degree to which these objectives are achieved.

STATING ORGANIZATIONAL OBJECTIVES

Ideally, objectives should be established in broad areas for the entire company. Then, objectives for the various components of the company—a division, a department, a section, or a unit—should be established as a means of obtaining the broad company objectives. Some objectives can be established for the immediate future, others may be set up for achievement within periods ranging from five to fifty years. The process of obtaining these objectives should be examined in terms of the time limits placed upon achieving them. Again, in a growing and dynamic organization, objectives themselves are not static. Because of technological and marketing advances, a reasonable objective with a reasonable time limit may become obsolete before it is attained. Objectives, therefore, must be reviewed constantly and changed in terms of changing circumstances.

Now, let us tie this down more closely to the problems of organization analysis and the determination of training needs. Unless we know what we are trying to accomplish in a company, we have no sound criteria on which to base our organization analysis. We are simply collecting data for which we have no bench mark. Suppose, for example, we look at our sales organization. We find it is composed of X number of people located in Y areas and selling Z number of dollars per year of our products at N cost per unit of sales. We may know the percentage of the market our competitors are getting and have a general idea of his selling costs. We may know a good many other things about our own sales organization and that of our competitors. This information is of little value unless we are willing to state certain goals—in terms of volume, geographical coverage, sales force, unit costs of selling, etc.—and the time limit for achieving these objectives. With a clear statement of objectives, we can than examine the operations of the sales organization to determine the pluses and minuses in the organization as they are reflected by our stated objectives.

The first step in organization analysis for training purposes is a clear understanding of organizational goals. Whether or not these objectives are achieved is a function of many factors in addition to training. However, failure to obtain a given objective should be an immediate signal for a manager to ask, among other questions, whether or not training has any relationship to the failure.

Purposes of Organization Analysis

Thus, in analyzing an organization, managers should insist on an answer as to whether or not training is adequate in terms of "the survival and prosperity of the business":

1. To insure that the human resources of the enterprise are adequate for present and future operation of the business.
2. To insure that the most effective performance possible takes place in all functional areas of the company such as utilization of physical resources, productivity of personnel, quality of the product, customer relations, services, etc.
3. To insure that the climate of the organization is such that employees can perform their assignments in an efficient manner.

This kind of analysis should be made beginning with the unit level of a company, continuing through department and division levels until an adequate picture of the training situation of the entire organization is available for the study and action of general management. It must be emphasized that this is not a once-in-a-lifetime endeavor but is as continuous as taking inventory of the physical assets of a corporation. The use of training as a management tool requires continuous scrutiny of training needs.

ANALYSIS OF HUMAN RESOURCES

The second step in organization analysis is the determination of the adequacy of the human resources of a company. It requires concise analysis of accurate data to determine whether or not training is required and what kind of training is needed.

A few large corporations (Dale, 1952), such as General Electric, R.C.A., Westinghouse, and Standard Oil of California, have recognized the necessity for experts in the analysis of human resources and have established departments of manpower planning. Other companies have gone only part way in systematically reviewing their manpower needs, usually concentrating in the area of managerial manpower only.

Most companies ignore the problem of determining the adequacy of their human resources, although the same companies undoubtedly conduct routine physical inventories. This lack of manpower planning is not too surprising, especially if such planning is directed toward long term needs. As Cordiner (1956) indicates, "many business organizations in the United States are just now beginning to learn to plan five years ahead." It *is* surprising, however, that industrial organizations fail to inventory their *present* work force with any regularity. Only after a crisis in manpower is attention usually given to human resource inventories or is resort made to training as a means of securing and maintaining an adequate work force.

A Manpower Inventory

Certain basic information concerning the employees and their assignments is necessary, if an inventory of human resources is to serve as a basis for planning training in a company. Let us consider the data required for one job or position in the company (Table 2.1).

We will momentarily ignore the steps and problems involved

Table 2.1

DATA REQUIRED FOR MANPOWER INVENTORY

1. Number of employees in the job classification
2. Number of employees needed in the job classification
3. Age of each employee in the job classification
4. Level of skill required by the job of each employee
5. Level of knowledge required by the job of each employee
6. Attitude of each employee toward job and company
7. Level of job performance, quality and quantity, of each employee
8. Level of skills and knowledge of each employee for other jobs
9. Potential replacements for this job outside company
10. Potential replacements for this job within company
11. Training time required for potential replacements
12. Training time required for a novice
13. Rate of absenteeism from this job
14. Turnover in this job for specified period of time
15. Job specification for the job

in obtaining these data [2] and see what they would mean in terms of organizational planning and training in the case of just one job classification (Table 2.2).

An analysis of the data in Table 2.2 indicates that there is an immediate need for training of one new employee (items 1 and 2) and retraining of at least four of the present employees (item 7). Assuming mandatory retirement at 65, training needs for the next two years exist for at least seven additional employees (items 3 and 14). Two of these can come from other job classifications within the company (item 10), but at least five will have to be trained completely (items 9 and 12). The absentee data indicate an average of .85 employees absent each working day (item 1 times item 13). Someone will have to do the work of this fractional employee.

We can derive further implications from this table. The age level in the department is high (item 3), and disability from disease or death is potentially greater than in a department with younger employees. Other departments can expect little help from this department in terms of replacements (item 8). Absentee data on individuals can lead to investigating possible physical disabilities among the group. Furthermore, the data used to supply the numbers in the skills, knowledge, attitude, and performance areas can be used as a basis for remedial action. For example, one of the workers whose performance is questionable (item 7) may be one of the workers possessing skill and knowledge for one or more other jobs (item 8). One by-product of a manpower inventory is the discovery of people who are doing poorly in one job but are transferable or, in fact, promotable.

We have temporarily ignored the problem of collecting these data. It is obvious certain of this information can be secured easily if adequate personnel records are kept. It is a more difficult and exacting task to secure accurate and adequate information on the skills, knowledge, attitudes, and performance of the employees in this department. This problem of evaluating individuals against job demands will be presented in Chapter 4, "Man Analysis." Data on potential replacements from within the company would come from a similar manpower audit made in

[2] Methods of obtaining these data are considered in Chapters 3 and 4.

Table 2.2

MANPOWER ANALYSIS OF ONE JOB CLASSIFICATION

1. Number of employees in the job classification: 37
2. Number of employees needed: 38
3. Age levels:

Age levels:	29	33	45	47	50	51	53	55	63
No. per age group:	2	8	7	10	3	2	2	1	2

Factors	Level Satisfactory	Questionable	Unsatisfactory
4. Skill	32	2	3
5. Knowledge	33	3	1
6. Attitude	36	1	0
7. Performance	33	2	2

8. Skill and knowledge levels for other jobs:

Classification	No.	Jobs
No other jobs	33	x
One other job	3	Job Z, Dept. Y
Two or more other jobs	1	Job Z, Dept. Y; Job A, Dept. B

9–11. Potential replacements and training time:

Outside company	Within company	Training time
0	1	Less than 1 week
0	1	3 weeks to 6 weeks
10	0	12 weeks to 16 weeks

12. Training time on job for novice: 12 to 16 weeks
13. Rate of absenteeism (Two year average): 2.3%
14. Turnover (Two year period): 5 employees; 13.5%
15. Statement of job specifications

other units and departments of the organization and coordinated through a central source.

Admittedly, this is an extremely simplified picture of the problems of determining the adequacy of human resources in an organization. As jobs increase in complexity, the problem of man analysis which is basic to human resource analysis becomes increasingly complex. Yet, corporations spend millions of dollars in planning for physical expansion and for maintenance of existing physical facilities. The need for maintaining the human resources of an enterprise is equally important and requires as careful planning. We believe that an analysis along the lines suggested, continuously carried on throughout a company, will reveal significant training needs and contribute materially to overall company efficiency. The initial analysis is the most difficult one. Subsequent analyses become easier with experience and development of efficient procedures.

A word of caution is in order here. The burden of paper work and forms can make impossible the determination of training needs. Managers are harassed with reading materials, reports, and other time consuming printed matter. Complicated forms and reports proliferate overhead costs. Continuous effort must be made to keep reporting as simple and as clearcut as is consistent with the accuracy required.

Simplicity is also required in reporting the results of manpower audits once the data have been gathered. In management audits it has become fashionable to ignore simplicity in the design of forms and reports. There has been an epidemic of management replacement charts of many colors with an impressive array of cabalistic symbols. These charts make the originators happy but frequently confuse the consumer. And they do not convey any more information than the simple straightforward presentation of identical data on human resources as is shown in Chart 2.1.[3]

Analysis of human resources of an organization indicates where training is needed to improve the performance of the present job incumbents or to prepare for replacements. It does not indicate that training is the sole answer to the problems revealed by the analysis. It is entirely possible that the foreman DEG

[3] We are indebted to Dr. William Holmes of Lever Bros. for the basic idea for this chart.

Chart 2.1

MANPOWER STATUS CHART—MILL A

Positions and Incumbents

Assistant Foremen	Foremen	Assistant Superintendents	Superintendents	Managers
				MWL(63-1)
			DAC(64-1)	
		FEJ(82-1)----------	------→	
	MEM(73-1)			
	DEG(62-2)			
	RAH(75-1)			
	ETF(78-1)			
	RAD(83-1)			
BES(85-1)———	——→	----------	------→	
AES(78-1)				
VFH(64-1)———	——→			
MCV(65-1)				
MWM(86-1)———	————	——→	----------	------→
RAP(80-1)				
ENN(80-2)				
JLC(80-1)------	------→			
POD(69-2)				

Legend:

——————→	Promotable to position indicated
- - - - - - - - →	Possibly promotable to position indicated
72, etc.	Retirement year
1	Job performance satisfactory
2	Job performance questionable

in Chart 2.1 should be encouraged to take early retirement, and assistant foreman ENN should be relieved of his duties. DEG may be too old to profit from training, and ENN may be a monument to poor supervisory selection procedures. The chart does show that it is imperative to secure a replacement for manager MWL and for superintendent DAC within a reasonably short time span. This may or may not require training. The answer as to whether or not training is required depends on subsequent analysis of operations and of men in this particular organization. An analysis of the human resources of an enterprise simply helps to direct attention to potential training efforts without specifying the nature of these efforts.

Human Resources Analysis—A Continuing Activity

We have been discussing the analysis of human resources as if a company were a static entity. Projection of training needs must consider not only what the company is now, but also what the company may be in five, ten, twenty, or more years. Changes in technology, products, and organizational structure will require changes in the number and types of employees required to man the organization. One large corporation recognizes that its planned expansion and consequent change in structure will require an estimated 10,000 additional members of its management group in the next ten years. Another large corporation, because of a change in its merchandising program, expects to have an entirely different kind of salesman selling its products in the future. A recent survey (Aprecella and Thompson, 1957) indicates that there is a general shift in the nature of the work force in American industry due to the addition of new and improved equipment. This will cause an increase in the number of employees engaged in indirect labor and a decrease in the number employed in direct labor. These examples of future trends have direct implications not only for selection of employees but also for training new employees or retraining present workers. Only by forward planning and organization analysis can these needs be met adequately. A training director, however competent, cannot plan training to meet a need known only to the top echelon of a company's management. A training director who is a member of this upper echelon is the exception rather than the rule in American industry today.

The analysis of the human resources of a company is the second step in determining the direction of training efforts as a management tool. It is concerned with determining what people and how many people must be trained for the present and future effectiveness of the organization.

ANALYSIS OF EFFICIENCY INDICES

Certain functions must be carried out effectively in any individual organization, if it is to continue to produce goods and services that customers will buy and use. How effectively these functions are performed can serve as indices to the general effectiveness of the enterprise. Management has developed many indices for evaluating these various functions. Usually the indices are expressed in terms of cost accounting concepts. Frequently, they represent the ratio between actual performance and an established ideal or standard of performance. In organization analysis, these indices or ratios can serve as valuable guides for directing training efforts.

The exact nature of these indices vary from company to company but generally they involve such factors as:

1. costs of labor required to produce the goods or services
2. the costs of materials required to produce the goods or services
3. the quality of the goods or services
4. utilization of machinery and equipment in producing goods and services
5. costs of distribution of goods and services.

Most modern companies have, as part of their system of records and controls, data which indicate whether or not the company as a whole and its various departments and units are meeting, exceeding, or falling short of the expected performance in these five areas. Careful and continuous scrutiny of these records can give significant leads to determining training needs. Generally, however, the data secured from the cost department or from the industrial engineering division are overall figures and ratios and do not pinpoint the cause of imbalance between performance and standard. Effective use of this information requires careful analysis based on sophisticated observation of operations. It may even require building of additional records or the use of a well-designed experimental investigation (Coakley, 1950).

Direct Labor Costs

First, let us consider the matter of labor costs. In this index of organizational productivity it is assumed that, for each unit produced, the exact amount of money paid to the employees who produce this unit can be established. If the unit costs for labor on a carded percale sheet is $1.10 per sheet, based on accurate analysis, and the actual cost is $1.11, the labor cost is too high for efficient operation. This is particularly true if the competing companies are producing this item at $1.09 per unit. Certainly, this fact is a starting point for determining the reasons for this situation. There could be many reasons for high production costs which have no or very little relationship to training, that is, condition and speed of machinery, prevailing wage patterns in the area, union agreements, and many others.

Assuming our investigation has eliminated these nontraining factors, the problem then becomes one of determining at what point or points in the manufacturing process more is being spent for labor than should be spent. This consists of analysis by department and job of the labor costs of manufacturing the article. Once the source of excessive labor costs is found, the reasons can be investigated. This investigation will include operations analysis and man analysis which are discussed in subsequent chapters. Whether the cause or causes turn out to be something which training can remedy will depend on the results of the operations and the man analysis. Whether or not the solution is dependent on training, there is little room for argument that a training program to reduce the labor costs in producing an article should not be started prior to establishing the need for training. Furthermore, efforts in other directions may prove relatively futile, if the basic reasons stem from inadequate training of personnel.

Indirect Labor Costs

This, of course, is an oversimplified example. Analysis of labor costs is not only the analysis of costs of direct labor, but also that of indirect labor, including supervision, staff services, and managerial costs. These data are much more difficult to obtain accurately and to pinpoint. Their relation to productivity is more difficult to analyze. Yet, where direct labor and other factors leading to excessive labor costs per unit are ruled out as causes, these additional labor costs must be analyzed, if the problem is serious enough to justify the effort. Certainly, if a training remedy in this area is contemplated, it should be undertaken with something more than the simple pious belief that training is a good thing and can do no harm. Remember that training, whether effective or not, costs money.

The example just used might imply that a global analysis of the entire organization is necessary to determine whether or not excessive labor costs can be reduced by training. Actually, such an analysis can be made in regard to a division, a department, a section, a unit, or a specific operation. Excessive overtime, a greater number of employees than authorized for the operation, excessive learning time for novices, and many other indices may be signs that carefully planned and executed training is necessary, if labor costs are to be kept within the required standards or reduced.

Other Indices

The other indices, listed on page 39, require analyses similar to those required of labor costs, if we are to determine whether or not a training problem exists. The costs of materials, for example, may become excessive, if the waste in their use is higher than normal or standard for the particular production process. Excessive seconds or defective goods can increase materially the costs of operating a business. Services which fail to satisfy customers require adjustments and reduce the margin between outlay for these services and the price the customer pays for them. Excessive waste and defective products certainly arise from many causes other than defective training of employees. Too frequently the wrong kind of training, rather than the lack of training, is a causative factor in the increased costs of doing business. This is especially true when we reconsider our definition of industrial training as encompassing not only skills and knowledge, but also attitudes. We have no evidence of a statistical nature, but our experience leads us to suspect that the major problems of waste and quality control are frequently attitudinal rather than problems of skill and knowledge.[4]

In utilizing machinery and equipment not only is proper scheduling important, but also efficient maintenance and repair are necessary. Records of idle time and downtime as well as costs of maintaining and repairing machinery are indices which should be investigated as clues to training needs. Replacements required, studied against normal life expectancy of machinery and equipment, are another source for determining training needs. Actually, excessively low costs for maintenance and repair may be as effective indicators of training needs as are excessively high costs. This is particularly true if low costs for maintenance are combined with excessive replacements.

The problem of proper utilization of machinery and equipment emphasizes an aspect of determining training needs which we may seem to have neglected. It might appear that the analysis of efficiency indices includes determining training needs only for those individuals who operate, maintain, or repair machinery and equipment. This, of course, is far from the point. Poor utilization of machinery and equipment is the responsibility not only of the operator, but also of his supervisor, and the supervisor of his supervisor. A thorough analysis of the causes of poor machinery utilization might lead to the conclusion that it is not the machine operator but the company president who needs training. The point, however, is that analysis of labor costs, material costs, quality, machine utilization, and costs of distribution can lead to establishing training needs not only among first line operators, but also among any of the various levels of supervisors and managers of a company.

The costs of the distribution of goods and services include not only the costs of selling but also those of getting the goods or services to the customer and collecting for them. An error in

[4] There is some indirect evidence (McGehee and Livingstone, 1952) to support this suspicion in regard to waste. Similar unpublished investigations on quality are less clearcut and indicate that skill and knowledge may play a bigger part in quality control. Even here, attitudinal problems seem to be important.

shipping an order can cause not only a definite financial loss to a company but also possible future loss of orders from the customer. Late deliveries can bring about the same results. On the other hand, large errors of judgment in market trends, advertising approaches, and customer services can prove disastrous to a business. Again, we must emphasize that our enthusiasm for training has not warped our judgment to the extent of believing that even proper training would completely eliminate shipping errors, late deliveries, and poor judgment in merchandising. We are merely saying that continued analysis of this functional area may reveal that training can be used effectively to increase the achievement of organizational goals in these various areas.

Efficiency

Organization analysis in terms of productivity and utilization of capital represents only one aspect of organization analysis to determine the *efficiency* of the organization. As Ryan (1947) has pointed out, productivity or "output" is only the numerator of the expression which characterizes the efficiency of an activity. The denominator is the input or effort of the activity; it is the cost of work to the individual performing the act or series of acts. This means that efficiency is a ratio of output to input. The usual cost accounting procedures and indices of productivity found in an industrial organization rarely if ever are efficiency indices in this meaning of the term.

In analyzing an organization to discover training needs, it is extremely important to study not only the productivity and cost accounting data but also the input required of individuals to achieve the results characterized by these data. An imbalance between output and input may indicate that tasks are so organized that training has not or cannot develop the required behavior in the employees to perform these tasks in the manner expected. It may also indicate that the tasks required are such that only a low input is required, and that increased output with accompanying increase in input can be effected by task reorganization and training. An excessively high or excessively low efficiency ratio in an organization can be a symptom of organizational ill health. A low ratio continued over a long period of time can threaten the ultimate survival of the organization by depletion of the energies of its employees. High efficiency ratios may mean that the employees of the company are not being utilized in a manner conducive to attainment of organizational objectives.

As Ryan (1947) has indicated, input is not to be considered synonymous to physical exertion. In addition to physical exertion, it has also psychological aspects involving the individual's feelings, beliefs, emotions, and attitudes. At the present stage of measurement of human behavior, it is admittedly difficult to obtain adequate measures of the input factor in efficiency. This is one of the many areas in the determining of training needs which requires systematic research. Some indications as to the kinds of measures used to determine the nonphysical costs of work are discussed in the next section on the analysis of organizational climate. The training specialist, as well as line management, in studying and analyzing what are usually called "efficiency indices" in industry, should be aware that he really is analyzing only one-half of the ratio, that is, production or output. He should know and strive to secure data on input in order to make an adequate analysis of efficiency in an organization as a basis for determining training needs. It is entirely possible that new and different measures from those now found in industry need to be devised, if the training analysis is to be done adequately in terms of "efficiency" as discussed here.

ANALYSIS OF ORGANIZATIONAL CLIMATE

Training has been described in Chapter 1 as being concerned not only with skills and knowledge but also with the attitudes of employees. Contrary to beliefs occasionally found among supervisors, attitudes are not innate. Employees do not come into the world with ready-made predispositions to react favorably or unfavorably to a specific situation or situations in the factory or office. An attitude or a pattern of attitudes arise from the specific experiences an individual has had and his interpretation of these experiences. Attitudes toward work, supervision, company procedures, goals, and objectives are learned just as is the skill required to handle an overhead crane or the knowledge required to analyze cost figures for a new product. It is true that the attitudes of employees are developed by many experiences outside a specific work situation. Attitudes toward authority may date back to childhood experiences. Attitudes toward quality may be a function of school experiences or experience in prior jobs. Many of the problems of training in the areas of attitudes are complicated by the necessity of changing or modifying already existing attitudes of employees. Development of attitudinal patterns *de novo* rarely occurs in a work situation.

Attitudes are rarely the results of deliberate planning on the part of managers, or of training procedures. They may arise from a single traumatic experience, be adopted ready-made from peers and associates, or develop through balancing the pluses and minuses of many experiences in a specific continuum.[5] They probably also result as the concomitants of formal training in industry without any intent on the part of the trainer to develop them or any provision for directing their growth. Even in providing training in a relatively simple skill such as packaging blankets, the operator learns not simply the manual task but also certain attitudes toward quality and quantity of work, punctuality, supervision, safety, and company policies. Rarely is a conscious effort made to develop specific attitudes toward these and other nonmanual aspects of work. We would like to suggest that formal efforts to modify attitudes are more successful within the framework of teaching a specific task than when efforts at developing attitudes are divorced from the specific job situation. Certainly, this is one area of training procedures which requires careful research. Acceptance or rejection of this hypothesis would affect materially the organization of a training program and the way training is conducted.

The climate of an organization is a function of the attitudes of its members. As Stagner has indicated, attitudes "can be characterized as generalized ways of perceiving certain classes of situations" (Stagner, 1956, p. 163). If employees perceive the com-

[5] A detailed discussion of the formation of attitudes is beyond the scope of this book. The interested reader will find the following sources, among many others, informative on this topic: Kretch and Crutchfield, 1948, pp. 149 ff; Asch, 1952, pp. 527 ff.

pany's policies, procedures, and goals as congruent with their own needs, goals, and aspirations, the attitudinal climate is one of cooperation, mutual confidence, and willing acceptance of the requirements for continued membership in the company. In contrast, if employees perceive the company as antagonistic to their needs, goals, and aspirations, the attitudinal climate becomes one of conflict, hostility, noncooperation, and unwillingness to accept requirements for continued membership. It is a rare industrial situation where there is complete congruence between employees' goals and company goals; similarly, complete lack of congruence is equally rare.

The attitudes of an employee toward various aspects of work and membership in a company are a product of his experience both within and outside his work environment. Similarly, the morale of the group or subgroup to which the employee belongs is a product of his and the shared experiences of his fellow employees. Since both employee attitudes and the morale of employee groups are products of experience these predispositions to act in certain ways can be developed or modified by training. Attitudes and morale, the ingredients of organizational climate would, therefore, be important factors in determining training needs and planning training, if evidence were adequate to indicate that a significant relationship exists between attitudes and morale on the one hand and the achievement of organizational goals on the other.

The Relationship Between Attitudes and Productivity

What then is the evidence in regard to relationship of employee attitudes and morale of work groups to the achievement of organizational goals? Brayfield and Crockett (1955), in fifteen comparisons of the relationship of the attitudes of individual employees to productivity, found only three instances of low although statistically significant relationships. They do find an indication from other studies "that morale, as a group phenomenon, may bear a positive relationship to performance on the job" (p. 405). The same investigators, in reviewing studies of absenteeism and labor turnover, found significant relationships with employee attitudes and morale.

A review by the Psychological Service of Pittsburgh (Herzberg, Mausner, Peterson, and Capwell, 1957) of employee attitudes and production indicates a closer relationship than found by Brayfield and Crockett. Fourteen of the twenty-six studies reviewed indicate that "workers with positive job attitudes show higher productivity than those with negative attitudes" (p. 99). In the remaining twelve studies, nine show no relationship and three show negative relationships between attitudes and productivity. The same report indicated that "a worker's job attitudes play an important role in determining whether he will report consistently to work in face of minor obstacles, and whether or not he will leave his job for avoidable reasons" (p. 107). There is also some indication in this report of a relationship between attitudes, accidents, and minor psychosomatic illness.

Both Brayfield and Crockett and the Pittsburgh group indicate the weakness of the research on which their conclusions are based. Furthermore, the differences in the conclusions of these reviews, as Katzell (1957) has pointed out, is partly due to their not covering exactly the same literature and in part to different standards for determining when a relationship is significant. We agree with Brayfield and Crockett's conclusions:

> . . . that satisfaction with one's position in a network of relationships need not imply strong motivation to outstanding performance within the system, and second, that productivity may be only peripherally related to many goals toward which the industrial worker is striving (1955, p. 421).

A careful examination of these two reviews does lead, however, to a fairly consistent conclusion. The attitudes of the worker do seem to be related to his survival on the job. To the extent that negative attitudes breed high turnover and consequent selection and training costs, we can point to adverse effects of attitudes upon the attainment of organizational goals. The inconsistency of the findings with respect to attitudes and morale as they relate to production is, if nothing else, a clear indication that the relationship may vary from company to company and plant to plant. Given such inconsistent results, management must be made aware that this is a question for research in their own organization and that an assumption of a positive, negative, or zero relationship is unwarranted. To make decisions aimed at furthering organizational goals on the basis of any of these assumptions is to court the possibility of gross mistakes.

The research of Kahn and Katz (1953) also points up the necessity of surveying organizational climate in determining training needs and planning training. Two bases of evidence are found: first, these studies show the close relationship between the quality of leadership and productivity, and the effect of the nature of the work group relationship on productivity; and, second, these studies emphasize the influence which the social-psychological environment of the organization has upon the behavior of individual employees or upon primary work groups. As these authors indicate, "many an unsuccessful training program testifies to the almost insurmountable difficulties in producing changes by means which fail to take adequate account" (1953, p. 627) of the social-psychological environment. In other words, a human relations training course is doomed to failure in a company whose management has little or no interest in employees as individuals and perceives of them as a commodity called "labor."

We maintain that a careful evaluation of the organizational climate is essential if training is to be used adequately as a management tool. Such an evaluation should indicate, first, whether or not training can produce changes in behavior which will contribute to organizational goals, and, second, it will indicate the changes in behavior which training should attempt to accomplish, given a climate which will permit changes in behavior as a result of a training program.

Analyzing Organizational Climate

If the analysis of organizational climate is necessary to determine training needs and the possibility of training being effective, the problem becomes one of how this analysis can be made in an objective and accurate manner. Two general types [6] of data can be used to analyze the organizational climate of a com-

[6] Over twenty years ago Blankenship (1939) presented a very similar analysis of methods of measuring industrial morale. Other methodological and statistical improvements have taken place in the use of these methods yet no really new techniques have been invented in the interim although terminology has become more complex, that is, "organizational climate."

pany or the unit of a company under consideration. The first of these is the use of existing data concerning certain conditions in the company and inferring the status of employee attitudes and of morale from them. Among these data are (1) indices of labor-management conflict, that is, strikes, lockouts, sabotage, slowdowns, disciplinary problems, complaints, and grievances, etc., (2) labor turnover, (3) absenteeism, (4) employee suggestions, (5) productivity, (6) accidents and short-term sickness.

The second general type of data must be obtained by various methods since it does not already exist in the organization. The methods consist of some direct effort to analyze organizational climate rather than infer its nature from other data. One of these methods is direct, planned observation of employee behavior. A second method is that of interviews with employees. The third is the use of printed materials—schedules, questionnaires, attitude scales, indirect and projective techniques. These three methods have in common the assumption that observed behavior, whether verbal or nonverbal, is an index to the attitudes of employees. This assumption is made, of course, with regard to data secured from existing situations such as labor-management conflict, labor turnover, etc. The major difference between the two general types of data is that the latter is collected deliberately for the purpose of analyzing organizational climate; the former occurs in the course of the on-going operations of producing goods and services.

Indirect indices. It would seem that data secured in the course of the on-going operations of the company would be more valid and reliable for inferring the organizational climate. Unfortunately, this is not necessarily true. Indications of labor-management conflicts such as strikes, grievances, and complaints depend on many factors other than the individual employee's attitude toward his company. Stagner (1954), among others, has offered some evidence of a dual system of loyalty by employees to company and union which would support this statement. It is also well known that an increase in grievances frequently occurs as the time for contract negotiations approaches.

In contrast, the absence of overt signs of labor-management conflict cannot be assumed to be an indication that morale is high and employees are satisfied with their work or their company. This is particularly true in companies where no recognized means of bringing grievances into the open are available. Even the much vaunted "open door" policy does not guarantee an employee immunity from reprisals if he by-passes his immediate superior in stating a grievance.

What is true of labor-management conflict is true also of other indirect indicators of employee attitudes and morale. Turnover and absenteeism are functions of economic conditions and job opportunities as well as of employee attitudes. Employee suggestion systems, as Whyte (1955) has shown, have inherent limitations as barometers of employee attitudes. Productivity depends on departmental organization, machinery conditions, quality of raw materials, and many other factors in addition to the willingness of the individual employee to work. Furthermore, the absence of excessive turnover, absenteeism, and accidents in a company is not positive evidence that morale is high. High productivity and many suggestions from employees are not clear indicators of industrial harmony.

What, then, can be said about these indirect indicators of worker satisfaction, attitudes, and group morale? First, as an index of organizational climate, they can be considered only as possible symptoms of attitudes and morale. They are a starting point for investigations to determine whether or not psychological factors are major determinants of the conditions found. Investigations of this type frequently must be carried out by careful study of other possible causes and their elimination before ascribing the conditions to undesirable organizational climate.

Whether or not grievances, complaints, absenteeism, turnover, accidents, psychosomatic illness, or low productivity are functions of low morale and undesirable attitudes, these conditions require the attention of management in their own right. Their excessive occurrence renders it more difficult to achieve organizational goals. It is also possible that analysis of the causes of these conditions will indicate training needs in skill and knowledge areas as well as in the attitudinal area.

Observations: Significant data on attitudes and morale have been secured in industrial situations by trained observers. Since Mathewson's (1931) classical study of restriction of output among unorganized workers, the methods and techniques of di-

rect observation have been improved and refined. Jahoda, Deutsch, and Cook (1951), in a clear description of the methods of direct observations, indicate two major advantages of this method: (1) it permits the recording of employee behavior simultaneously with its spontaneous occurrence and (2) it is independent of the employees' ability and willingness to report. The same authors state that its primary limitation is that the extended time required to make observations is uneconomical. It seems to us, however, that an additional important limitation is that of the theoretical orientation of the observer. No matter how objective and scrupulously accurate an observer is, he will be observing events in a factory or a store with a certain frame of reference. He not only will report what he sees within this frame of reference but also will interpret it within the same frame of reference. It is entirely possible that an observer of the Mayo-Rothlisberger persuasion will perceive in the same situation something different from that perceived by an observer trained by William F. Whyte or E. Wight Bakke. Still another limitation, not completely eliminated by the proponents of this method so far as the industrial situation is concerned, is the effect on the behavior of the individuals observed by the presence of the observer.[7] In spite of its limitations, however, it is a powerful data-gathering method for analyzing organizational climate.

An illustration of the kinds of information and their implications for training which can be obtained from direct observation of a work group is found in Zaleznik's (1956) [8] study of a machine shop in a manufacturing plant. He reports that this work group had developed into a "fairly effective social group" but this effectiveness was not directed toward the achievement of organizational goals. There was little personal job involvement in work, and the employees were carrying out the minimum requirements of the job. Zaleznik concluded that positive leadership was necessary, if the group were to go beyond merely per-

[7] One of the authors has some evidence to show definite changes in the behavior of a group of sewing machine operators when they were observed without knowledge of observation and when they knew they were being observed and were aware of the observation.

[8] Zaleznik's principal method was direct observation although he also used informal interviews and personnel records.

forming these tasks in a routine way. From a training standpoint, the implications of this study are clear. (Implementation of the implications, of course, is another matter.) Systematic efforts are required to change the attitudes of the members of this group, if their goals are to become more congruent with company goals. It is possible, as Zaleznik indicates, that this requires a change in the leadership pattern for the group with full support of the administrative environment. This change in leadership pattern includes training administrators "beyond sheer verbal facility about leadership of groups" and bringing about changes in actual supervisory behavior.

Verbal statements. Analysis of organizational climate on the bases of indirect indices and direct observation has a common disadvantage. We are inferring either from statistical data or from overt behavior the feelings and sentiments of employees toward the company for which they work. We have no direct evidence as to how an employee feels or the intensity of his feelings. In order to secure a verbal statement of attitudes of employees, there has been an increasing use in industry of interviews and attitude questionnaires. It should be pointed out that the crucial problems in the use of interviews and attitude questionnaires concerns the validity of verbal reports (Jahoda, et al., 1951, p. 153). In other words, if a worker says he loves his boss, his company, and his work, can what he says to the interviewer be taken as what he really feels, or is it what he wants his boss to think he feels? The problem of validity is not only a problem of truth and nontruth but also the problem of ability of the employee to put into a verbal form what he really thinks and believes. Psychoanalytic literature suggests that many of an individual's important beliefs and attitudes are not at the conscious level. Since the individual is not aware of them he cannot report them.

In spite of their limitations verbal reports can give insight into attitudes and morale if these reports are obtained under conditions which protect the individual employee against the folly of his own truthfulness. They are of little value "when the circumstances in which the report occurs lead us to suspect that the subject's motivation or the pressures to which he is exposed are such as to prevent a candid report" (Jahoda, et al., 1951,

p. 154). The inability to report can be reduced to some extent by skillful interviewing and careful questionnaire construction.

Projective techniques and disguised methods of investigating the motivational structure of patients are widely used in clinical psychology and psychiatry. There has been an increasing interest and use of these methods in assessment of social attitudes (Campbell, 1950). These techniques primarily attempt to reduce invalidity of verbal reports by disguising from the respondent the true purpose for which he is being asked to respond. Although these methods may have promise for analyzing organizational climate they are not well developed for this purpose at present.

Generally, interviews and questionnaires used to analyze attitudes of employees and morale are not employed primarily to determine training needs. This means that careful analysis of data from these sources must be made from the standpoint of training if clues to planning training are to be found. An unpublished investigation of organizational climate which was undertaken primarily for determination of training needs illustrates how interviews can be used for this purpose.

This study was made in a small mill several years ago when economic education for employees was the current training rage. Considerable pressure was being exerted on training personnel to give this sort of training to rank and file employees in the mill. As a preliminary step, it was agreed that an investigation of what employees knew about economics of the mill, what they wanted to know, where they got their information, and where they wanted to get their information, would be made by interviewing a sample of production employees. At the same time, certain questions were to be used to attempt to gauge overall morale in the plant.

The results of this investigation were reasonably clearcut insofar as economic training was concerned. The employees knew little or nothing about broad economic issues; they knew almost as little about the specific economic issues in their company and mill. Furthermore, they were not greatly concerned with economic issues either within or outside the company. All they wanted to know was when they were to work and what they were to be paid for their work. On the other hand, questions about job satisfaction and morale indicated that no serious problem existed in these areas, unless it was one of apathy.

Training implications are equally clear from this investigation. The usual economic education program might have been a complete failure in this mill. Employees did not seem sophisticated enough economically to understand or benefit from this type of training. The problem here was one of creating interest in how the specific economic system in their limited economic world was related to their aspirations for steady work and adequate pay. It was not a problem of communication media but a problem of interest in receiving communications. This is true even though there is definite evidence that the limited economic information these workers had was positively related to job satisfaction and morale.

The training implications of a survey of employee attitudes and opinions which are implicit in the reported results but are not made explicit are found in Mann and Dent's (1954) study of accounting department employees in the Detroit Edison Company. The investigation is of special interest because it was possible to study the relationship between the evaluation of first line supervisors' job performance by their supervisors and the attitudes of the supervisors' subordinates toward the supervisors.

Supervisors considered satisfactory or superior in their job performance by their superiors were more frequently perceived by their subordinates in the following ways:

1. Subordinates felt free to discuss both job and personal problems with their supervisors.
2. The subordinates were kept informed as to what the supervisors thought of their work.
3. The supervisors held frequent group meetings.
4. The supervisors used general supervision.
5. The supervisors would go to bat for an employee who had a complaint.

Again, the training implications are clear even though it is possible that inferior supervisors may not change their behavior as a result of training. Training is indicated in both techniques of supervision and in modification of basic attitudes of supervisors towards employees. On the other hand, the attitudinal problems may be so complex as to require a modification of selection procedures.

Additional examples of the possible use of morale and attitude surveys as leads for determining training needs could be given. Usually this would point to the same conclusion: if the results of such surveys are studied with respect to the problem of effectively using training as a management tool, significant and valuable leads for planning training and determining training needs will be derived. Because most studies of employee morale are oriented toward job attitudes and occasionally toward human relations, it will usually be necessary for the training director to assert the desirability for studying directly *production* training needs as perceived by employees. Even then, it will be necessary to go beyond the immediate data and into the area of operations and man analysis if training needs are to be fully ascertained. However, if the possibility of using surveys as a source of uncovering all kinds of training needs is kept in mind during the design of an attitude survey, more direct evidence of problems in training can be uncovered.

Combined methods. We have indicated both the indirect and direct methods of analyzing organizational climate as if they were used separately and independently. This, of course, is not true. Actually, the most effective way of assessing organizational climate is to use these measures in conjunction with each other. The General Electric Company's ERI (Merrihu and Katzell, 1955) is one promising form this combination of indices may take, particularly the indirect measures.

Still another approach to combining indices has been called an "operational attitude" survey. This is the use of the indirect measures discussed earlier, direct observation, and interviews, and/or questionnaires. An example of this type of investigation will illustrate how it can be used to assist in determining training needs. In one department of a large mill, there was consistent low production among a group of operators, absenteeism was high, and grievances were numerous. An unstructured interview with a sample of the operators in this department indicated low morale and little effort to work toward attainment of organizational goals. In addition, complaints were frequent about the arrangement of materials in the department and lack of consistent standards of inspection. Direct observation in the department substantiated these complaints. Further investigation indicated that the inspectors were not adequately trained to make the judgments required of them. This led to reorganization of inspection procedures and to retraining of inspectors.

Generally, the careful use of both direct and indirect methods of analyzing attitudes and morale of employees is an essential step in determining the training needs of an organization. Careful assessment of organizational climate also will indicate whether or not efforts to develop or modify skills and knowledge of employees have a reasonable chance of success.

VALIDITY AND RELIABILITY OF MEASURES USED IN ORGANIZATION ANALYSIS

We have outlined the problems and some of the approaches possible in organization analysis as a basic step in planning and utilizing training in industry. This discussion has implied the use of measures and measuring devices as a prerequisite to adequate organization analysis. These measures may be relatively simple, that is, the number of employees in a specific job classification in a single department of a company. Many of the measures and the methods of determining them are complex and intricate. It is our position, however, that quantification of data is a necessary step not only for determining training needs but also for all aspects of utilizing this management tool efficiently. Adequate quantification is necessary if accurate decisions are to be made in training as well as in the many other facets of industrial management. Quantification is no guarantee as to the quality of decisions but without it decisions are less likely to be based on the available data.

This brings us to the question of the characteristics of measures and measuring devices which are necessary if our quantifications are to aid us in planning, administering, and evaluating training. Measures must have at least two basic characteristics if we are to use them; they are validity and reliability.

A measure is valid when it measures what it purports to measure and not something else. In the simple quantifying of the number of employees in a specific job classification, the concept becomes almost synonymous with accuracy. Most measures used in organization analysis are not this simple. It is not uncommon, for example, to think of the efficiency of an employee in terms of the number of units he produces in a given period of time. The number of units may have been counted with perfect accuracy but be an invalid measure of efficiency if efficiency is considered as a ratio of input to output (Ryan, 1947, Ch. 2). Many factors in industry besides the input of the individual employee determines the number of units he produces. We have raised the question concerning the validity of measures in the section of this chapter dealing with interviews and questionnaires as means of measuring attitudes. Cost figures, especially standard costs, are sometimes viewed as a valid index of the efficiency of an organization. Yet the temporal nature of a cost system ending at measured intervals of time can make a unit or a department of a company the hero at one time and a villain in the next act. Figures on absenteeism and turnover may be accurate but not involve measures either of morale or of training needs. Persistence in the employment of a company of large numbers of employees may be a monument to inertia rather than an index of organizational health.

The question of the validity of measures becomes, to some extent, a question of valid for what. In using the methods and resulting measures suggested in this chapter on organization analysis, managers and others concerned with determining training needs must examine them first to determine if the measures actually measure what they purport to measure. Then, the measures must be examined to determine if they represent a condition serious enough to justify the efforts required to correct it by training.

The degree of reliability of a measurement procedure is determined by the consistency of the measures which are obtained by the procedure. For example, if three competent people, using the same information, reported twelve, eighteen, and twenty-two employees in a job classification in a department of a company, the measurement procedure would be, to a rather high degree, unreliable. If an attitude questionnaire administered to the same employees on two successive days showed markedly different results, the reliability of the instrument would be questionable.

It should be pointed out, however, that spurious reliability can be obtained by the failure to get independent measures of the same phenomena. For example, if only one of the three people actually counted the employees and the others copied his results, we would have spurious reliability. The problem of reliability in evaluating training is treated in some detail and in its broader aspects in Chapter 9 of this text. It is also discussed in connection with measurement procedures in operations and man analyses. It should be pointed out here that for many measurement procedures which are used in organization analysis the question of consistency of the procedures is a pertinent one. This is particularly true of data describing production, quality, machinery, and material utilization, as well as the other indirect and the direct procedures for analyzing organizational climate. Unreliable and spuriously reliable procedures give data which are of little value either for determining training needs or for utilization in any other kind of management decisions.

ORGANIZATION ANALYSIS AND TRAINING NEEDS

Training is the procedure used for developing or modifying the skills, knowledge, and attitudes of employees. In discussing organization analysis, the impression may have been created that any malfunction of the organization can be cured by adequate training procedures. An industrial organization is a complex social situation. What happens in an organization is the result of many factors both within and without the organization. Restrictive governmental regulations, pressure from external agencies such as unions, availability of risk capital, economic conditions in the general community, and many other factors over which management has little or no direct control can lead to conditions within the organization similar to those we have suggested as indications of training needs.

It is possible that the very nature of organizational structure and managerial controls may result in an organizational climate inimicable to the continued health of the organization. Argyris

(1958) has described and analyzed this kind of situation in a plant that is part of a large national corporation. In the plant, the objective indices of morale—absenteeism, turnover, grievances, production—are all on the favorable side. Corporation officers and plant officials consider the plant as one of the best in the company. The employees seem to have the same feeling about the plant as the officials of the company, for 92% of them "state that the company is a good place to work, that they are satisfied with it as a whole, and that they have no desire or plans to leave" (1958, p. 103).

Yet a further analysis of the attitudes of the employees indicates that the majority were favorably disposed toward management because "it pays good wages, provides secure jobs, and hardly ever bothers them." Further, 79% do not want jobs of greater responsibility; and 91% said they could not think of any information they wanted about the plant or the company. Argyris describes these employees as "apathetic, indifferent and alienated" and as individuals who have lost their maturity. He claims that dealing with immature employees results in managers becoming less mature because they must use "immature leadership patterns (i.e., those that emphasize money and deemphasize human values)."

Argyris further maintains that psychological conditions in this plant and similar conditions in other plants which he has studied "are the natural and logical results of an organizational pattern which places the employee in such a submissive, dependent position—an organizational pattern typical of the great majority of our business enterprises today" (1958, p. 116).

Whether or not we agree with these conclusions, the data presented by Argyris should make us cautious about assuming that all organizational ills are subject to a training remedy. These data also point to the need for further research to develop more adequate means of organization analysis to determine training needs. It should make us even more cautious in spending the company's money on a training program unless there is clear evidence that a training need does exist.

There is, of course, certain housekeeping training which must go on continuously if an efficient work force is to be maintained. But major training efforts to improve quality, reduce costs, or improve the organizational climate of a company are justified only when management is convinced by factual data that training can contribute to the achievement of these organizational goals.

SUMMARY

In brief, training needs must be determined before training starts. The determination of these needs is made through organization analysis, operations analysis, and man analysis.

Organization analysis focuses upon the business enterprise as a whole and consists of the following:

1. a statement of the organization's objectives
2. analysis of human resources
3. analysis of efficiency indices
4. analysis of organizational climate through
   (*a*) indirect indices
   (*b*) direct indices.

The results of steps 2, 3, and 4 are then compared to objectives of the organization as determined in step 1. These comparisons then point to the specific areas in which operations and man analysis are needed.

Operations and man analysis are closely related to each other and to organization analysis. Consequently, they are frequently done concurrently. Operations analysis is discussed in Chapter 3 and man analysis in Chapter 4.

3 OPERATIONS ANALYSIS

WHY OPERATIONS ANALYSIS?

If we are to use training dollars wisely, we must know:

1. where training is needed in the organization
2. of what training should consist
3. who should receive training.

Organization analysis (Chapter 2) is concerned with determining where training is needed in an organization. This chapter is concerned with the problem "of what training should consist." This is the problem of operations analysis.

It is trite to say that a modern builder would not attempt to build even a small house without blueprints and specifications. In spite of its triteness, the analogy is applicable to planning and carrying out a training program for any job in industry. Yet training is frequently initiated and carried out without much consideration as to its content in terms of job requirements. The experienced operator and the seasoned executive are so habituated in their job performances that they are usually unaware of exactly what they do to obtain the results for which they are paid. A supervisor of a group of employees with varying job assignments finds it is impossible to know in detail what each operator does and how he does it. Unless a careful operations analysis of a job is made, it is very easy to overlook critical behavior required by the task and even easier to overlook the details of how the task is performed.

The necessity for a careful operations analysis to indicate critical behavior in training is illustrated in a program to train sewing machine operators. In this job, an operations analysis using motion picture techniques showed that the crucial factor in determining the quantity of production was the rapid positioning of the cloth in the machine. Prior to the operations analysis, emphasis was placed on other aspects of the job in training operators and not on this critical element. Tiffin (1952) emphasized the need for determining the specific behavior required of inspectors if improvement in job performance was to come from training. Charters and Whitley (1924) report that many job duties of an apparently clearcut job are overlooked by experts. Their experts listed 106 duties of a secretary. When 125 secretaries kept a record of their daily activities, the number of different duties increased to 871.

Failure to perform an adequate operations analysis of a job can result in unneeded effort in developing skills or inculcating knowledge which are not essential to the performance of the tasks in a job. It became evident early in World War II, that a person did not have to acquire an aeronautical engineering education to become an effective fighter pilot. Yet, because of uncritical prewar assumptions, there was a continued emphasis on many aspects of aeronautical engineering in the training of aviators. These facts were nice to know but not particularly relevant to flying a military aircraft in combat. Adequate training requires careful blueprints and specifications.

There is a second factor which makes operations analysis a prerequisite to efficient training—the way a job is performed is not necessarily the way it should be performed to make the maximum contribution to the attainment of organizational goals. An analysis of the duties which a supervisor performs, and how he performs these tasks, could well indicate that the job of a supervisor was not constituted in a way which resulted in the desired contribution to organizational goals. In fact, one such analysis has resulted in restructuring certain supervisory jobs in one of the units of one of America's largest corporations.[1] This means that training for supervisors must be planned in terms of the changed nature of their jobs. An operations analysis is necessary to determine whether or not job content is in line with company objectives. Until it is known that the job content is that required from an organizational standpoint, training in the existing content is a waste of time and money.

We could have used the more conventional or widely used term of "job analysis" as a descriptive term for this phase of determining training needs. We have chosen, however, to introduce the term "operations analysis" for three reasons. First, as Kershner (1955) has indicated in his careful review of the literature on job analysis, there is no agreement among experts as to what the term means. Second, job analysis has become associated with many personnel endeavors including selection and placement of personnel, job evaluation, methods improvement, and others, including training. It is our belief that this instrument cannot serve all masters. An adequate job analysis for the purpose of job evaluation rarely furnishes the information needed for training purposes. Third, the product of the traditional job analysis is historical. It shows what the job is now and does not describe the job as it should be if it is to make a maximum contribution to organizational goals. Finally, no provisions are made for describing jobs yet unborn but for which training may be required next week, month, or year. Therefore, we will use the term "operations analysis" and give it specific meaning in a training context.

Operations analysis is the orderly and systematic collection of data about an existing or potential industrial task or a cluster of tasks usually called a "job." Its purpose is to determine just what an employee must be taught in order to perform the task or job so that he contributes maximally to the attainment of organizational goals. An operations analysis will result in the following data concerning a task or a task cluster:

[1] Private communication.

1. standards of performance for the task or job
2. if a task cluster or "job," the identification of the tasks which make up the job
3. how each task is to be performed if standards of performance are to be met
4. the skills, knowledge, and attitudes which are basic to the performance of each task in the required manner.

ELEMENTS OF AN OPERATIONS ANALYSIS

Standards of Performance

Conventional job analysis omits or treats as an afterthought the problem of standards of performance. From a training standpoint, it seems to us that the first step in determining the content of training is finding out the objectives of the task or the job from an organizational standpoint and the standards by which their achievement is to be judged. This step is analogous to that of stating organizational objectives in organization analysis. If the unit of behavior being analyzed is a single task, it can be determined whether or not it is necessary for the achievement of organizational goals and whether or not it should be taught to an employee. If it is a cluster of tasks that are organized into a job, it can be determined if all the tasks are necessary for achieving the purpose of the job in the organization. We can also determine which cluster of subtasks comprise the necessary and sufficient conditions for adequate performance. If we know the standards by which results of performing a task or a job are measured, we are in a better position to know whether or not the task is being performed in a correct manner. This knowledge concerning tasks is a prerequisite for determining the skills, knowledge, and attitudes the employee must acquire if he is to perform the tasks adequately. Furthermore, without standards of performance we have no means of determining whether or not the training provided for the task or job is accomplishing its purpose.

Standards of performance in the majority of production jobs in the operation of machines are usually defined by the machines and machine-man system (Miller, 1955). This is also true of many clerical jobs. Standards would be expressed in terms of units of output of a specific quality in a specified amount of time. Even where operation of machinery is not a part of the job, the concept of a work system, of inputs to the employee and outputs by him in terms of amount, quality, and time, is a reasonably sound basis on which to establish standards for the performance of a task or a task cluster. In this, as well as in a man-machine system, there will always be an element of judgment as to the standards of performance expected. This judgment must ultimately rest on the member of line management who is responsible for the achievement of task objectives and who can relate these results to overall organizational goals.

Identification of Tasks

It is customary in analyzing a job to consider related behaviors which achieve a specific objective as a task. Tasks are frequently the units which are used in instructing employees in the behaviors required to meet the standards of the job. For example, in the job of spinner there are tasks which are known as "creeling," "piecing up," "patrolling," "cleaning," etc. In the job of a retail store salesman are such tasks as "showing merchandise," "persuading the customer," "taking stock," "writing up and registering sales," and many others. The job of a supervisor includes not only "giving instruction to employees" but also "planning work assignments," "reviewing payrolls," "improving methods," and many others.

If an employee is to be taught to perform a job satisfactorily, it is necessary to know what tasks constitute the job. It is also necessary to know the relationship of the correct performance of these tasks to the standards for the job in order that proper emphasis may be placed on them in teaching the task. "Closing a sale," for example, might be much more significant in achieving the purpose of the job of a salesman than "making out an expense account." "Securing cooperation of employees" may be a more significant part of a foreman's job than "requisitioning employees from personnel." An adequate operations analysis not only lists the tasks involved in performing a job but also gives some indication as to the relative critical nature of the various tasks.

It should be emphasized that the simple listing of tasks which have become part of the job would contribute little or nothing to achieving the purpose of operations analysis. There may be tasks which were initially important but are no longer necessary because of changes in the operations of which the job is a part. In determining what tasks should constitute a job, the individual who makes the operations analysis should constantly be aware of the necessity of relating tasks observed to the job standards.

Space does not permit us to explore at any length how a given task becomes a part of a job or how a given cluster of tasks is designated as a job. From the available evidence, tasks become associated as a job through engineering considerations, custom, and perhaps sheer chance (Davis and Canter, 1955). Carefully planned experimental investigation as a basis for determining optimum job structure in terms of organizational goals is the exception rather than the rule (Marks, 1958). The task of training employees, however, would be lightened if we knew more about the proper task structure for jobs in industrial organizations. It is possible that one of the earlier steps in an operations analysis is that of securing data derived from experimental procedures on this important question of job design.

How Each Task Must Be Performed—Job Methods

The next step in an operations analysis, after that of task determination, is to obtain an adequate description of how each task should be performed. It is not adequate to indicate merely that a weaver must start up a loom or that a machinist set up a lathe or that a sewer hem a sheet. The actual steps required to perform these operations must be determined as well as the order in which this behavior must occur.

This is also true in analyzing supervisory and managerial jobs. It is not enough for training purposes to say that a foreman is required to maintain discipline among his work force. It is necessary to know what procedures the foreman is to follow in maintaining discipline and in performing his other duties. Furthermore, if we simply assume that a manager is required to make a decision on whether or not to buy a certain piece of equipment, we are overlooking the fact that in decision making there are specific steps in collecting and evaluating data.

In operations analysis it cannot be assumed that just because a task is performed in a specific way, this is the most efficient way of doing the task. It sometimes seems as if human beings have an affinity for doing things the hard way. If the hard way accomplishes the purpose of the task, the response is reinforced each time it is repeated. It soon becomes the individual's habitual way of responding to the task situation. In many industrial situations the way an individual performs a given task, within certain limits, is left up to him. Sometimes he stumbles upon the most effective way of performing the task. More frequently his performance of the task falls very short in employing methods which are the most efficient for achieving the task objectives. It is essential in this phase of operations analysis to determine what methods are optimum.

We are not, however, advocates of "the one best method" concept. People differ and so do they when they become employees. Methods which are efficient for one employee may be inefficient for other employees unless they are modified in some way. Yet in developing a training plan for a job it is necessary to establish a certain best way for the majority of trainees to perform a task. Modification of the best way to fit the individual characteristics of a specific employee is the prerequisite of good instruction and of effective supervision.

Skills, Knowledge, and Attitudes

Operations analysis is by no means complete with the statement of the tasks which constitute a job; more is required than a description of the proper methods used in performing the task. Underlying the performance of each task in a job are skills, knowledge, and attitudes which the employee must either have or acquire. As we have indicated earlier, the development and modification of these human capabilities and sentiments are a part of training. A thorough operations analysis indicates what skills, what knowledge, and what attitudes must be developed in an employee if he is to perform a given task or tasks. It also must indicate the degree to which a skill must be developed and the amount of knowledge required if economy in training is to be achieved. Overtraining, as well as undertraining, is costly.

This point can be illustrated by examining the following items taken from a job description of an engine lathe operator:

5. Shapes cutting tools to correct contour, *angle of rake,* and clearance by holding and manipulating them against the surfaces of a power grinder. Checks the grinding of each tool with a scale to determine the correct shape for the kind of cut and kind of metal for which the tool is to be used. (3–5%)

6. Lubricates and cleans the lathe parts and accessories as required to keep bearing surfaces working smoothly and to insure that all lathe surfaces and parts for tools are free from metal chips, grit and grease (U. S. Employment Service, 1946, p. 90).

It is obvious that, although the description of these two tasks may be adequate for the purpose of job evaluation and similar personnel administrative functions, it does not furnish sufficient information for designing training. We need to know just what responses must be developed and to what extent so that the tools are held against the surface of the power grinder with the right pressure and at the correct angle. Furthermore, we need to know just how much information about lubrication is required of the operator in order to train him to avoid errors of excessive or insufficient lubrication. We need some indication as to the necessary attitudes toward quantity, quality, and safety if these tasks are to be performed efficiently.

A similar problem is presented in the statement taken from a job description of a foreman:

Selects and places on jobs in his department employees who can perform their tasks efficiently or who can learn to perform the job tasks efficiently in a reasonable amount of time.

This is primarily a matter of determining what knowledge the foreman must have to make decisions concerning the suitability of an applicant for a specific job in his department. There are also elements of skill in decision making which may have to be taught. In addition, the foreman's decisions will be influenced by his attitudes not only toward applicants in general but also toward the source referring applicants, training employees, cost control, and many other factors in operating his department.

Adequate training for this single task can be planned only with specific data as to the skills, knowledge, and attitudes required to perform the task in terms of the job standards for a foreman.

OPERATIONS ANALYSIS FOR JOBS AT VARIOUS LEVELS IN AN INDUSTRIAL ORGANIZATION

We are taking the position that an operations analysis is the initial step in determining the content and nature of training for any industrial job. From practical experience we know that line personnel will not quibble too much about making such an analysis for production jobs such as weavers, millwrights, inspectors, and similar jobs. Yet, when it is suggested that a similar analysis be made of complex jobs such as plant manager, vice president in charge of purchasing, or company treasurer, business administrators usually consider this analysis as either unneeded or too complex. Admittedly, the process of making an operations analysis of a vice president's job is more complex than analyzing the job of mimeograph operator. Yet the basic ingredients of each of these jobs from a company standpoint are the same. Each job has, or should have, a reason for existing and a standard of performance as a basis for judging its contributions to the company's goals. Each job is made up of a series of units or tasks. Each task in both of these jobs requires for its performance certain skills, definite knowledge, and specific attitudes. The development time for each job is different. The skills, knowledge, and attitudes are different. Yet these are present in the job of the vice president and the job of the mimeograph operator. The results of analyzing these jobs in terms of the finished product will be more voluminous for a vice president than for the mimeograph operator. Yet this analysis is needed if adequate training is to be planned and implemented. Since it is possible that the results of a vice president's job behavior may have more direct and lasting influence on the achievement of organizational goals than the job behavior of a mimeograph operator, it is even more important to plan and carry out training for the higher level than for the lower level job. Of course, in some organizations vice presidents are above training and are the product of "Topsyism."

Yet where upper level jobs are subject to the influence of training, a prerequisite to an adequate training program is an adequate operations analysis.

Operations analysis of jobs at the production, clerical, technical, supervisory, and executive levels in an organization, may be simplified to some extent by the use of multiple factor analysis. If a common factor such as "mechanical comprehension" exists in jobs such as machinist, millwright, electrician, provisions for developing this comprehension can be made in the training for all of these jobs. Although the work of Fleishman and his associates is primarily concerned with psychomotor performance on tests used in the Air Force, it is suggestive of the kind of analysis which might be made in carrying out an operations analysis (Fleishman and Hempel, 1956).

PROCEDURES FOR AN OPERATIONS ANALYSIS

Generally, the techniques used in conventional job analysis are the ones which will be used in making an operations analysis. Horst (1941), Thorndike (1949), Ghiselli and Brown (1955), among others, have classified these methods into several categories. These categories may be reduced to the following:

1. review of literature concerning the job
2. performing the job
3. observing the job
4. asking questions about the job.

Before discussing these commonly used techniques, we should indicate the limitations in our presentation. Little exists in research investigation which deals with the validity or reliability of these methods when used either in conventional job analysis or for an operations analysis. The lack of attention to reliability and validity of methods used for job analysis is indeed surprising since as Kershner (1955) has indicated "for roughly the last forty-five years job analysis activities have taken on an increasing importance for a variety of personnel, counseling, and manpower functions." The few research investigations of these methods available are concerned with their use for omnibus job analysis purposes and not specifically for training purposes. The lack of research on methods of job analysis for training purposes was pointed out by one of the authors over ten years ago (McGehee, 1949). A careful search of published research on training since that time indicates little or no change in this situation.

Therefore, we will be forced to express opinions concerning the various methods used in making an operations analysis. These opinions are based both on our experience with certain of these techniques as well as the opinions of other users.

Review of Literature and Performing the Job

An examination of the first two methods makes it clear that they are really supplementary rather than primary methods of securing data for an operations analysis. Review of the literature concerning a job serves two purposes. It can furnish an analyst clues as to what to observe in a job and what questions to ask about a job. It can assist the analyst in understanding what he has observed and the answers he has received to his questions. Even here, the literature concerning a job may have some limitations if the job is highly technical and complex. It may be so technical that only an expert can understand it. Yet reviews of existing manuals, descriptions of machinery and equipment, operating procedures, and even job descriptions written for purposes other than training may give the analyst some insight into the job he would not have gained otherwise.

Performing the job may not seem to be as clearly a supplementary procedure as a literature review. It would seem that ideally the most effective way of determining what tasks make up a job would come from actually doing the job. Practically, performing the job in order to analyze it has certain serious limitations. Except for relatively simple jobs, the learning time required to master many jobs would be prohibitive both in time and expense. Higher level jobs require much training both within and outside the company in order to perform them. A research chemist, for example, must have something more than a casual acquaintance with the subject of chemistry. Furthermore, the opportunity to learn a job by performing becomes more limited the higher the job is placed in the industrial hierarchy. A company vice president would probably object to being replaced by an analyst just so the analyst could analyze his job.

Certainly, where an individual can be found who knows a job from performing it and who can do an acceptable analysis, his talents should be used. Even here his expertness in the job may lead him to overlook critical aspects of the job. Despite this limitation, from some experience we have had analyzing jobs for training purposes at the operator level, we believe that performing certain critical tasks has given us a better understanding of what the operator must learn to perform the tasks adequately. When it is possible, an operations analyst can profit from trying to perform certain aspects of the job which he is analyzing. Yet even here there is no research evidence that either a literature review or performing the job results in increased reliability and validity of the analysis.

OBSERVING THE JOB

It should be made clear that we are discussing job observation and asking questions about a job separately for convenience in dealing with these methods. In practice, they are frequently used together and complement each other. Some observation of a job is usually necessary if the analyst is to ask meaningful questions. Similarly, the analyst, in observing most jobs, must ask questions to understand exactly what is taking place. Unaided observation, except when used by an individual with a great deal of familiarity with the job, leaves unanswered many questions as to what is happening.

In general, there seem to be two plans for observing a job: one, the continuous method; the other, a sampling method. In the first method, the analyst observes the job continuously over a given period of time—an hour, a day, a week, or a month. The sampling method, on the other hand, is a planned system of observation usually of relative short duration, randomized over several days, weeks, or months and over several employees performing the same job.

It has been our experience that, except in the case of relatively simple jobs, the continuous method is a time consuming procedure and is less likely to detect the rare but crucial tasks which do not occur hourly or daily in the job. For example, in the weaving of rugs the weaver is required occasionally to make what is called a "pick out." This occurs when the yarn making up the woof of the cloth breaks and is not caught until the needle travels the width of the rug. A weaver might be observed continuously for weeks before this occurs. A careful sampling of a large number of weavers is more likely to reveal this task than is the continuous observation of one or two weavers.

Work Sampling

The sampling plan also lends itself to the observation of jobs at the technical and managerial level where it would be very difficult to make continuous observation. Certain tasks in technical and managerial jobs may occur daily. Yet many tasks occur at irregular intervals. To isolate and study the major tasks in a high level job might require continuous observations over many months. The job incumbent, who might not object to the occasional observation of his activities, certainly would develop a certain amount of antipathy to the presence of an observer over a relatively long period of time.

Work sampling must be planned carefully both in terms of the number of observations, the length of each observation, and the time schedule for making the observations. If a foreman is observed each morning only at 8:10 A.M., little would be added to our knowledge of the tasks which he performs during the rest of the day. There is also some point in the observation process at which nothing new is being observed. In some types of jobs, observation of a few minutes at a time may prove the most efficient procedure; in long-cycle jobs or jobs of a technical or managerial nature, long periods of observation would be indicated. The interested reader will find an excellent treatment of the entire problem of work sampling by Barnes (1957).

An application of work sampling to the problems of supervisory job behavior has been made recently in the General Electric Company (1957). Although the primary purpose was not to determine job content for training, the study has direct implications for the use of this method not only in determining what first line supervisors do on the job and how they perform these tasks, but also for determining the more effective methods used by these foremen in furthering the achievement of organizational goals. As was indicated earlier, we believe operations analysis should be concerned not only with how a job is now being done but also with how a job should be done in terms of maximum contribution to the advancement of company objectives. This type of analysis gives a lead to improving job performance by determining how the job can be performed in a more effective manner.

Since the General Electric study illustrates various problems in observing jobs in order to analyze their content, we will present it in some detail. From approximately 100 first and second shift production foremen, the 12 highest rated and the 12 lowest rated day-shift foremen were selected for detailed observational study. Designation as highest or lowest rated foremen was on the basis of a composite of four criteria. Each of the 24 foremen was observed during eight 2-hour periods. The total 16 hours of observation were spread over a 4-month period "to assure a representative sampling of each foreman's on-the-job activities." The observer was an individual who had just completed an assignment as a manufacturing foreman.

The procedures used in making the observations and the estimation of the adequacy of the observations can best be described in the language of the report:

> The observer followed closely each foreman and made detailed notes as to the nature of all activities and the duration of time encompassed by each activity.
>
> The foremen, who had been told the general purpose of the study, were asked to follow their normal procedures and, as much as possible, to ignore the presence of the observer. While a few observation periods had to be repeated because the observer felt that his presence had significantly changed the foremen's behavior, for the most part the "velocity of work" in the foremen's jobs did not allow them to alter their usual patterns of activity.
>
> It is felt that the behavior reported here is a truly representative sampling of these 24 foremen's normal on-the-job activities. A comparison of data collected during even-numbered observation periods with that collected during odd-numbered periods indicated that this

sampling of foreman-behavior had a high degree of reliability and stability.

In order to check on the accuracy with which the observer was able to analyze and record the observed foreman-behavior, nine of the 24 foremen were observed by the regular observer and, simultaneously but independently by a second observer. Close agreement between the two independent observers indicated a high degree of reliability for this method of observation.

In order to identify *effective foreman-behavior* and to investigate the role of the foreman as a *communication link* in the manufacturing process, the following information was coded and recorded by the observer each time the foreman changed activity:

I. *Topic of Activity* in which the foreman was actually engaged, such as establishing job priority, determining work progress or job status, working on production schedules or production records, dealing with some aspect of personnel administration or health and safety, etc.

II. *Foreman Contacts*—the people who contacted or were contacted by the foreman in the performance of his job. These included personnel from service groups, management personnel, employees reporting to him directly and functionally, etc.

III. *Initiation of Contacts*—was the contact initiated by the foreman or another party?

IV. *Reason for Communication Flow*—did the foreman request information, was information requested from the foreman, or was information volunteered without request by either party?

V. *Nature of Flow of Communication*—did the information flow primarily from the foreman to the person contacted or from the other person to the foreman, or did a true two-way exchange result from the contact?

VI. *Nature of Work Direction and Communication to Foreman's Own Employees*—did the foreman issue a specific work order, did he explain "why" something was to be done, did he issue a general work order delegating the details of planning and carrying it out to the employee, or did he pass on information solely to keep his people informed?

In addition to the above, certain biographical and background information was gathered on each foreman (General Electric Co., 1957, pp. 7–10).

The results of this study are incidental to our purpose of illustrating the use of sampling in observation of behavior on a job. It is interesting to note, however, that the more effective foremen engaged in fewer activities, spent more time on planning, and spent more time with staff or service personnel than did the less effective foremen.

Certain aspects of this study, however, are pertinent to analyzing job content by observation. First, sampling was used effectively. Second, it was believed, although no final evidence was available, that the behavior of the foremen observed was not markedly modified by the presence of an observer. Finally, there is some evidence as to the reliability of this sampling method, that is, comparison of results of even and odd numbered observation periods and agreement between independent observers. This study suggests that a similar type of investigation could be used effectively in an operations analysis at both the operator level and at higher levels in a company.[2]

Recording Observations

An operations analysis by observation can be made by having an observer present who records the tasks performed and how they are performed. The same analysis may be made by obtaining a permanent record of task performance through motion pictures or similar recording techniques. Each of these procedures has its advantages and disadvantages. Neither is equally efficient in all types of jobs found in an industrial situation.

Individual jobs at the operator level which have short cycle, high speed elements are difficult for an observer on the scene to analyze. Micromotion techniques, other motion picture techniques, or other recording devices [3] provide records which can be analyzed at a slower tempo than the tasks actually occur. The tasks can be reviewed until an adequate analysis is made. Such recording techniques are applicable, however, only when the main object of analysis is that of perceptual motor responses. Furthermore, taking motion pictures of job behavior can be an expensive process, and their analysis is usually time consuming.

[2] An earlier observation study of job content although not using strictly sampling techniques also suggests the same conclusion. See Wallace and Gallagher (1952). Also see Wirdenius (1958) for a detailed description of methodology in time-sampling study of supervisors.

[3] Lindahl's work (1945) is an example of a graphic analysis technique which indicates how a task is being performed.

The same problems of interpretation when using an observer on the scene arise when using recording devices. The resulting operations analysis depends not only on adequate recording of the job by the device used but also on the adequate interpretation of the records by a human observer. The problems of validity and reliability of the analysis of job content when using records does not vanish automatically because the analysis was made by viewing the product of a camera.

Certain jobs can be analyzed by observation only by having an observer on the scene. These jobs as a rule have a minimum of perceptual motor skills and invoke a maximum of covert as opposed to overt activity. The job of a first-line supervisor is one example of the type of job which can be analyzed by observation only by having an observer on the scene. This is true also of the laboratory technician, the private secretary, the development engineer, and in fact, the majority of white-collar jobs.

Many blue-collar jobs which have long cycle elements, which do not proceed at an extremely high tempo, or which require relatively simple perceptual motor activity, can be analyzed more economically by having an observer present than by the use of an elaborate recording apparatus. Most mechanical trouble-shooting and repair jobs are of this type as well as jobs which are essentially machine watching and servicing.

It is possible in certain jobs that a combination of recording by machines and using an observer would be the most economical way of analyzing a job. An example of this would be the job of a spinner in a textile mill. The various tasks could be determined by an observer. Those which require gross bodily movement such as cleaning, putting up roving, creeling, and patrolling could be analyzed by an observer on the spot. One task of the spinner called "piecing up" is, however, a very short, complex, perceptual motor response sequence. Adequate analysis of this aspect of the spinner's job would require micromotion or some similar form of recording the movement sequence of the task.

Generally, therefore, whether a job is analyzed by an on-the-spot observer, by analysis of films, or through other recording devices will depend entirely on the nature of the job to be analyzed. Regardless of the method used, we are confronted with the related problem of the effect of the observer upon the performance of the job. Time study observers make the assumption that job behavior either remains the same or can be adjusted by leveling for differences due to the observer's presence. This is simply an assumption and in absence of proof is a highly questionable assumption. There is no evidence concerning what is added to or omitted from a job that may be crucial to quality, waste, or other aspects when the operator is being observed. At the supervisory level, human relations may become more human if the foreman is under observation. The problem of consistency of behavior on the job when a person is being observing is the heart of the validity problem of this type of analysis. A valid analysis secures accurate information as to what the employee does on the job. This problem needs careful attention to determine the conditions under which an observer, human or mechanical, does or does not change job behavior significantly.

At our present state of knowledge, we can only try to assure that the presence of an observer does not change job behavior by carefully structuring the observation situation. A full explanation of the purpose of the observer, a concise indication of the possible effects of the observer's presence on the employees in the future, and circumspect behavior on the part of the observer should help to reduce to a minimum deviations in job behavior.

ASKING QUESTIONS ABOUT THE JOB

Asking questions about a job in an operations analysis can be done in several ways. These ways, however, narrow down to essentially two: 1. interviews with job incumbents or others who know the job content and 2. questionnaires. It is not pertinent to our problem to discuss techniques of interviewing or the construction of questionnaires. The interested reader is referred to standard texts on these subjects.[4] Both the interview and questionnaire approach on the surface would seem more economical in time than either observing a job or performing it. Yet these methods are limited by the capacity of the respondents to make

[4] Among others: Kahn and Cannell (1957) and Payne (1951).

accurate and full responses to the questions asked.[5] Furthermore, these methods would not seem to be capable of eliciting the type of information which could be secured from a micromotion analysis of a job in which there were complicated perceptual motor responses. On the other hand, it would seem that the interview and the questionnaire methods would have certain advantages in the analysis of jobs in which there was a minimum of overt activity *and* where the job incumbents were endowed with fair verbal facility.

Unfortunately, there is a lack of research on the validity or reliability of either interviews or questionnaires in an operations analysis. An extrapolation from data on the validity and reliability of these two methods, as used for purposes other than analysis of job content, would lead us to be wary about blindly accepting the job-content data secured by these methods.

It is entirely possible that we are belaboring this point too much. As pointed out earlier, it is rare that any one method is used alone. The real problem is not the relative reliability and validity of an interview or questionnaire alone. It is rather a question of how reliable and valid a given method of operations analysis is for a given job. The method could be any possible combination of variations in the four basic methods listed earlier.

Combination of Methods

Recently a series of investigations was completed which deal with the relative utility of certain techniques used to ask questions about jobs. Although the results of these studies may be limited to the organization in which they were made and the jobs studied, they indicate the type of research needed to evaluate all forms of job analysis. These studies were conducted in the Air Force and concerned analysis of 16 jobs judged to be representative of the different Air Force career fields (Rupe, 1952; 1955a; 1955b; 1956). The methods used were: questionnaire-survey; group interview; individual interview; observation interview; and, technical conference. The analyses of these jobs were made by noncommissioned personnel trained in the task of job

[5] See Chapter 2 for related comments on the strengths and weaknesses of interviews and questionnaires.

analysis. A careful experimental design was followed so that no one method had an advantage over any other method due to analyst, job, and circumstances of conducting the analysis.

The relative adequacy of the various methods was determined in terms of data yielded by each method with regard to: 1. work performed in carrying out the job; 2. equipment, machinery, and material used; 3. skills, knowledge, and physical requirements of the job. In addition, these methods were compared in terms of costs as estimated by the amount of time required of analyst, job incumbents, and their supervisors for securing or giving the job information. An exhaustive statistical analysis of the data secured was made and the investigators arrived at the following conclusions:

1. None of the methods provided enough information on skills, knowledge, and physical requirements to justify comparison of the effectiveness of the five methods used.

2. All five methods were about equal in furnishing data on machines, equipment, and materials used on the jobs. The investigators suggest these data might be obtained more effectively and/or less expensively by other methods such as stock lists.

3. As to cost, the questionnaire survey was the least expensive, the technical conference the most expensive. The remaining three methods listed in terms of increasing costs were group interview, individual interview, and observation interview.

4. In terms of effectiveness in reporting work activities, the least effective was the group interview. The questionnaire survey was the least consistent and ranked fourth in effectiveness. The individual interview and the technical conference were equal in effectiveness. The individual interview was the most consistent and most effective method in reporting work activities. It's cost was about the average of the five methods.

5. In the military situation, the analysts differed more in effectiveness than did the methods used.

The final conclusion is of particular interest to us because it bears on the question of reliability of the various methods. Rupe does not resolve the question as to whether or not the analysts in this study were competent or whether the instruments used lacked the basic characteristics which make for reliability. It is evident from his description of the training of these analysts that they were selected carefully, motivated, and trained to the extent that job analysts were customarily trained in the Air Force. It appears, however, that Rupe considered the methods as having unreliable elements which rendered them of questionable value for ordinary job analysis activities in the Air Force. In fact, he advocates the development of a method which consists of a check list survey method of job analysis. Although he advances forceful reasons for the use of this technique, he offers no empirical evidence as to its superiority over the methods which he had investigated. Even more disturbing, from a training standpoint, is the failure of these methods to produce adequate data on the skills and knowledge required for performance of the jobs studied.

It is true, of course, that this investigation was carried out in a military situation and on jobs which in civilian life would be either blue-collar or low level white-collar jobs. We would be rash if we generalized these conclusions to private industry as a whole or even to jobs at comparable levels in private industry. These studies do suggest, however, that the usual question techniques for analyzing jobs should not be accepted as reliable instruments just because they are in common use. They also suggest that additional research on question methods as well as on other methods is imperative if we are to know what degree of dependence can be placed on currently used methods of analyzing jobs.

Critical Incident

Flanagan (1954) has introduced a refinement to the method of asking questions about a job which is pertinent to operations analysis. This technique "consists of a set of procedures for collecting direct observations of human behavior" in various situations. Generally, the technique is to ask competent observers to describe the behavior of persons performing tasks which make a real difference in effective task performance. An incident to be considered critical "must occur in a situation where the purpose or intent of the act seems fairly clear to the observer and where its consequences are sufficiently definite to leave little doubt concerning its effects" (p. 327).

The critical incident technique can be used for many purposes other than operations analysis. Its major value here is that it focuses on those aspects of the job where performance is of a make or break nature. It relegates nonessential aspects of the job to a minor position and concentrates on the vital tasks in the job. The critical incident approach could also define research programs aimed at determining whether or not the behaviors are indeed critical. As Kershner (1955) has pointed out, the use of critical incidents in job analysis does not automatically solve the problem of the validity of the analysis. A necessary step in establishing validity of the results of a critical incident job analysis is validation of the results against some measures of criticalness other than the judgment of the observers who supply the incidents.

The discussion of the critical incident technique leads to the suggestion that an additional method of operations analysis would result, perhaps, in more valid and practical results if its use became widespread in industry. This is what might be called an experimental approach to operations analysis. Let us assume that certain outcomes are expected from a job and that there are standards to determine the degree to which these outcomes are secured. Assume further that this job could consist of tasks 1, 2, 3, 4, 5 or tasks 1′, 2′, 3′, 4′, 5′. Experimental operations analysis would then consist in having the job performed by competent incumbents with one group using task sequence 1 to 5 and the other group task sequence 1′ to 5′. Comparison of outcomes against standards for the two groups should give a more adequate answer as to what tasks should constitute the job than any of the methods discussed previously. The same approach could be used in determining not only the tasks which should constitute a job but also the methods for performing these tasks. This is drinking "Scotch mists" as far as the present day approach to operations analysis is concerned. But someday, somewhere, this approach may become practical when experimentation in the field of social behavior becomes as respectable as it now is in producing ICBM's.

Consumer Research and Operations Analysis

Thus far, we have been concerned with the problem of asking job incumbents or their supervisors about the content of a job. For jobs in which there is contact with others who receive the services of the job incumbent, we can ask questions of the recipients. In sales situations, for example, we can ask the public about the specific behavior of sales people which pleased them, displeased them, led to a purchase, led to a cancellation of an order, led to a refusal to buy, etc. Nuckols (Life Insurance Agency Management Assoc., 1959) has conducted consumer research which points out a number of things salesmen do which create a favorable impression on the public. In addition, by carefully comparing life insurance holdings, plans to purchase in the future, and the nature of previous contacts by life insurance agents, he has come up with specific recommendations as to sales and advertising approaches which would most likely lead to the purchase of life insurance (Life Insurance Agency Management Assoc., 1959; Nuckols, 1959). He found that people whose present holdings, needs, social security benefits, etc., had been analyzed and a definite program had been explained to them had two characteristics which differentiated them from those who had not received this service: (1) they carried more life insurance and (2) they had set higher insurance ownership goals for themselves. In addition, those respondents whose present ownership fell far short of their goals were more likely to state that they planned to buy additional insurance in the future than those whose present ownership came close to their goal. On the basis of these results, Nuckols recommends a "programming" approach to the sale of life insurance and a consideration of public relations campaigns which would raise the ownership goals of the public.

This research and its interpretation illustrates a number of points concerning the use of consumer research in determining job content. First, we need not rely on the simple answers to single direct questions in analyzing data from this source. An examination of the interrelationships of responses to several questions can supply fruitful hypotheses as to the most appropriate job content. This point leads to the second. We must be cautious in examining these interrelationships and realize that a high relationship between responses to two items does not necessarily mean that one causes the other. Nuckols (1959), for example, points out that the positive relationship between having been programmed and insurance ownership is not necessarily a causal one. Both of these factors could be related to another variable which causes each. However, the discovery of these interrelationships leads to a number of interesting hypotheses which can be investigated through a longitudinal or experimental approach to the problem.

In the use of consumer responses in operations analysis there are other problems, however—validity of responses, reliability of questions, interviewer bias, sample construction, and others. Readers concerned with jobs of consumer contact might well refer to Jahoda, Deutsch, and Cook (1951) for a detailed discussion of the limitations of consumer research techniques.

SPECIFYING SKILLS, KNOWLEDGE, AND ATTITUDE

Too frequently, when the usual analysis is completed for a job, only two kinds of information result:

1. the tasks which constitute the job
2. how these tasks are to be performed.

For example, an analysis of the job of a weaver would consist in indicating that the job was made up of (1) starting up the looms, (2) stopping the looms, (3) patrolling the loom set, and (4) recognizing defective weaving. A statement of how to start up a loom would be as follows: "start loom with lay on back center. To get on back center turn hand wheel but be sure the cylinder is not turned. Pull brake hand to release brake. Pull shipper handle."

This type of data is probably sufficient for most administrative purposes. It is not sufficient for an adequate operations analysis. In training, we are trying to develop or modify skills, knowledge, and attitudes. In order to do this, we must know just what skills are required to make the motions required "to get on back center" and to "pull brake handle." We need to know what knowledge is required to make the decisions necessary to start up the loom. Likewise, we need to know what attitudes toward quality, safety, supervision, and other aspects of employment are necessary if the employee is to become an efficient worker.

Gagné (1955) has pointed out that the crucial problem in analyzing a job for training purposes is describing the job in a manner that is meaningful for the persons who are planning and conducting training. Gagné further states that many schemes for analyzing jobs fail to use concepts which are meaningful, unambiguous, and convenient:

Let me give two examples of descriptive terms which are inadequate in one way or another. There is one school of thought which makes immediate inferences from observations to underlying abilities. According to this method, jobs are described in terms of *abilities,* such as numerical facility, verbal fluency, color vision, ability to recall details. These terms are not readily understandable, they are subject to different interpretations and they are not reliable (from job to job, that is). The presence of colored signals in a job situation does not immediately prove that color vision is involved. One must, in fact, return to the observable behavior before deciding this. If the job requires the individual to discriminate colored signals, that is one thing; if he must react to the presence of light regardless of color, that is quite another. The point is that the decision is made on the basis of a behavioral description; the word "discriminate" is crucial here. Furthermore, if the job is initially described in terms of color vision, it is quite apparent that one cannot get back to the original behavior from such a description.

Another descriptive method is, if anything, older. This is the one used in motion and time study, which employs such terms as "Transport loaded," "Transport empty," and so on. This method meets all the criteria except one. It is convenient, understandable, reliable. Unfortunately, it is behaviorally meaningless, as many psychologists have long realized. Essentially, it is a physical description of movement, which provides no indication of the behavior involved at the beginning and end of these movements. The woman who pushes a lever forward to start the washing machine may perform a physical movement highly similar to that made by a helicopter pilot in changing the pitch of his rotor blades. But the *behavior* which begins and terminates these physical movements is very different (Gagné, 1955).

He suggests that the description of the behavior required in task performance in terms of the following requirements would give the training specialist specific guides as to the training required: discrimination, recall, use of symbols, decision making, and motor skills.

Gagné is concerned primarily with jobs of production or maintenance employees. The same schema for describing other jobs at the clerical, supervisory, technical, and executive level might be adequate and practical with some elaboration. A supervisor, in handling a discipline problem, is required to exhibit behavior which can be described in terms of discrimination, recall, use of symbols, and decision making. Motor skills in this instance probably would be at a minimum. The decision of an executive to promote or not promote a given subordinate also could be described in similar categories.

It is in translating the task into meaningful behavioral patterns that the training specialist can make one of his major contributions to industrial training. If he can describe the job requirements in terms of behavior such as discriminating or using verbal symbols, he can establish specific things which must be learned. He can then see that the training is so organized that the employee has a maximum opportunity to develop the responses required by the job. This requirement for the training specialist will lead to developing skills, knowledge, and even attitudes among this group of industrial employees which today are noticeably absent. Furthermore, if the managers of enterprises required the ability to analyze tasks into meaningful behavior components as a prerequisite for activity in industrial training, training specialists without this ability would be conspicuously absent from the field of industrial training.

SUMMARY

Operations analysis is the procedure for determining (1) what tasks constitute a job, (2) how these tasks are to be performed, and (3) what behavior is required of an employee in order to perform the tasks as specified. It is the blueprint for organizing and conducting training for a specific job.

In spite of the critical nature of the data secured by an operations analysis for effective training, scant research has gone into developing and evaluating methods for securing this type of information. Research is needed to establish a theoretical foundation for operations analysis. It also is needed to develop valid and reliable instruments for this purpose.

Finally, the training specialist needs to become aware of the contribution to efficient training that can be made by reliable and valid operations analysis. Furthermore, he needs to convince line management that operations analysis is a major prerequisite for sound training for any job.

4 MAN ANALYSIS

In the preceding chapters, we have discussed two steps in determining training needs and planning for the economical use of the training dollar. Organization analysis and operations analysis are essential first steps if we are to focus our training efforts upon the individual who is the recipient of any training—the employee. He is the learner; it is he who will modify his behavior either to meet, or to circumvent, organizational requirements. The final step in determining training needs, man analysis, is directed toward finding out (1) whether the individual employee requires training and (2) what training he requires. It is focused directly on the individual employee.

SUMMARY AND DIAGNOSTIC MAN ANALYSIS

Man analysis is concerned, first, with determining how well a specific employee is carrying out the tasks which constitute his job. Second, it is concerned with determining what skills must be developed, what knowledge acquired, and what attitudes engendered if he is to improve his job performance. It may also include determining what new skills, knowledge, and attitudes are required if an individual is to perform a new or different job. The term, summary man analysis, will be used when we are concerned with determining on a global basis how well an employee is performing his job. When dealing with skills, knowledge, and attitudes, we shall refer to diagnostic man analysis. Diagnostic man analysis concerns two things: (1) determining the specific quality of behavior of the individual in the job situation leading to his performance and (2) the extent of this behavior must be changed to meet the requirements of the job as defined by organizational goals.

Man analysis, and especially diagnostic man analysis, is the most difficult phase of determining training needs. The difficulties of man analysis arise, in the first place, from the nature of the activities which must be measured. It is trite, of course, to say that human behavior is complex. Yet this complexity becomes even more evident when an attempt is made to obtain accurate measures of a person's skill, knowledge, or attitudes.

Diagnostic man analysis, if anything, is more complex than summary man analysis. We are not just asking what are the results of an employee's performance, but why these results occur. We are trying to determine the degree of skill possessed, the amount of knowledge available, and the specific attitudes involved. Furthermore, we need to know whether poor performance of a task is the result of insufficient skill or knowledge or some other factor which determines the quality of behavior. Merely securing a summary measure of job performance may seem a reasonably easy task until we realize that we need to know the nature of the job performance directly attributable to the individual and not contaminated by the many factors which are beyond his control.

Compounding the problems of making accurate man analyses is the fact that the measurement of a given person's job behavior usually has to be made by another person. Supervisors and managers are fairly free with unrecorded judgments of both subordinates and superiors. However, they show a certain reluctance in making precise, recorded judgments. It is entirely possible, as McGregor (1957) contends in discussing performance appraisals, that the reluctance arises from an "unwillingness to treat human beings like physical objects." We suspect, however, that the reluctance to appraise and examine closely the job performance of employees at all levels arises from some other source than this unwillingness. First, no continuing and constant demand is made on a supervisor by his superior that he furnish objective measures of the performance of his subordinates. Second, the individuals who should make concise man analyses usually have received only minimal training in performing this managerial task. They have acquired only small skill in performing this difficult assignment. Finally, techniques of measurement in this area are not precise. Caution in utilizing those techniques available is laudable but crudeness of available techniques should not serve as an excuse for avoiding this basic managerial task and retreating into vague generalities about employee job behavior.

TIMING OF MAN ANALYSIS

Both summary and diagnostic man analysis should be automatic and continuous during the period an employee is learning a new task or new methods of performing the tasks which constitute his job. There is ample evidence that immediate knowledge of results facilitates learning.[1] Delay in correction of mistakes and emphasizing correct behavior can result in establishing habits which persist and result in ineffective job behavior. Once an employee has reached an acceptable level of performance, man analysis is required from a training standpoint only when there are indications that his job performance has retrogressed or there is a change in the standards of performance expected of him. However, from the standpoint of sound personnel administration, and for determining whether or not an employee is making his maximum contribution to the organization, a summary man analysis should be made periodically. The summary analysis will then indicate whether or not a diagnostic man analysis is necessary.

[1] See Chapter 6.

METHODS OF MAN ANALYSIS

The methods of man analysis can be classified in three major categories:

1. objective records of job performance
2. devised situational measures
3. observational measures.

It will be obvious to the reader that methods used for man analysis can assist in organization analysis and operations analysis. For example, data on amount of production when secured from departments in an organization can indicate where training is needed, that is, organization analysis. The same data when secured on individual employees in a department can be a basis for man analysis. Techniques for observing a job when directed toward discovering job content can be used for operations analysis. The same techniques when focused on an individual employee to determine how he performs the tasks of his job can be used for man analysis.

OBJECTIVE RECORDS OF JOB PERFORMANCE

Any job which exists in an industrial organization exists to accomplish certain purposes which are related to the attainment of organizational objectives. When a careful operations analysis has been made of jobs, these purposes may be stated in standards of performance. These standards can usually be expressed in the amount of work done, the quality of the work done, and the cost of the work done as related to materials, machinery, equipment, manpower, and the effect upon the continuing survival of the enterprise. When these results can be expressed in units produced which meet a given standard, in dollar costs, or in some other unit of numerical measure, such as days lost due to absenteeism or hours of downtime of machines, we call these resulting figures objective records of performance.

It should be pointed out that in asking for standards of performance for various jobs in an organization, we are not suggesting that either organizational structure or organizational goals are static. In a dynamic economy rigidity of structure either in goals or organization is certainly a way to oblivion. One of the important functions of management is a constant re-evaluation of objectives and resetting of goals when needed. This may require, and frequently does, organizational changes.

Objective records available in an industrial organization generally are not entirely relevant, reliable, or free from bias. A sales manager may find at the end of the year that his gross sales are off 10% due to economic conditions in the country over which he has no control. A foreman may find grievances up 50% in his department because of a new company policy on establishing work loads. A spinner may find that the hanks produced per hour by his machine are reduced or increased because the mill has changed the quality of the cotton it is using.

Records in an industrial organization may be inadequate with respect to accuracy. A report (Life Insurance Agency Management Association, 1953) based on an investigation in seven large ordinary insurance companies illustrates this point. These companies contributed the names of 1166 men who were under contract as fulltime agents. A careful follow-up of these men revealed that of this group, 11% had already terminated their contracts, the status of 13% was unknown, and 6% were in military service. Of the remainder, only 70.8% were actually fulltime agents in their activity and major source of livelihood. Yet all of these men were considered fulltime agents!

In spite of the problems of relevance, reliability, and freedom from bias in objective performance records, they can, when carefully used, serve as a basis for summary man analysis and, in turn, lead to a decision as to whether or not a diagnostic man analysis should be made. When definite standards of job performance are established and where the standards are stated in terms of objective measures, consistent deviations below this standard by an employee should be a signal to his superiors that a diagnostic man analysis should be made. The diagnostic man analysis would show, then, whether or not training of the employee or some other type of administrative action is indicated. If training is required, the same analysis would reveal the nature of the requisite training.

When an employee is responsible for a single outcome or a few relatively simple outcomes as a result of his job performance, one or more objective indices of job performance can be used in arriving at a summary man analysis:

1. units produced in a given period of time
2. quality of units produced
3. costs of materials in producing a unit, that is, waste, scrappage
4. cost of maintenance of equipment and machinery used by the employee
5. absenteeism and tardiness
6. grievances and complaints from the employee
7. accident frequency and severity
8. disciplinary actions.

Each of these items will not carry equal weight in determining the overall job performance of the individual. Weights should be assigned in terms of the considered judgment of management which establishes the standards of performance for the job if one objective index is needed.[2] Even without a composite figure, the individual factors could be used as a basis for determining whether or not a diagnostic man analysis is required.

Objective Performance Records for Managerial Personnel

The problems of securing objective performance records for a summary man analysis increase as the outcomes for which the employee is responsible multiply both in number and complexity. Yet it is this group of employees (supervisors, technical and professional personnel, and executives) who can and do influence the achievement of organizational goals in a more significant manner than that of an employee responsible for a single and comparatively simple outcome. Consider the areas for which many foremen are held responsible insofar as the performance of their department is concerned—personnel, machinery, production, costs, quality. The works manager is responsible for these

[2] The problem of weighting different indices of job performance for a given individual does not differ from the problem of weighting criterion measures and is discussed in detail in Chapter 9.

aspects of the business and many others for his entire plant. Similarly, company officers have broad and more complex responsibilities than those employees who fill middle and first line management positions.

The difficulty in obtaining objective performance records for summary man analysis of supervisors and managers as well as technical and professional employees is accentuated by the time span problem. Usually among production employees the performance record is available weekly. Among managerial employees, these data may not appear in the company records for months and sometimes for years. Profit and loss figures for units of a company usually are available on a monthly basis but these figures must be used in terms of their trends over a reasonable period of time if they are to be an index of job performance of the persons who are held responsible for profit performance of the organization.

In Chapter 9 we discuss at some length the contamination of records used to evaluate training by factors beyond the control of the employees being trained. It is pertinent, however, to indicate that objective records on the performance of employees used in man analysis are subject to similar contamination. A plant manager may be held responsible for the profitable operation of his plant. Yet profits from the operation of the plant may shrink, disappear, or increase due to conditions beyond his control, such as an economic recession or a boom. This renders it even more imperative that we examine carefully any objective record of job performance used in man analysis to determine if it is contaminated by factors beyond the control of the individual whose job behavior is being analyzed.

The difficulties of securing a current objective job performance index for supervisory and managerial employees usually have resulted in abandoning such measures in favor of ratings and similar observational techniques. As will be shown later in this chapter, these kinds of measures present special problems in terms of relevance, reliability, and freedom of bias. In fact, there are some pessimists, or perhaps realists, who take the position that adequate objective or observational indices of managerial performance are impossible to obtain. Yet superiors constantly evaluate their subordinates and, on the basis of these evaluations, make decisions which affect the individual employee in a vital way, including whether or not to continue him on the payroll. It seems to us that rather than accept the pessimistic viewpoint or continue the present kind of evaluation of managerial personnel characteristic of most American industry, careful research for better objective and observational instruments and methods is indicated.

A possible approach to acquiring data of this kind has been reported recently by Merrihue and Katzell (1955). Their Employee Relations Index was not developed to secure objective performance records on individual managers, supervisors, and staff personnel but rather to measure "the extent to which groups of employees accept and perform in accordance with the objectives and policies of the company" (p. 91). It seems to us, however, that the approach described and the methods used in developing this index are useful in developing an objective job performance index for specific managerial, supervisory, and staff jobs in a specific company. We, therefore, will summarize in some detail the construction of the ERI.

These investigators in constructing the ERI, on the basis of preliminary research, selected from thirty-three proposed indicators some eight indicators. The eight were selected because of "their convenience, objectivity, and demonstrated relationship to a general factor" (p. 95). The indicators selected were: periods of absences, separations, initial visits to dispensary for occupational reasons, suggestions submitted through the suggestion system, actions incurring disciplinary suspension, grievances submitted through the formal grievance procedure, work stoppages, and participation in the insurance plan. Data on these eight indicators were collected for a period of 13 weeks. They were then summarized for work groups and plants as a whole on a per capita basis. A factor analysis showed that these eight indicators tend to fluctuate together. The eight indicators were then combined into a single index by means of a multiple regression equation.

Next, an investigation of the validity of the ERI was carried out by establishing its relationship to other indicators of organizational effectiveness. Profitability figures were found to be related to the ERI in seventeen plants. In a comparison of four work groups having a higher efficiency record with three groups having a low efficiency record, the ERI score was significantly greater for the high efficiency work group. Scrappage and ERI scores for fifteen work groups were negatively related. Average rankings on quality of seven production groups were positively related to ERI scores.

Merrihue and Katzell are fully aware that they have not developed a perfect index for measuring the status of human relations management in a given work group or a total plant. They recognize the need for further improvement and refinement of the index. It seems to us, however, that they have suggested one possible approach to constructing an index which would point not only to the status of a group or a plant but also to the quality of the job performance of a supervisor in charge of a department, a manager in charge of a plant, or an executive in charge of a division of a company.

The construction of an individual job performance index would require even more careful research than that required to develop the ERI. The indicators which would go into this index, however, should have similar characteristics to those required of the indicators in ERI:

1. Each indicator should reflect behavior of the individual which affects the accomplishing of the objectives in his job either adversely or favorably. The utilization of labor in accomplishing a given amount of production might serve as an indicator for a supervisor to the extent that labor utilization is a decision which he can make.

2. Figures used in each indicator should be comparable for and applicable to other employees filling similar jobs in the organization. Production figures, for example, would not be suitable unless they are expressed in comparable units and are adjusted for conditions which make them comparable from department to department or from plant to plant.

3. The relationship of each indicator to the other indicators should be known.

4. It is highly desirable that the data for these indicators be easily collected. They should be data which are or can be made

easily available in the usual records kept by the company. There should be a range of variability in these statistics from individual to individual and there should be no question about their accuracy.

With modern methods of data processing, once such an index has been established for measuring specific supervisory, staff, and managerial jobs, the problem of computing them is reduced. Such an index, as Brogden and Taylor (1950) have suggested, might be expressed in dollar figures both in securing comparability and acceptance by managers.

We do not pretend that construction of an index for measuring individual job performance such as we are suggesting is a casual task. It will require careful research and fruitful insights if the index is to be relevant, reliable, and useful. If its usefulness were restricted simply to determining whether or not the employee requires diagnostic man analysis for training purposes, the efforts required to construct it might be greater than its ultimate value. Such an index, however, would have many uses other than the analysis of training needs. The effort required in its development certainly would be justified where many comparable jobs exist or where the jobs under consideration contribute substantially to the attainment of, or the failure to attain, organizational objectives.

Diagnostic Man Analysis

We have indicated that objective job performance measures are useful primarily as a summary man analysis technique. Yet the same measures occasionally can give clues to specific training needs of an individual employee. Careful examination of a piece of cloth for defects may give some lead as to skills, knowledge, or attitudes required of the weaver. Similar examples of the uses of articles fabricated, assembled, or inspected could be given but it is our opinion that more adequate diagnostic man analysis can be secured by use of the other two methods of man analysis—situational and observational methods. We consider, therefore, the problem of diagnostic man analysis at greater length in the next two sections of this chapter.

DEVISED SITUATIONAL MEASURES

If we are to modify an employee's behavior, we need to know precisely what changes must take place and what the employee must learn if his behavior is to change. A starting point in acquiring these data is ascertaining what the employee knows, what he can do, and his motivational structure in regard to his assigned company tasks. This in turn provides data as to what he must learn in order to perform his assigned tasks efficiently. The process of determining the specific training needs of an individual employee we call diagnostic man analysis.

One method of making a diagnostic man analysis is that of observing the employee as he performs his assigned tasks during the regular course of his day-to-day behavior on his job. These procedures are discussed later in this chapter. A second method is to expose the employee to a carefully structured situation which requires him to utilize the skills and knowledge which are essential to the performance of his job. His behavior in the devised situation is analyzed to determine what skills are deficient or what knowledge is lacking.

There are several reasons for utilizing devised situations for the purpose of a diagnostic man analysis. First, in many jobs in industry, nonstandard situations frequently occur which would result in securing irrelevant and unreliable data on the job performance of an individual employee. Second, the pressure for production or for completing an assignment in the regular job situation would preclude the employee from repeating behavior which requires several occurrences to analyze adequately. Third, certain critical behavior may occur only infrequently in the course of performing a job, and repeated observation would be necessary to analyze behavior of this type. A rug weaver may not have to pick out a broken shot over two or three times a year; a foreman does not discharge a man every day; and, an executive does not make decisions daily to change a product design or begin an intensive advertising campaign. Finally, the devised situations can measure the nature of a specific skill and the amount of a certain knowledge possessed uncontaminated by the possession or nonpossession of other skills or knowledge by the employee.

Devised situational measures are not unknown to industry (Tiffin and McCormick, 1958, Ch. 7). Generally, they have appeared as achievement tests—either as job knowledge or job performance tests. They have been used as selection devices, as a means of measuring the general outcomes of training, and, infrequently, as a means of diagnostic man analysis. In addition, certain devised situations, which are not tests in a true sense, have been used in industry as training techniques (role playing, business games, case study) which could be used as methods of obtaining data for diagnostic man analysis. We plan first to discuss the use of achievement tests as methods of man analysis and then look at possible measures which could be secured in other devised situations.

Achievement Tests—Knowledge and Performance

Achievement tests generally are constructed for use in a particular company; published information concerning specific tests of this type is therefore rather infrequent. There are, however, certain commercially available job knowledge tests such as the Purdue Vocational Tests primarily concerned with machine shop tasks (Tiffin and McCormick, 1958). Job performance tests which are commercially available are found more frequently for clerical jobs (Seashore and Bennett, 1946). Tiffin and Greenly (1939), however, have a miniature punch press performance test which was used in selection of punch press operators.

It is beyond the scope of this book to present data on the construction of achievement tests for industrial use. Although published descriptions of the use of these tests in industry are rare, there exists, however, extensive published data on how to construct and to administer achievement tests. The interested reader is referred to the treatment of these problems by Adkins (1949) and others (Regans and Frederiksen, 1951; Stone and Kendall, 1956; Stuit, 1947; Cronbach, 1949; Stead, et al., 1940). Rather, we plan to discuss the nature of these tests, their use and limitations as well as indicate the direction required to utilize them in diagnostic man analysis.

The primary purpose of job knowledge tests is that of determining whether or not an employee has the necessary knowledge to perform the tasks to which he is assigned. These tests are very similar to the achievement tests used in the educational field. In industry, it is essential in many jobs that an employee know certain facts in a subject matter field. An electrician needs certain basic information concerning electricity; a secretary should have some understanding of the rules of grammar and punctuation; and, an accountant should know the basic principles of accounting. In the usual everyday performance of job duties lack of information fundamental to efficient job performance can be the reason for below standard performance. It is difficult, however, in the usual job situation to determine whether or not a low level of results comes from lack of knowledge, low skills, or motivational sources. The job knowledge test when properly constructed can pinpoint the source of ineffective performance as being or not being the result of a lack of knowledge basic to performing the job. Furthermore, when the test is constructed as a diagnostic instrument, it can pinpoint the specific deficiencies in knowledge.

A job knowledge test, however, does not furnish data on how well an individual will perform a given task or group of tasks. It is entirely possible for an electrician to have a thorough knowledge of the principles of electricity and yet not be able to splice properly two strands of wire together. A foreman may make a perfect score on a human relations knowledge test yet so carry out his duties that his work group is in a constant state of turmoil and low morale.

Job performance tests are used to determine how well the individual employee can perform a given part of a task, a task, or a group of tasks. To use our electrician example again, a job performance test or a part of such a test would require the electrician, under standard conditions and standard instructions, to splice two strands of wire together. In job performance tests, both skill and knowledge are being measured in the way the task is performed and the end product of performing the task.

Relevance and Reliability of Achievement Tests

Achievement tests in industry, whether used for summary or diagnostic man analysis, must meet the usual requirements of any measuring instrument. They must be relevant, reliable, and free from bias. In industry, they must also be practical from the point of view of administration and scoring. Furthermore, if the results from such tests are to be accepted and used by industrial personnel the tests must have "face validity." They must look as if they are instruments which really measure what they are supposed to measure.

Again, evidence on the relevance, reliability, and freedom from bias of industrial achievement tests is scant in published form. Generally, relevance is determined by one of two methods. The first is on the basis of the judgment of experts in regard to the content of the test. Second, if the test discriminates adequately between individuals of known levels of knowledge or skill, it is considered a relevant test. Tiffin and Greenly (1939) considered the miniature punch press test as being sufficiently relevant because punch press operators performed more efficiently on the test than did insulation stripping machine operators and students.

We question whether these two methods of determining relevance of job knowledge tests are sufficient. Both expert judgments and discrimination between skill levels can merely reflect established (and perhaps incorrect) training programs. Thayer, Antoinetti, and Guest (1958) summarized research which indicated that a test of insurance knowledge was both adequate in the judgment of experts and discriminated between managers, assistant managers, and agents. On the other hand, this test has repeatedly shown little or no relationship to sales volume. They wondered whether product knowledge was an essential part of the training program for agents, at least to the extent measured by the test under study. If it were unrelated to other criteria, too, the appropriateness of intensive training in the technical details of insurance would be questionable. They did, in fact, find support for earlier, tentative findings which showed a relationship between the test scores of agents and the persistency with which the insurance they sold remained in force.

In one sense, they were asking a question similar to that asked in selection research—is this test valid? In a training sense, they were asking if a test which met the usual standards would indicate whether or not technical training was essential for the agent's job. We contend that before any achievement test is used for summary or diagnostic man analysis, we should know whether the knowledge measured is related to job performance. If it is not and the test is used, we may initiate unneeded training.

Reliability of a test is determined by various means including test-retest data and analysis of internal consistency. Since achievement test scores are particularly susceptible to variation due to differential learning, test-retest data on reliability must be interpreted carefully. Internal consistency data do not have this problem, but present special problems of their own. Freedom from bias may affect either the relevance or the reliability or both of a test. It is suggested that assistance of an expert in test construction be obtained in devising achievement tests for both summary and diagnostic man analysis in industrial training.

Fewer job performance tests than job knowledge tests are constructed for general industrial use. Accordingly, there is even less published information on the relevance and reliability of job performance tests than is available on job knowledge tests. During the past decade, the armed services have become interested in the construction and use of performance tests both for use in training and in other phases of manpower management. Several publications have given detailed information on the relevance and reliability of tests developed by the Army, Navy, and Air Force.[3] Although the military situation is not a replica of the industrial situation, data on tests used in the former can indicate something concerning the possible relevance and reliability of performance tests in general.

Baker, Scott, and MacCaslin (1955) have described the steps and rationale present in constructing performance tests for use in evaluating the outcome of basic combat and light infantry training. In addition, they have discussed the necessary precautions in the administration, scoring, and interpretation of these tests. Two batteries of tests each consisting of seventeen subtests were constructed. One battery was concerned with measuring the results of basic combat training and the other with measuring the results of light infantry training.

[3] In addition to the work of Baker, Scott, and MacCaslin (1955), Machie, et al. (1953), Siegel and Courtney (1953), and others have reported work on performance tests in the armed services.

Relevance of the performance tests was established by two approaches. First, to insure "face validity" the opinion of military experts as to the areas which should be covered by the tests were obtained; then items for the tests were carefully selected from the training program and lesson plans used in instructing trainees. The second approach to establishing the relevance of the tests was determining whether they differentiated between trainees at different levels of instruction. Data are presented which show that the tests do differentiate between trainees prior to any instruction, after 8 weeks of instruction, and after 16 weeks of instruction.

The reliability of the tests was estimated in several ways:

1. test-retest using the same form of the test
2. using comparable but different forms of the test
3. internal consistency analysis
4. determining degree of agreement between scoring of two independent testers.

The authors concluded that "on an overall basis" each test battery had sufficient reliability for work with company-size units.

Based on the meager published data, the reliability of job knowledge tests generally is higher than that of job performance tests. Data on the relevance of these two types of achievement tests as used in industry are so sparse that no firm conclusion on this characteristic can be stated. As summary measures of job performance they seem, however, to be as relevant as aptitude tests and to have higher relevance than many personality and interest schedules.

Diagnostic Achievement Tests

The utility of achievement tests as diagnostic man analysis techniques generally has been overlooked in industrial training. It seems to us that their real value lies here rather than as a summary man analysis technique. Taylor (1952), for example, was able to reduce training time from 12 to 8 weeks for certain trainees in an automotive mechanics school by the use of a series of diagnostic achievement tests. Either a job knowledge test or a job performance test should be able to indicate the degree of skill or amount of knowledge basic to job performance possessed by an employee. Generally, achievement tests need to be constructed to yield reliable subscores for the various job areas if they are to be used to indicate weaknesses in either skills or knowledge. Unfortunately, most achievement tests do not meet this requirement.

Achievement tests used in industrial training, however, can furnish more adequate diagnostic data if they are constructed specifically for this purpose. The contents of the test must be of such a nature that critical job behavior is adequately sampled. In performing the tasks required by the test, the employee will indicate the degree of skill or the amount of knowledge (relevant to his job) which he possesses. These requirements for a diagnostic achievement test can be illustrated by considering the requirements for a job performance test for a loom fixer in the textile industry. This job is a trouble-shooting and preventive maintenance job.

An operations analysis of the trouble-shooting phase of this job shows four major and critical areas of job performance: (1) analysis of machine malfunction; (2) verification of the analysis; (3) elimination of the malfunction; and (4) verification of the elimination of the malfunction. Implicit in the performance of the tasks in this job are certain skills in handling tools as well as skills in problem solving. Implicit, also, is the need for specific information concerning the operation of looms and the kinds of malfunctions to which the machines are subject. Furthermore, since the loom fixer is competent to make only certain repairs and must refer others to maintenance personnel, he must decide whether or not to make repairs.

An adequate diagnostic performance test would include test tasks in which the loom fixer would demonstrate his competence in each of the four critical areas of job performance. The task would be varied enough to show whether or not the skills and knowledge exhibited were restricted to only one type of malfunction or were characteristic of the fixer's handling of a wide range of malfunctions. The tasks would be so designed that the behavior in the diagnosis, elimination, and verification of elimination of the malfunction could be recognized and evaluated in terms of their adequacy.

In addition to the above requirement, the job performance test for a loom fixer would be so designed that it could be administered, scored, and analyzed by line personnel who are not sophisticated in test administration and interpretation. There are two obvious reasons for this requirement. First, line personnel would use the results of the test. If the testing situation were so complex that they would have difficulty in understanding the test results, very little use would be made of the results in subsequent training of the employee. Second, since the supervisor or instructor would normally administer the test and analyze the results, the test would have to be one that could be used without formal training in tests and measurements. Finally, the test should have the characteristics of all efficient measuring instruments—relevance and reliability. This means that a certain amount of careful research will have to go into the design and construction of the test.

These requirements for a diagnostic job performance test for loom fixers apply to job performance tests for other industrial jobs. In fact, they are applicable to job knowledge tests as well. It is true that an employee in taking a diagnostic achievement test will not do exactly what he must do to perform the tasks of his job in his daily work. On the other hand, the major advantage of an achievement test is that the employee is exposed to a standardized situation and standardized situations rarely exist on the actual job. The standardized situation allows for the diagnosis of skills and knowledge not contaminated by extraneous factors such as variability in materials and servicing frequently found in the actual job situation. Achievement tests give an index of what the employee could do if his work situation were ideal. He can demonstrate more adequately his true skill and knowledge. Furthermore, if the employee performs adequately in the standardized situation, a comparison of that performance with his on-the-job performance might reveal inadequacies in untested performance phases, job content, the test itself, or all three.

Achievement Tests for Managerial and Staff Personnel

As a general rule, job knowledge and job performance tests, when used as industrial training aids, have been used in connection with training for hourly rated production and lower level clerical employees. Occasionally, job knowledge tests have been used in connection with specific formal courses given to first-line supervisors. One of the authors has found job knowledge measures used as pre- and post-tests have assisted materially in conducting courses in cost accounting, time study, and basic mechanics. Such tests help to determine points which need special emphasis for various persons in the class as well as to provide measures which indicate whether further training is needed after the completion of the formal course.

An interesting variant of the job knowledge test as used with foreman trainees has been described by Rood (1956). Each trainee must qualify in each phase of supervisory performance before he is allowed to perform the complete assignment of a foreman. As part of the process, each trainee must go through a "Qualification" session with someone who is an expert in the area in which he is being qualified. The expert questions the trainee to ascertain what he knows about the particular area and recommends additional training if knowledge is deficient. Although the quiz session is not highly structured nor does it have the usual provisions for objectivity and reliability found in the better written job knowledge tests, careful utilization of a procedure of this kind should produce diagnostic data on the training needs of individuals at various supervisory and management levels in a company.

Peterson and Wallace (1955) have combined a series of interviews with a product knowledge achievement test and a series of standardized performance records to be used in evaluating and guiding life insurance agents in their careers. After the agent has gained considerable experience in the business, he is tested and then interviewed by four different home office executives on four separate areas: his background and experience, his sales knowledge and skills, his attitudes and knowledge regarding the job of supervision, and his supervisory skills as applied to a situational performance measure. The interviewers are trained to follow a carefully developed guide and are required to explore only that area to which they are assigned. When all interviews and tests are complete, the interviewers make independent judgments as to whether the agent should move toward a managerial career or continue as a career agent. The judgments and evidence are then pooled in a career conference conducted by a fifth executive who has not interviewed the man. Regardless of the decision reached, in the final phase of this conference there is a careful delineation of a training program for the individual to assist him in his development as a manager or agent. Research on relevance and reliability of this procedure is now underway, but the careful integration of an achievement test, standard performance records, background interviews, and skill interviews make it an interesting approach to diagnostic man analysis. The fact that it requires a training plan based on the analysis marks it as fairly unique.

An attempt to use a more highly structured test situation at the supervisory-administrative level has been reported by Suttell (1955). This use of a situational test was with Air Force officer candidates and can be considered only very roughly equivalent to use of a similar kind of test in industry. Her report can give, however, some indication as to the relevance and reliability of this kind of performance test. The situational test consisted of sixteen problems which tapped five major areas of behavior of junior administrators. These problems required behavior on the part of each participant in which he showed his skill in handling administrative situations involving other individuals. The entire test was administered to 343 officer candidates. Reliability data were obtained in terms of interobserver agreement and in terms of internal consistency of the test.

The data on the reliability and relevance of this test indicate that it is inadequate as a summary measure for man analysis. It would not be useful for anything but group work. If, however, both the reliability and relevance of situational tests of this kind can be improved for use in industry, they offer definite possibilities for use with supervisory and administrative personnel as a tool for diagnostic man analysis. This use of situational tests has received little or no attention in industrial training.

Another testing procedure, the "In Basket" test, recently developed as primarily a managerial selection device, has possible use as a diagnostic man analysis test for determining training needs (Foundation for Research on Human Behavior, 1958). The "In Basket" test is basically a performance test. The individual being tested is confronted with the usual assortment of notes, memoranda, reports, and correspondence a busy executive may find on his desk at any time during the working day. The test task is to handle these communications in the most effective way possible. This test is still in the stage of development but suggests possibilities for diagnosing typical executive actions such as delegating authority and decision making.

Both ingenuity and research can develop useful achievement tests at the staff and management level in industry. As a matter of fact, the entire area of achievement testing in industry as a training aid has received little systematic attention from training directors. Efforts spent here would improve immensely the training directors' contributions to the wise use of the training dollar in industry.

Other Devised Situational Procedures

Although achievement tests usually result in some sort of a score characteristic of the performance of the employee taking the test, a score *per se* is not necessary, if the purpose of the devised situational procedure is diagnostic. During the past decade or so, certain methods for training personnel have been developed which are essentially devised situations. Generally, these methods have been used as a means of bringing about changes in the behavior of individuals who are exposed to these situations. Sometimes, however, they are used as a means of analyzing the strengths and weaknesses of the participants. We believe that if those who use these procedures would plan them, not only as training methods but also as diagnostic man analysis techniques, they would serve both purposes.

Among these devised situational procedures are role playing, case study procedures, the incident method of Pigors, conference leadership training sessions, and business games. In most of these devised situations, the participants must demonstrate certain skills and knowledge. They are also believed to exhibit certain attitudes which are indicative of the attitudes which characterize their day-to-day job performance. To utilize these sessions for diagnostic man analysis would require the presence of observers trained to spot and record the behavior of the participants.[4] It would require a careful guide as to what behavior to observe and how to record the observations. The observers would use certain instruments such as rating scales or behavior check lists which are discussed in the next section of this chapter.

A major advantage of these kinds of devised situational methods over actual observation of job performance is that in a relatively short period of time behavior can be observed and analyzed which would require weeks and months of on-the-job observation to spot. It is possible, also, that an individual observed in the devised situation might be more willing to accept the diagnosis of his behavior than he would if a diagnosis actually were made on the job. Acceptance of the needs to modify behavior is the first step in learning. Furthermore, trained observers should be able to make a more adequate diagnosis of the behavior of employees in devised situations than the usual supervisor or manager would make.

In the course of his evaluation of a film series of simulated sales situations, one of the authors has developed two highly reliable check lists to be used by the trainer to record the trainee's behavior. Only items which yielded high inter-rater agreement are included on these lists. Their purpose is to permit the trainer to record what the agent does, spot his strengths and weaknesses, and use the lists to help the agent improve his sales effectiveness. Although we do have data on the reliability of the check lists, we are only now beginning to get sufficient data to help establish the relevance of these items. Perhaps the most interesting result of the development of these lists was the elimination of a number of behavioral descriptions frequently found on less rigorously developed forms. Observers could not accurately classify trainee behavior using these descriptions.

We have no evidence on either the relevance and reliability of the measures resulting from the use of devised situations of the kind listed at the beginning of this section. It is true that partici-

[4] See DiVesta, Roach, and Beasley (1951) for one suggested approach to recording behavior in devised situations. Kennedy also (1959) has reported methods of studying behavior in business games which could be adapted for diagnostic man analysis.

pants in sensitivity training programs, pioneered by the National Training Laboratory (1953) report significant self-insight from this experience. Although such reports are of interest, they do not qualify as adequate evidence. However, the use of these various devised situations offers enough promise to justify careful research on their application to diagnostic man analysis. Certainly, they should represent significant improvements in man analysis for training purposes with a group of employees where techniques for this purpose are scarce and inadequate—staff, supervisory, and managerial personnel.

OBSERVATIONAL MEASURES

The third type of measures which may be used in making a man analysis is what we have called observational measures. The measures are based directly on the observation of the behavior of an employee as he performs the various tasks of his job. They differ from objective records of performance in that both the behavior of the employee and the results of the behavior are observed and recorded. In objective records of performance only the results of job behavior are available. These measures differ from devised situational measures in that they are records of what takes place on the actual job and are not behavior occurring in a situation which simulates some aspect of the job.

Observational measures are of two kinds—those which are recorded as the behavior occurs or immediately thereafter and those which are recorded some time after the occurrence of the behavior. The data obtained on the behavior of General Electric foremen described in Chapter 3 are an example of the former. Data secured by rating methods, diaries, and interviews with job incumbents are examples of retrospective observational measures.

Advantages and Disadvantages of Observational Methods

It would seem that observational measures should be superior to either objective records of performance or devised situational measures both in relevance and reliability. Unfortunately this does not seem to be true. Observational records have many of the same kind of contamination found in objective records. They share, also, with many devised situational measures, errors that grow out of the necessity of having to have an observer in order to secure observational data. Since the observer is human, his observations are subject to errors of perception, attention, and memory. His observations are influenced also by his own attitudes, beliefs, and theories concerning the phenomena observed. Even where the behavior is recorded by some mechanical device such as a camera, the film must be observed and interpreted by a human being whose judgment usually contains errors. Furthermore, observational measures are made usually under circumstances which, unknown to the observer, can and usually do influence the nature of the behavior observed. To use an extreme example, an employee assembling parts of a rheostat may seem to be bungling and completely lacking in the perceptual motor skills required of the task. The reason may not be a fundamental lack of skill but the physiological effect of an alcoholic weekend. Training may be indicated for either reason but certainly not the same kind of training.

For diagnostic man analysis, observational measures potentially are superior to objective records of performance. As indicated earlier, they furnish data not only on the outcome of the employee's behavior but also on what he actually does to produce this outcome. They may be even superior in certain situations to devised situational measures, since in no way is the behavior observed a reaction to an artificial situation. Certainly, observational measures are superior to devised situational measures in that they cause less interruption of the main purpose of a business—the production of goods and services.

It would seem, therefore, that one of the tasks of improving man analysis for training purposes is that of increasing both the relevance and reliability of observational measures. Considerable research has gone into improving rating techniques in the last quarter of a century. Even more research is necessary to develop relevant and reliable procedures for observational man analysis.

Immediate Observational Methods

An observer should know what to look for in trying to determine the training needs of an employee by watching him as he works. A careful operations analysis, which shows what the employee should do and how he should do it, is a basic starting point for determining what should be observed. Even an individual thoroughly familiar with a task may overlook crucial elements without such a guide. Generally, when an operations analysis of any but the most simple job is reduced to writing, the results comprise a rather bulky document. In actual practice, when systematic observation of employees' behavior is made for a training man analysis, the crucial requirements for performing the tasks of a job are reduced to a check list.

Check Lists

A check list is a tool for obtaining measures of the job behavior of employees. Like other tools for measuring training needs, it must be relevant and reliable. Its relevance and reliability should be determined prior to its use as a means of man analysis. The usual check list, made by a training expert in the odd moments between coffee breaks, meets these requirements of relevance and reliability only by sheer chance. In developing a check list for use in life insurance sales training mentioned earlier, it took 7 weeks of intensive research before it was possible to eliminate unreliable items and develop a reliable instrument for recording trainee behavior. The relevance of these items is as yet undetermined.

A search of the literature reveals a minimum of data on the relevance and reliability of the check list when used as a guide for observing and recording employee behavior during actual performance of the tasks of his job. There are some data available as to its use as a rating method for summary man analysis but it is unsafe to generalize concerning the characteristics of an instrument when used under different conditions. It seems to us, however, that carefully constructed check lists emphasizing diagnostic analysis of employee behavior have real potential for determining training needs of employees.

Employee Performance Record

We have implied, perhaps, that observing the job behavior of an employee to determine his need for training is a special situation and should take place only at appropriate times. Certain situations do arise in an industrial organization which require special observation of an employee or a group of employees to analyze behavior and determine what training, if any, is required to remedy deficiencies in performance of their jobs. It is, however, our position that it is the responsibility of management to determine the adequacy of the job performance of his subordinates. If this is true, it follows that the manager, whether he is a first-line supervisor or the president of a company, should be continuously alert to the training needs of his immediate subordinate. This means that he is observing their job behavior continuously to assist them in improving their job performance. Managers, even those at the lower end of the management hierarchy, have many other duties and responsibilities in addition to discovering training needs of individual subordinates. Since these training needs do not demand the immediate attention that is required by lagging production, off-quality goods, a union demand, or the potential loss of an important customer, the manager can and frequently does fail to observe his subordinates in terms of training requirements. Tools and procedures are needed to assist him in making this task as much a part of his daily routine as reading his mail and going to lunch.

Flanagan and Burns (1955) have described an employee performance record which has as its purpose assisting foremen to make daily observations of behavior of an employee which is considered critical in the performance of his job. The Employee Performance Record card was developed for use at the Delco-Remy Division of the General Motors Corporation using the critical incidents approach. This approach, developed by Flanagan (1949), has been used for a variety of purposes in the area of personnel administration and employee evaluation. Generally, the foreman records on a prepared form either critical behavior indicating a need for improvement or critical behavior which shows outstanding performance. This critical behavior is associated with sixteen critical job requirements under two general headings: physical and mental qualifications, and work habits and attitudes. This performance record, of course, was not instituted at Delco-Remy merely for the purpose of determining training needs of individual employees but from the type of data recorded on the form on each employee, it would not be difficult to determine specific training needs.

The Employee Performance Record was the result of several years of research and trying out of the instrument. The steps which led to the development of the form began in 1948, and the form was used first in a plant in 1951. Information about the use of the performance record was not released to the general public until after it had been in use for four years. The authors caution that the record requires careful training on the part of the users if proper use of it is to be made. This is just another line of evidence that solid advances in the field of industrial training and personnel administration in general require persistent long-range work based on sound research and development procedures. This Employee Performance Record, in our opinion, has real potential for determining on a day-to-day basis the training needs of individual employees.

Retrospective Observational Measures

We have been discussing the observation of employee behavior by an observer on the scene who records his observations at the *time* of the occurrence of the behavior and/or immediately *thereafter*. Often it is not possible or desirable to make a record of employee performance at the time of the performance. We then resort to observations which are recorded in retrospect, that is, several hours, days, weeks, or even months after the occurrence of the behavior. This observational record can be made either by the employee himself or by some third party observer such as his supervisor, subordinate, or one of his peers. Perhaps the most frequently used retrospective observational measure is some type of a rating technique. Moreover, employee diaries, as well as interviews and questionnaires, are occasionally used to determine training needs of an employee. Properly used, each of these techniques can contribute significant insights to training needs.

Rating Methods

Rating methods have a long and somewhat checkered history in American industry. Mahler (1947) reviewed their use and abuse in a monograph entitled *Twenty Years of Merit Rating.* Most books on personnel administration and industrial psychology have at least a chapter dealing with rating procedures. More recently, especially in the assessment of management personnel, the term "rating" has lost favor and has been replaced by the milder terms "appraisal" and "evaluation." Under whatever name ratings appear, their use in American industry represents an attempt to secure quantitative statements of judgments concerning job performance, or traits underlying the job performance, of employees.

The use of ratings in industry has grown, in part, out of the need for accurate data upon which to base personnel decisions. For many jobs, objective records of performance either are not available or are available after too long a time to be of use for administrative purposes. In many jobs it is not possible to observe and record significant job behavior. When administrative action becomes necessary in such situations, we fall back on judgments made by people who are or should be in a position to make accurate evaluations of the behavior of an employee. Efforts to make these judgments relevant and reliable by minimizing the sources of error have led to the use of ratings.

As Ghiselli and Brown (1955) have indicated "there is no such device as an objective rating procedure. . . . ratings always involved personal estimates and subjective judgments" (p. 87). This means that particular care must be taken to see that ratings used in personnel administration are relevant and reliable measuring instruments. Published reports on the use of rating techniques to secure data for man analysis alone are relatively few. However, the basic factors leading to relevant and reliable ratings are the same whether the rating procedure is used in connection with making salary increases, promoting an employee, validating a test, or determining which employees require training. Therefore, we shall first present a brief outline of the general problems in securing relevant and reliable ratings. Then we shall discuss their specific use in man analysis.

Ghiselli and Brown (1955) have indicated the basic problem in establishing the validity (relevance) of a rating:

> Through subjective estimates, ratings make possible a quasiquantification of these complex behaviors. The validity of these ratings needs to be determined by comparing them with more objective measures. But here is the dilemma. Ratings are used because such objective measures are not available or are very difficult to obtain. It is doubly necessary that factors known to affect the validity of ratings be thoroughly investigated (p. 88).

These authors list and discuss seven factors which are related to the relevance of ratings:

1. the nature of the behavior being rated
2. the rater's knowledge of the behavior to be rated
3. the rater's knowledge of the behavior of the workers to be rated
4. the bias of the rater
5. the purpose of the ratings
6. amount of time available for making the rating
7. the characteristics of the rater.

In addition to these seven factors, the problem of relevance in ratings used in training needs analysis concerns also the problem of whether or not the behavior which is to be rated is behavior which is crucial or critical in the performance of a task. We could probably get reasonable agreement as to whether or not an employee's hair is red, black, or brown provided we screened our raters for color blindness. But unless we could demonstrate that hair color is related to job performance, a rating of hair color would have no relevance in a man analysis for training purposes.

The reliability or consistency of ratings concern the degree with which the rater can observe and report accurately the behavior which he is rating. Part of the problem in securing reliability is the selection of items of behavior to be rated; part is the control of the environment in which the rated behavior is elicited; part is the training and indoctrination of raters in making ratings. Still further improvement in reliability can be achieved by using as raters persons who are capable and willing to make required ratings.

Characteristic of many prewar rating scales was the use of trait names such as honesty, initiative, persistence, and leadership. As indicated earlier, trait names caused certain semantic difficulties among raters which led to unreliability. Furthermore, these trait names had certain emotional and moral connotations, as well as social acceptance values, which made even well-intentioned raters hesitant to use the negative side of a rating scale. There was rarely any effort made to determine whether or not these traits had any relationship to the quality of job performance. A heightened interest during World War II in obtaining more accurate evaluations of the behavior of military personnel both for research and administrative reasons led to intensive work on rating procedures in the armed forces. Growing out of these activities came two developments which show promise of increasing the relevance and reliability of ratings—critical incident procedures [5] and forced-choice methods.[6] Both techniques have been adapted to industrial use, and continued research and refinement of these procedures have taken place.

Critical Incident Procedures

The critical incident method has contributed to the construction of relevant rating scales in two ways. First, the items which make up a critical incident rating procedure are statements of the behavior of employees which, in the judgment of competent observers, differentiate between effective and ineffective task performance. They are actual observed actions of employees in task situations which are critical to successful and unsuccessful task performance. In the second place, the specific behavior to be rated is described in such a way as to make it readily and reliably observable in contrast with vague and poorly defined trait names. This helps to reduce the semantic problems which lead to unreliability and eliminates items which have no demonstrable relationship to job performance. It is true that the crucial test of relevance of rating forms constructed along critical incident lines is rarely made, that is, statistical relationship between rat-

[5] Flanagan (1949), (1954) and many other publications.

[6] Staff, A.G.O. Personnel Research Section (1946), Richardson (1949), and many other publications.

ing results and an objective measure of job performance. Yet the relevance of the critical incident evaluation procedures should be greater than that of the typical World War II ratings by the insistence that the behavior evaluated is that which, in the judgment of experts, differentiates between effective and ineffective task performance.

Forced-Choice Ratings

The basic approach to obtaining items for a forced-choice rating is not radically different from that used in securing behavior items for a critical incident evaluation procedure. Generally, they are drawn from the description of the behavior of employees who differ in effectiveness in carrying out their job requirements. These descriptions are secured from supervisors and others who are in the position to observe this behavior and describe it.

At this point, the procedure for developing a forced-choice rating becomes different from that used in the critical incident methods. The items which ultimately become a part of the forced-choice form are selected on the basis of their discrimination between employees differing in job competence; job competence is determined by the judgment of observers or by some more objective criterion. The items are then scaled in terms of their social acceptability. Only items of approximately the same social acceptability are paired together in a final scale. Furthermore, the individual who makes the rating is not informed of the discriminative power of the items in distinguishing between employees judged superior or inferior in job performance. The proponents of this form of rating claim that it minimizes the factors which result in lack of relevance and reliability and lead to extreme bias common in the earlier rating methods (Highland and Berkshire, 1951).

Recent research indicates that no forced-choice questionnaire or rating device thus far tested has fulfilled the early promise hoped for. Maher (1960) finds that not only can the responses on a forced-choice study activity questionnaire be distorted under instructions to respondents to get the highest score possible, but also that the validity of the questionnaire for predicting grades drops to zero under such instructions. If continuing research on the sources of transparency in such devices does not reveal ways to overcome the possibilities of distortion of ratings, the forced-choice approach may have to be abandoned. Some sources are being identified, however, which hold out some hope for this approach.

Although neither the critical incident nor the forced-choice approaches to the construction and use of ratings are a panacea for the faults inherent in any attempt to secure relevant and reliable judgments on human behavior, they appear to be a definite advance over the older or more conventional approaches to employer ratings. First, they require that items appearing on the rating forms be statements of behavior not trait names. Second, they require that these items be descriptive of behavior which differentiates the job behavior of employees who perform their job tasks in an acceptable and an unacceptable manner. Third, they demonstrate that if relevant and reliable rating instruments are to be secured, careful research and development is required. Fourth, the forced-choice forms of ratings attempt to guard against such sources of unreliability as the "halo" tendency.

Diagnostic Ratings

Generally, rating methods have been used to obtain a summary measure of an employee's behavior. Even though critics grant that the forced-choice rating form may provide adequate summary analysis, they frequently contend that it is of no help in diagnostic analysis. Wherry (1959) has begun research to answer these criticisms by developing a diagnostic forced-choice rating device. Starting with a 150-item check list, he had managers describe good, average, and poor salesmen. The results of these ratings were then factor analyzed and yielded a general factor and five specific factors: "quantity of output," "compliance with rules," "job knowledge," "identification with company," and "interpersonal relations" (p. 229). Blocks of five items were constructed so that each item in each block had a high loading in a different specific factor. The items in each block were also matched on discrimination index, preference index, and loading on the general factor. In this way, the rater is presented with blocks of apparently equally attractive items and must rank the man's standing on each. In doing so, he gives the man scores on each factor which may reveal areas needing training.

Although this instrument is still in its developmental stages, the Wherry format has a definite advantage. The first half of the form consists of the usual forced-choice form designed to evaluate the man's overall performance. The items which are scored are those which have been shown to discriminate between good and poor employees. Thus, we have a summary analysis. Given a low score here, we then go to the second part which enables us to spot possible areas needing work. These features combined in a single instrument represent a major advance even though the particular form described by Wherry still needs refinement. In addition, the use of several items representing each area as a basis for deciding that training is needed is a sounder procedure than that typically used—the analysis of the rating form item by item. The latter procedure is fraught with danger as it is only rarely that the reliability of an item is known. Where it is known, the reliability is typically low—much too low for individual diagnosis. (Nor does intuitive grouping of items in the process of this item-by-item analysis offer *any* guarantee of increased reliability.)

Forced Choice in a Training-Needs Study

Roach (1958) of Nationwide Insurance has supplied the authors with a report of an interesting and carefully executed research project which utilized a forced-choice rating scale in determining supervisory training needs in his company. This study clearly indicates that determining training needs requires research of a rather high order. It further illustrates the fact that real determination of the training needs of individual employees requires something more than a talented crystal ball.

The procedure followed in the construction and use of Roach's forced-choice questionnaire can be briefly summarized. Division managers wrote essays describing the behavior of the best and the poorest supervisors they knew. Statements taken from these essays were developed into a 401-item questionnaire. Division managers then rated their supervisors by means of this questionnaire. The results of these ratings were then submitted to a factor analysis, and fourteen basic dimensions of supervisory behavior were extracted. A forced-choice questionnaire was then constructed with items covering each of these fourteen dimensions of behavior. District managers filled out the forced-choice questionnaire on each of their supervisors. These results were analyzed to determine group and individual needs for training.

Although this attempt to develop a forced-choice rating form for use in determining training needs cannot be considered 100% successful, it represents a distinct advance over typical rating procedures. Roach's approach at least assured relevance to the extent of incorporating in his questionnaire items of observed supervisory behavior. Again, a combination of the summary and diagnostic approach as suggested by Wherry might make Roach's scale even more useful. Although the reliability of the latter's scale was not sufficiently high to permit individual diagnosis, he at least knew how reliable the scale was.

It is this kind of approach to determining training needs, whether the measures used are objective records of performance, devised situational measures, or observational measures, which eventually will succeed in taking training out of the realm of inspiration, guesswork, and intuition. Once facts can be secured as to the actual training needs of an employee or a group of employees, then training can be conducted effectively and economically. The research approach to determining training needs requires time and costs money, and training also requires time and costs money. Unless research and research results are used in planning and implementing training the time and money spent on training is easily wasted.

Diaries

A common technique used for diagnostic man analysis for salesmen or others who work outside of the plant or office is the diary, sales record, or similar record. In the life insurance business, for example, the *Sales Method Index* (Life Insurance Agency Management Association, 1957) has been developed to permit an agent to record the details of each sales attempt he makes whether successful or unsuccessful. He can record the source of the prospect, what he knew about him before the sale, his occupation, income, what was covered in the interview, the policy discussed, etc. The thirty-four questions permit the agent to go into considerable detail and then to contrast his relative success in various markets and in using various sales methods. More typically, simple records dealing with the number of calls a salesman makes, how many interviews he obtained, and his number and size of sales are kept. The man and his supervisor then analyze these figures and decide whether he needs more training on the closing of the sale, approaching a prospect, and other aspects of life insurance selling. Although such records permit the supervisor to get a more complete picture of the man's activities in the field, they suffer from several inherent weaknesses. First, the man himself must keep the records. To get him to do this at all in the face of his selling duties is difficult, to say the least. Second, even if he is required to complete the necessary records, the supervisor must rely on the man's honesty and ability to follow the recording instructions. Despite these weaknesses, it seems to us that such records can be helpful—if properly developed—if only because they cover an essential part of the job for such people. Joint calls in which the superior accompanies the salesman can supplement such records but can cover only a small sample of the total activity of the man. In addition, that small sample is probably biased by the presence of the supervisor.

Unfortunately, very little research has been done on the relevance and reliability of such devices. Despite the intensive work done on the *Sales Method Index* no reliability data are available (because the main data upon which the reliability could be determined are not available). We have already pointed to the questionable accuracy of such self-reports. On the other hand, some data on the *Sales Method Index* (Life Insurance Agency Management Association, 1955) suggest that they are valid when used properly.

Because of the numerous jobs which take the employee to places where other methods of diagnostic man analysis cannot be made or can be made only infrequently, research designed to improve self-reports for such people could make a substantial contribution to the whole area of diagnostic man analysis.

Interviews and Questionnaires

The use of interviews and questionnaires in the assessment of organizational climate has been discussed at length in Chapter 2. Again, the same techniques can be directed toward determining the needs of individuals for training as well as for determining where in the organization training is required. They would, however, go beyond acquiring information about attitudes and would probe the problem of training in the areas of skills and knowledge. The problems in using these techniques to secure relevant and reliable data on the training needs of individuals do not differ from the problems in their use in the analysis of organizational training needs. Since these were presented in a previous chapter, we shall not discuss them here.

One of the authors has made effective use of both interviews and questionnaires in the determination of training needs of managerial personnel. In a training program for college graduates, he has used as a regular procedure interviews both with trainees and their superiors to determine areas of training which should be emphasized for these men as they progress in their training program. Questionnaires directed to supervisors and their superiors about training needs have served as one basis for developing formal classes in such subjects as cost accounting and time study.

The use of interviews in conjunction with employees' diaries to determine training needs was suggested in the previous section on diaries in this chapter. Mann and Dent's (1954) study indicates a possible use of interview techniques to obtain data on training needs from an individual's superior and subordinates. The nominating technique developed under Jenkins' (1948) guidance in World War II could be extended to secure data on training needs of an individual from his peers by the judicious use of "why" questions.

It would seem to us that either the interview or the questionnaire may have two unique advantages over other means of determining the training needs of an employee. These advantages exist only when the employee himself is being asked concerning his own training needs. First, the individual employee is the only source of information as to what *he* believes he needs to learn to perform his job adequately. Only by asking by interview or questionnaire can this introspective data be secured. Second, self-insight can serve, in some instances, as a powerful motivating device for modifying behavior. It is possible that an employee who recognizes and accepts defects in his behavior on the job will be more willing to make an effort to eliminate this defect than if the defect were merely pointed out to him by an instructor or a supervisor.

Interviews and questionnaires as a means of securing information from an employee in regard to his training needs have been relatively neglected both in industrial practice and in the literature on training. Maier (1958), however, has recognized the value of the problem-solving interview in one aspect of industrial training, that is, the employee-appraisal programs. With this exception, little has been done to utilize these promising tools in determining individual training needs.

As is true of all procedures used in determining training needs, careful research and evaluation are required to determine when and how these two means of asking questions can be used most effectively in the delineation of the training needs of individual employees. We reiterate that effective training including adequate determination of training needs will advance only so fast as we substitute research for the present standard equipment of training directors—hunches and the crystal ball.

SUMMARY

Because it is ultimately the behavior of the individual employee which is modified by training, we must focus upon *his* training needs. This determination of individual training needs we call *man analysis* and consists of two major steps: *summary* man analysis and *diagnostic* man analysis.

The objective of summary man analysis is to find out how well an employee is carrying out the tasks which comprise his job. If his performance is deficient, diagnostic man analysis is then employed to determine what skills, knowledge, or attitudes must be developed for improvement. Diagnostic man analysis would also be used for similar determinations in preparing an employee for transfer or promotion.

Three major sources of information are examined in man analysis:

1. objective records
2. devised situational measures
3. observational measures

The first of these sources is used primarily in summary man analysis, whereas the latter are used for both summary and diagnostic man analysis.

5 LEARNING AND INDUSTRIAL TRAINING: I

THE PURPOSE OF INDUSTRIAL TRAINING: LEARNING

The central process in industrial training is *learning*. When we establish and implement a training program for employees, we do so with the expectation that the experience in the training situation will modify the behavior of the employees who have participated. As we have indicated in Chapter 1, this modification of behavior is the result of the process known as learning. Whether our training program is for a production employee, a secretary, an engineer, a supervisor, or a vice president, the program is directed to change the behavior of the individual so that he can meet the demands of his job more adequately.

Since learning is the central purpose of any training in industry, we discuss, in this and the following chapter, the importance of learning theory and the principles of learning for industrial training. We examine in Chapter 7 certain of the numerous techniques used to facilitate learning in industrial training activities: on-the-job training, lectures, role-playing, vestibule schools, visual aids, etc. An understanding of learning theory and principles is essential to the critical evaluation of techniques used in modern industrial training.

LEARNING THEORY AND INDUSTRIAL TRAINING

There are two major groups working in the field of learning. One group is made up of those persons who must meet daily the pressing, practical problems of guiding and directing the learning of others; teachers, parents, foremen, and industrial trainers are a large part of this group. They also have been working with problems of learning much longer than the other group.

Generally, these people are empiricists. They try something, and if it works or seems to work, they try it again. What they try may eventually become an established method of training. Some of these methods are excellent and some worthless. This group of practitioners has neither the time nor the inclination to ask any questions about the "why" of their methods. They work on a rule of thumb basis, sometimes with excellent results. After all, children were taught arithmetic and artisans their skills long before any formal experimental effort was made to investigate the learning process.

A second group has appeared within the last 100 years. It is made up of the learning theorists. The theorists generally have little interest in the practical problems of teaching a mechanic his trade, or a salesman to sell life insurance. They are concerned with the nature of learning, how learning takes place, and the variables which facilitate and retard learning. The theorists have attempted to solve the riddle of learning through the use of the standard methods of science—controlled experiments and mathematics. Nor have they restrained from telling the world what they have and have not learned about learning. A selected bibliography on the subject of learning covering the period April 1, 1957, to April, 1958, lists 204 journal articles and books (Kendler, 1959).

Unfortunately, communication between learning theorists and learning practitioners is comparatively rare. The practitioner usually practices without the benefit of the discoveries of the theorist; the theorist theorizes and researches without adequate knowledge of the learning problems which practitioners must solve. The theorist is partly responsible for this lack of communication. As McGehee (1958) has pointed out this has arisen for several reasons:

First, these men are trying to develop "scientific" theories, i.e., generalizations which closely approximate the phenomena under consideration. Consequently, they have to adhere to procedures in their experiments which hold all variables constant except the experimental variable(s). This has resulted in too many reported studies which appear to the practical trainer as almost puerile. Yet it is only by the careful addition of this bit of knowledge gained from studying the maze learning behavior of the white rat or of that bit from pursuit meter responses of college sophomores, that precise knowledge concerning learning is developed. This naturally has led to difficulties in applying these bits of knowledge to everyday problems of training. An experiment which demonstrates conclusively that white rats tend to repeat "rewarded" responses in learning an elevated maze does not lead easily to the generalization that Rosie the Riveter responds in a similar manner. So the research, on which many theories of learning are based (since they deal with rats, chimpanzees, pre-school children, and college students) are not easily assimilated into the mores of the individual who must plan a training program to cut learning time for a group of operators assembling electrical relays or sewing seams on towels.

Second, the language used by learning theorists is esoteric and often (what is worse) mathematical. Again this is a penalty of their trade. Not only must generalizations be discovered but they must be stated in unequivocal terms. Much of the English language is vague and pluralistic. Common words have multiple meanings and each hearer interprets in his own way. For example, Hull states "reaction-evocation potentiality is the product of a function of the habit strength multiplied by a function of the strength of the drive (5,242)." This can mean different things to different listeners. However, if the same principle can be expressed (as Hull does state it) ${}_sE_R = f({}_sH_R) \times f(D)$ and these symbols are substituted for mathematically, everyone understands precisely what Hull means. Or do they? Actually, where common everyday concepts are used, considerable misinterpretations arise. Thorndike, for example, revived the old Hedonistic controversy with his law of effect by using everyday terms like "satisfaction" and "annoyance." It is unfortunate that the necessity for exactness in terminology has obscured (except to the initiated) the general principles of learning postulated by learning theorists like Hull and Tolman.

Finally, these searchers after fundamental truths are human, even as you and I. They bring to their search for underlying principles their own predispositions and they become enmeshed in their own theories.

Accordingly, not only do they interpret the results of their experiments in terms of their theoretical orientation, but also they design experiments which serve to test their theories in terms of their theoretical orientation. Again, the hypothetical man from Mars, provided he was a non-connectionist, non-reinforcement theorist, and non-Gestalter, could find definite evidence to support each of these theories in the famous study of the learning of simians reported by Köhler. The dispute among theorists concerning the learning process has increased the confusion of the layman without an appreciable gain in controlling the process (p. 305–306).

The practitioner, however, is not blameless. He often wants a quick answer to a problem for which there is no simple answer. He seeks panaceas instead of solutions. He uses theory in a limited way even if it is merely a theory as to what his boss would like. Careful study of the results coming from the work of the theorist would give the practitioner in industrial training a broad understanding of training problems and a more adequate approach to finding answers to them.

We do not attempt to discuss in detail the various theories of learning which have been developed during the past 100 years. We merely suggest that the training specialist in industry familiarize himself with these theories in the excellent summaries which are available. We are suggesting this not as simply a stimulating intellectual exercise, but as a source of sound ideas concerning planning and directing industrial training. For example, careful study of the works of Skinner will suggest to the training specialist that his responsibility for training an employee does not end after the employee acquires new behavior. Providing for the maintenance of this behavior over a period of time is equally as important as bringing it about initially.

Familiarity with learning theory and principles may also help training specialists and those with supervisory functions to work out new and better ways to handle informal day-to-day training situations. Although we are primarily concerned with formal training in this book, we believe that the points discussed below should enhance supervisory effectiveness in informal training settings. Instead of presenting a detailed theoretical discussion of learning, we discuss certain discoveries which various investigators have made about the learning processes. We emphasize those aspects of learning theory and principles which seem particularly pertinent to industrial training including:

1. the nature of the learning process
2. motivation and learning
3. factors affecting learning efficiency
   a. practice and conditions of practice
   b. individual differences
   c. nature of material to be learned
4. transfer of training and maintenance of behavior.

Data Limitations

The reader must remember, however, that much of the data presented on learning come from experiments conducted in other than industrial situations. Research on learning has been conducted in two major settings. First, and most extensive, data have come from investigations initiated in universities. The subjects used in these experiments were students, monkeys, rats, and pigeons. A second source of data is from studies conducted by the research organizations of the armed forces using military personnel as subjects.

Basic research sponsored or conducted by industry is noticeably lacking. Therefore, despite the title of this book, what "principles" of learning we can describe have been developed for the most part in settings other than industry, using subjects other than employees. It is impossible to tell the extent to which principles so developed can be generalized. Even if we grant that the principles are valid, the problem of application is tremendously difficult. Granted that motivation is important to learning, what are the relevant, manipulable motives in the industrial training situation? Once identified, how can they be increased in strength to an optimum point but not to the point that learning again becomes inefficient? It is a simple matter to deprive a rat of food and make food the relevant goal object. What are the relevant motives and goal objects which can be used in industrial training?

There is an additional limitation to the data derived from the experiments of the learning theorists. They rarely investigate learning tasks requiring complex knowledge and skills. Experimental investigations of the development of attitudinal behavior are only recently becoming less rare. It is entirely possible that principles derived from the investigation of a short-cycle learning task such as that presented by a pursuit meter exercise are not valid for acquiring the complex skills necessary to operate a turret lathe. Learning to program a computer may involve different principles from those in mastering a list of nonsense syllables. Research, however, may show that complex behavior is developed or learned in ways similar to that of learning lower level skills and knowledge. We must be cautious, however, in extrapolating conclusions from experiments of pursuit meter learning to learning to manage a production department of 500 employees.

Yet the only sizeable amount of data we have on learning comes from nonindustrial subjects performing relatively simple learning tasks. We believe that some of these principles are better guides to planning industrial training than the folklore of training. In fact when they have been used in industrial training, observational rather than experimental data suggest that they are effective. The reader should realize that the discussion which follows is a heuristic guide based upon incomplete information.

THE NATURE OF LEARNING

When observing a person acquiring a new skill, what do we see? At first, there is a good deal of confusion, or apparent confusion. The person makes numerous errors consisting of the wrong responses and of right responses at the wrong time. As he continues to practice the task, many of the errors cease and his responses become smoother, more precise, and better timed. At later stages, responses which were at first clearly distinguishable from each other now become molded into a fairly continuous, complex response. Finally, only occasional errors occur, the intervals between subtasks are shortened, less self-instruction ensues, and the performance becomes almost automatic. After much practice, the individual may be able to carry on conversations and look away from his work while still performing smoothly. We are concerned with how this transformation takes place and with ways to keep the smooth, polished performance at a high level. What happens? What variables operate to bring about this change?

The changes which take place in developing a skill are perhaps more obvious than those in acquiring knowledge and in developing the ability to solve problems and to make decisions. Certainly, the subtle changes in behavior which take place when an individual develops an attitude toward a given person or object are very covert. Although our information about behavioral changes which take place as an individual learns a conceptual or attitudinal response is not as well-documented as the changes in learning an overt motor response, it seems that a description of behavioral modifications as the result of learning is similar for the many forms of learning which occur daily. Uncertain and inappropriate responses diminish; specific and appropriate responses replace them. Behavior becomes organized and coordinated.

Learning and Performance

It should be obvious to the careful reader that our description of learning is a description of behavioral changes which result from experience. We never observe directly the process which we call learning. It is a process we infer from an individual's behavior prior and subsequent to experiences of specific kinds. It is a construct that we use to describe certain changes taking place in the organism. The exact nature of these changes is still unknown and subject to considerable speculation. At our present state of knowledge, it does not seem to be pertinent to our purpose to speculate about the nature of these changes. In fact, many theorists would hold that such speculation is unnecessary as long as we can adequately describe and predict behavioral changes.

This points up the fact that when we observe a trainee's performance we may or may not be observing the results of the process we have called learning. Experience can bring about behavioral modifications which are concomitants of processes other than learning. If a trainee becomes tired, his performance will deteriorate. After adequate rest, however, he may return to a high level of performance. If the skill no longer serves as a means to a goal, he will cease performing the task in a skillful manner. If he becomes bored with the task, he will perform in a perfunctory manner. He has not necessarily "unlearned" this skill. With an appropriate goal or a brief change in activity, he again will perform with skill.

When we say an individual has "learned something" we are inferring from his changed (usually improved) performance that some sort of relatively permanent change in his response repertoire has taken place. We can detect this change only by observing his behavior. The importance of this distinction between learning and performance should be clear. A temporary improvement in performance does not necessarily mean that the trainee has "learned" the task at hand. The improvement may be the result of a number of fortunate chance occurrences; and, unless additional practice is provided, we may stop training too soon. A decrease in the level of performance may be the result of many factors other than forgetting: fatigue, lack of motivation, boredom, change in motivation, and other causes. To assume that poor performance necessarily means little learning may result in wasted training efforts. Additional training or practice may result in further deterioration of performance. In such cases, time and energy might be better spent on a provision for rest, task variety, or an attempt to discover and increase the level of appropriate motives.

Briefly, then, we do not know whether an individual has learned until he has performed. Certain neural and other types of modifications may have taken place within the individual, but learning is demonstrated only by performance. A trainee demonstrates the acquisition of a skill by performing a skilled act. He demonstrates that he learned a body of knowledge by recitation or by answering questions about it. Certainly, any training method which does not provide ample opportunity for the trainee to perform allows little opportunity for the trainer to determine what the trainee has learned. Perhaps the most serious limitation of the lecture method as a training technique is its typical failure to provide ample opportunity for the learner to demonstrate what he has learned.

It should be pointed out that we generally think of the changes of behavior which result from learning as improving performance. Certainly, this is the goal for which we are striving. Yet behavior changes which result in deterioration of performance can be and frequently are the results of the process which we have called learning. Inadequate ways of performing a task, errors in information, and antagonistic attitudes are learned just as are responses which are considered adequate and appropriate. The circumstances which surround learning determine to a large extent whether or not the resulting performance represents an improvement in behavior. We shall discuss the factors which influence the results of learning—the behavior of the individual which comes from experience. The major factors to be considered are: motivation, conditions of practice, individual differences, and the behavior to be learned.

MOTIVATION

Learning and Goal Orientation

Most students of behavior agree that the human being is a goal-oriented organism. Individuals want things and direct their activities toward obtaining the things they want. An employee wants more money for whatever more money will give him—prestige, a new fishing reel, or to pay off an installment on his car. He directs his activities toward getting more money in any of many different ways. He may work faster if he is being paid on a piece rate, he may get additional training in order to qualify for a higher paying job in his company, he may seek higher pay in a job in some other company, or he may "moonlight," shoot craps, or put in a grievance to get the rate of his job increased. In fact, he may do several of these things, or many others not mentioned here, to achieve his goal for more money. This example of the goal-directed activity of human beings could be multiplied indefinitely with examples from the work-a-day life of employees. It is sufficient to say, however, that both common sense and experimental evidence substantiate the goal-directed nature of the behavior of human beings.

Learning theorists generally agree that an individual will learn most efficiently if he is motivated toward some goal *which is at-*

tainable through the learning of a particular sequence of acts and/or a body of knowledge. Although all theorists do not regard motivation as a *sine qua non* for learning, all would agree that it is most efficient where the learner's behavior will achieve a desired outcome. It is necessary that both the outcome must be desired and the behavior must appear to the learner as having some relation to achieving that outcome. The relation may be as simple as temporal contiguity between a response and achieving the goal. If the behavior-outcome relationship is obscure and the learner is striving toward his desired goal, he may ignore attempts to teach him the new behavior and try other kinds of behavior which appears to be relevant to his goal.

In conducting a training course for foremen on the union contract, for example, it is imperative that we realize that a number of things may happen. Some men may feel that they have more important production problems to worry about and will spend training time thinking about them and complaining about being taken from the job to learn a lot of "legal nonsense." Or they may enjoy the opportunity to get together with "the boys" and swap stories. Still others may see the training class as an opportunity to show how much they already know, and to strive for greater recognition in the eyes of the trainer and fellow trainees. A few may see that a thorough grounding in the contract may aid them in handing out job assignments, settling disputes, explaining vacation policies, and avoiding grievances.

At the risk of oversimplification, this illustration emphasizes a number of interesting points. First, the behavior of people is oriented toward relevant goals, whether these goals are increased recognition, production, or simply socialization. People will attempt to achieve those goals which are salient at the moment, regardless of the trainer's intent. Second, the motives of the individual foreman, the change of work setting from the line to the classroom and his fellow foremen will change his behavior. Whether this behavior becomes typical for him in this setting in the future will depend on the consequences of his behavior. If the foreman, striving for recognition, achieves his goal by bragging about the number of units produced last week, he will learn quite a bit in the classroom—that this is a place where he can get ego-recognition and the way to get it is to show off. In fact, he may find that the attempts of the instructor to engage in training thwart him in his efforts. He may resent the instructor's presence and avoid learning what is being taught. Third, despite the fact that the foremen are all adult males with similar jobs in the same company, they view the training meeting as a means to very different ends. Fourth, unless the trainer makes the relationship between the learning of the contract and the performance of the job quite clear, many men will do whatever they can in the classroom to achieve some desired goal, such as, talk to the man next to them, think of ways to meet a deadline, map out an approach to the new blonde, daydream. Points three and four are related. The foremen will view their jobs differently so that it may be necessary to show them how learning about the contract will achieve several goals–reduction of formal grievances, easing the job assignment problem, inducting new employees. Later we return to these points more formally. Until then, the reader might well ponder similar situations in his own experience which illustrate these points.

We may have created the impression that the motives, goals, and behavior employed to reach the goals are necessarily and obviously apparent to the behaving person. If so, we want to caution the reader that this is not our intent. The man, bragging about his production record to the detriment of a smoothly running class, may not be aware of his motives or the effects of his behavior on the class. However, as long as he gains recognition, he will continue to behave in this fashion. It is both unnecessary and incorrect to insist that a person is aware of the factors underlying his behavior.

Motivation Defined

The concept of motivation is so complex and so variously defined that it will be impossible to describe it as used by all theorists and practitioners.[1] In addition, it is almost as ambiguous as a term like "personality." Therefore, it frequently loses its usefulness as a theoretical concept. At our present state of knowledge, it would be foolish to tie ourselves to a rigid defini-

[1] For a brief, but very clear discussion of the many uses of such terms as motives, drives, and needs, see: Viteles (1955).

tion which, because of its precision, would necessarily restrict us to an application of the concept to a few well-defined situations. For our purposes, therefore, let us talk about a motivated person as one who is striving toward some goal. The goal need not be available at the moment to say that he is motivated. A man may be hungry in the middle of the morning but not appear to be, unless the relevant goal-object is present. If it is, he will eat.

Conflict of Motives

A person can be under the control of several different motives at the same time. The act of dining is pleasurable because it satisfies several desires at the same time: it assuages hunger pangs, provides pleasant taste experiences, gives one an opportunity to rest in a comfortable chair, provides an occasion for pleasant conversation with family or colleagues, provides an occasion which can be preceded by pleasurable libations, and may serve as an opportunity to move closer to some other goal in business or elsewhere. Thus, a person may want to eat for many "reasons."

Frequently, however, our motives are in conflict with each other (Miller, 1944). Because we have limited facilities to satisfy our desires, we may have to postpone the attainment of some goals in order to achieve others. A foreman may postpone his lunch hour despite his hunger in order to complete a rush job which will put him in good standing with his manager. A worker might agree to work overtime on opening day of the fishing season in order to earn money for better tackle. The lack of time, money, and physical facilities, as well as the impossibility of being several places at once makes it difficult to do all we want to do.

Not all goals toward which a person strives are completely positive in character. Where they are, the choice is simple. A hungry child confronted with a choice between two equally attractive pieces of candy has a very easy choice. Once he moves in the direction of one, he will choose it and choose it quickly. On the other hand, some goals have both a positive and negative character. A bachelor approaching marriage is both attracted and repelled. He gains certain benefits by marrying, but must also take on added responsibilities and lose certain freedoms. Under these conditions, he will move toward marriage at first while the attractive aspects are most salient. But as he gets closer, the negative aspects become apparent. If the negative are stronger and the situation is unchanged (no announcements are sent out, etc.) he will probably "chicken out" by postponing the wedding or backing out altogether. At the point when the positive and negative aspects are about equal, however, he will vacillate a great deal—first he will, then he won't, he will, he won't. If the positive aspects are stronger or the situation changes (parents, friends, and society make it more painful to back out), then he will probably go through with it. A similar analysis may be made of a new employee's behavior when he reports for work.

Finally, an individual may be confronted with two unattractive choices—he is "between the devil and the deep blue sea." As he is about to choose one alternative, its punishing characteristics become more apparent, so he turns to the other choice. An employee who has spoiled a piece of valuable stock may be tempted to conceal it to avoid the immediate wrath of his foreman. As he starts to do this, however, the possibility of the even more serious consequences of deliberate deception (if discovered) becomes apparent. He is confronted with a choice of making a clean breast of it now, or taking a chance on getting new stock without discovery of the ruined piece. As he starts to do one, its punishing characteristics become more salient; he starts toward the foreman and then stops or returns to his machine. Then he heads toward the stockroom, but suddenly becomes certain that the foreman is going there himself. So he returns to his machine again. This vacillation will continue so long as the individual is forced to choose and cannot avoid being confronted with the choice. If he can avoid it, he will do so rather than choose one or the other.

Of course, more complex situations can arise, such as being confronted with several choices, all of a positive and negative character. In cases similar to the last two examples, the human being will vacillate in his behavior, first deciding to do one thing and then the other. If all choices are repugnant, he will attempt to avoid making a choice at all.

The significance of this discussion to the trainer is obvious. He must recognize that people are multimotivated, that similar behavior shown by different people may result from different underlying motives, and that he must expect vacillation and indecision from people in the day-to-day work situation. The mere recognition of indecision and an attempt to discover the underlying cause may suggest solutions to the problem. An employee may have difficulty deciding whether to accept a transfer. The supervisor may recognize the importance of the transfer in terms of eventual promotion and be unable to understand the inability of his subordinate to decide whether or not to accept it. Perhaps the supervisor is aware that the employee's family wants to stay where they are, but feels that he has pointed to the benefits of the move in such a way as to override the disadvantages of pulling up roots. Stressing the positive aspects, however, may not be as effective as a careful explanation of the way in which the company training program will prepare him for the job and minimize the risks of failure in taking on a strange assignment. A recognition of competing pressures, and of the fact that the negative aspects of a choice become more apparent the closer one is to choosing that alternative, help considerably in understanding human behavior.

Reinforcement in Terms of the Perceptions of the Individual [2]

Any event which occurs in such a way as to change the probability of a given response is said to be reinforcing. We speak of rewards for certain behavior (positive reinforcers) which in-

[2] In discussing learning, reinforcement, perception, and similar technical concepts, we present a nontechnical picture of the organization and maintenance of these kinds of behavior. We shall not be bound by the rigid definitions of most theories and will probably repel some theorists by a mixing of constructs from several theories. Although recognizing that this may weaken our presentation from a technical standpoint, we hope to give the reader a sense of familiarity with such terms without burdening him with the weight of restrictive definitions.

crease the probability that this behavior will occur again. We also speak of various kinds of punishment (aversive stimuli or negative reinforcers) which, when removed, increase the probability of the reoccurrence of the response preceding their removal. Actually, punishment seems to inhibit the occurrence of response rather than eliminate or extinguish it. Instead the response which leads to the avoidance of punishment is reinforced. However, it should be emphasized that the role of punishment in learning is not completely clear as yet. Failure to reinforce a response, on the other hand, does seem to lead to the extinction or dropping out of that response. Knowing that not reinforcing a response leads to its extinction would suggest that the trainer can frequently eliminate undesired behavior which is directed at appropriate goals merely by failing to reinforce it. This is true as long as there are no other sources of reinforcement which would maintain the undesired behavior. Often, failure to reinforce a response may have a better long-range effect than a reprimand from the trainer, even though the reprimand gives the trainer some temporary relief or satisfaction. There are at least three reasons for this:

1. Punishment may suppress the response, but it may appear again if the source of punishment is not available at a later time.
2. Punishment can be disruptive and have its effects on larger behavior segments than the undesired response.
3. Repeated punishment from the same person may have the effect of altering the perception of the punishing person so that he is both avoided and also loses his effectiveness as a source of positive reinforcement.

Whether or not an event is reinforcing will depend upon the perceptions of the individual who is learning. This statement may appear to mean that we do not know what kinds of events will reinforce a particular individual's behavior. Literally, this is exactly what it means. What one person regards as a rewarding experience may be regarded by another as neutral or nonrewarding, or even punishing. In general, however, there are various classes of reinforcers—food, status recognition, money, companionship—which are reinforcing to almost everyone at one time or another.

This "one time or another" qualification carries us back to the perceptions of the individual. These perceptions will depend on the individual's past experiences with such events and the relevance of the event to his present motives. If a hungry man is given money as a consequence of his behavior and he has learned that food can be purchased with money, money will reinforce that behavior. If, however, he has not had this means-to-an-end experience with money, it will not. On the other hand, if money always had to be used immediately for highly perishable food and the man was not hungry, again, money would not be reinforcing. This example is admittedly artificial, but it emphasizes the point that whether an event is reinforcing or not will depend on the individual's experience with it and his motives at the time a given behavior occurs. The phrase, *motives at the time the behavior occurs,* is of key importance in understanding behavior. It emphasizes the fact that man is multimotivated and also emphasizes that a given motive may be salient at one time and latent at another.

But let us illustrate these last points in a training setting. We have all heard that praise is an effective means of reinforcement. This statement is probably true in general, but may not work out in practice. It is easy to imagine situations in which praise from a given trainer would not only fail to reward, but also may actually punish the trainee. If the trainer is held in contempt by his trainees, any man who gains favor in the trainer's eyes is obviously not worthy of acceptance by the group of trainees. To receive praise may be tantamount to ostracism if group acceptance is important to the trainee and, therefore, severely punishing. In other instances, where a trainer has no direct (line) authority over the trainees, his administration of praise and reproof may have little if any effect upon the trainees. It should be clear, therefore, that a change in the probability of a response being repeated depends to a very large extent on the perceptions of the trainee. These perceptions are, in turn, affected by his motivation and previous experiences in similar situations.

Getting the Trainee to Recognize the Need for Training

If we agree that learning is facilitated if the learner is properly motivated, we should then search for ways to motivate him. *One* way to do this is to help him recognize the need for training.

With a new man, this does not seem to be as serious a problem as it is with an experienced worker. For this reason, the motivation of new workers is frequently ignored. But let us put ourselves in the position of the young trainee and ask ourselves how we view the training situation. Specifically, let us ask what our motives are in this situation which resembles, in our now limited experience, the high school or college classroom. Miller (1953, p. 2) has pointed to a number of predispositions which the trainee probably brings with him to the training setting:

> The trainee approaches his first session . . . with a number of attitudes, ideas and probably prejudices concerning the value of the (training) device or training procedure and also his own abilities and capacities to master the learning "problem." Whether or not he is highly motivated to perform the operational job, he will generally search out in the situation which offers a challenge to him some means of rationalizing his failure if he is destined to "fail." He will look for a way out ahead of time in the event that he may need it. Every learning situation is, in some degree, a prestige situation for the learner.

Miller adds that the trainee has usually picked up gossip concerning the effectiveness of the training and the trainer. Even if he is favorably disposed toward the training and trainer, he will probably be initially concerned with the ways in which he can succeed in the situation and avoid failure. Even if the trainee is favorably disposed toward the training program, the trainer must recognize the trainee's perceptions of the situation and quickly provide the means for the satisfaction of the trainee's goals. Once having established ground rules congruent with training objectives, the trainer must abide by them or the trainees will attempt to achieve their goals through kinds of behavior which are undesirable from a training viewpoint.

But now let us assume that the trainee has not received the kind of indoctrination which would favorably dispose him toward the training technique, trainer, or training device. If he is not motivated "to try" in this situation, he will behave in accordance with salient motives and may sleep, get to know the rest of the boys, do the minimum amount of work without failing, or "knock" the course and trainer to rationalize his potential failure.

It will not only be necessary to show the trainee "why" he should submit to training—to reach standard sooner and thereby earn better wages sooner, or to prepare himself for a position with more prestige—but it will also be necessary to show the trainee how *this* training will help him reach his goals. Too frequently we assume that the connection between the training program and the goal is obvious. The means-end relationship between the various kinds of behavior to be acquired and relevant goals must be spelled out for the desired learning to take place. If not, learning will undoubtedly take place, but not that which is desired.

Hilgard (1956, p. 475) makes a related point very clearly:

> The understanding which the learner wishes in a problematic situation is knowledge of the essentials to economical goal-achievement, *and nothing more can be counted on.* The mistake is sometimes made in teaching school children (or college students) of assuming that they wish to understand what lies behind a process which is for them just a tool. They wish to know how to use the tool to reach immediate goals; the further curiosity is related to different goals, which may be goals for the teacher but not for them.

Lest we be misunderstood, we do *not* believe that our schools should become vocational training centers. But any student is justified in asking why he should study the arts, or sciences, or spelling, or mechanical drawing, or anything. There are meaningful and important answers to these questions other than getting good grades. Perhaps we should devote more energy to discovering ways to make the learning task more meaningful and interesting to the student. This point leads us to our next topic.

Development of Intrinsic Task Interests

If motivation is so important to learning, what kinds of motives and goals exist in the industrial situation which can be utilized by the industrial trainer?

Let us begin by discussing some of the incentives offered the employee. Various methods of compensation are the first things which come to mind: straight salary, piece rates, bonus systems, and fringe benefits. Undoubtedly, compensation is an extremely important incentive. But there are others available which are sometimes more important and sometimes less, depending on the job, economic conditions, and people involved. Data from numerous studies show how employees rank the importance of various job incentives (Herzberg, et al., 1957). Usually, we find that compensation ranks well below such things as job security, opportunity for advancement, and good supervision. Whether compensation is less important than these factors, however, is problematic. Many of these surveys were conducted during times of relative prosperity and in situations where compensation is both assured and adequate. If economic conditions were to change, it is possible that the importance of this incentive would outrank the others. Whether or not this is true, there seems to be little question that compensation is important.

The importance of compensation to the trainer, however, depends on the extent to which he can use this incentive to facilitate learning. Where individuals are on an hourly rate and the program for advancement within the rate schedule is out of the trainer's hands, there is very little he can do with this incentive. If he determines when the employee goes from the "learner's" to the regular rate and the difference between the two is substantial, this incentive can be a powerful one, if used carefully. Piece rates and various bonus systems can be powerful incentives, too, if other pressures do not exist to counteract their effects. Where the work group resists, however, they may not only slow the work of experienced workers, but also may create problems for the new employee who has been progressing rapidly under the tutelage of the trainer.

Because of the complexities of compensation schemes and the effects they have on other work variables, it is only infrequently that this serves as a manipulable incentive for the trainer. In addition, so many motives operate in the work setting as to make this a less important incentive than we formerly believed. It is possible, however, that new developments and new thinking about management theory may alter this condition (Nation's Business, 1959). Assuming for the present that compensation is only rarely available to the typical trainer as an incentive, what other incentives are available?

There are many: praise (sincerely put and from a valued person); good working conditions (lighting, warmth, ventilation, comfortable surroundings, etc.); pleasant relations with peers, supervisors, and subordinates; the acquisition of skills; status within the work group and community; and others. Of all these incentives, that most easily available to the trainer is expression of praise. The only other incentive in this list of importance here is that concerned in the acquisition and demonstration of skills. This *is* an incentive and one which can be powerful with certain inherent advantages. It is to this incentive that we shall devote the rest of this section.

There are several reasons for turning our attention to intrinsic task interest and demonstration of skills. First, a recent study by Herzberg, Mausner, and Synderman (1959) suggests that the contradictory findings as to the importance of various incentives may be the result of erroneous assumptions and methodologies. We have thought of factors affecting job attitudes as lying along a continuum, when in fact they may not. They suggest that there are certain conditions which surround the job which, if not adequate, will result in *dissatisfaction.* But if adequate, they will merely bring the worker to a neutral point. Herzberg, et al., call such factors "hygienic." Among these factors are equitable treatment, supervision, physical working conditions, and interpersonal relations. If these factors are favorable they may prevent the development of morale problems but not serve as curative for low morale. It is their contention that "The conditions that surround the doing of the job cannot give him (the worker) . . . basic satisfaction; they do not have the potentiality. It is only from the performance of a task that the individual can get the rewards that will reinforce his aspirations" (Herzberg, et al., 1959, p. 114). In brief, they feel that the real motivation to work and the real source of job *satisfaction* is an individual's achievement and the recognition of that achievement. As the trainer is frequently responsible for building the skills that eventually result in achievement, such theorizing may have great impact on training methods, if demonstrated to be correct.

Gagné and Bolles (1958) make a similar point when they state that task completion frequently serves as a goal in that people are generally motivated to complete tasks which they have started. In addition, if the trainee is ego-involved, successful completion of the task can become a powerful goal.

The foregoing does not deny completely the effectiveness of extrinsic task goals such as more pay, increase in rate, instructor approval, etc. However, Gagné and Bolles make a very cogent point when they say:

> . . . the idea that motivation should be intrinsic rests not so much upon the role motivation plays in learning or in performance during learning; rather, it reflects a concern with the transfer criterion (of efficient training). It seems reasonable to suppose that motives and goals intrinsic to the task are more likely to transfer to the job situation. One reason why training performance is frequently an unreliable indication of subsequent job proficiency may be that the trainee's motives so often change between the transfer (training) and the job situations (1958, p. 10).

It is our hunch that the failure of many executives to carry over skills learned in week-long or month-long training programs to the job is in good part due to the change in motivation between the training setting and the job. In the one case, competition among trainees, striving for peer and instructor approval are important and task-related. When the trainee returns to the job, however, the motivation changes markedly and no incentive is offered for an application of learning to the job. Gagné and Bolles indicate that their points are speculative and "To our knowledge, nothing has been done experimentally to demonstrate that motivation during training has *anything* to do with the degree of transfer to subsequent on-the-job performance" (p. 10).

We are forced to agree that our knowledge is extremely limited in the area referred to by these authors, including the area of developing or capitalizing on intrinsic task interest. We all agree that task interest is one form of intrinsic motivation and should be utilized when possible. It seems reasonable to assume that given two men of equal ability, the man who is interested in carpentry will learn faster than one who finds it dull, all other things being equal.

Our knottiest problem, however, is not how to capitalize on existing interests, but how to develop interests in tasks in the first place. At this point, we must become highly speculative. First, we might hypothesize that the completion of a task which leads to a desirable goal will eventually take on some reinforcing characteristics of its own.[3] Perhaps this is how interests develop. Thus, a trainee who is praised for the efficiency with which she learns to hem a towel comes to regard this task as desirable and interesting. This would be more probable if the task were originally perceived as a "tricky" or difficult one.

Another hypothesis exists in the possibility that the mere act of publicly performing a task may, under certain conditions, make it necessary for the individual to change his attitudes toward that task. Thus, in order to maintain his own self-concept, it may be necessary for him to find and accent favorable aspects of the task and alter his attitude toward it (Festinger, 1957). An employee who makes his living as a night watchman will frequently stress the importance of the materials he guards, fire prevention, and similar aspects of his job to enhance his own prestige. As he does this, he may find his own attitude toward the job changing. To the extent that we can supply the individual with supporting rationale for his attitude change, we may be able to help him develop and *maintain* "interest" in the task.

It is also possible that some tasks are intrinsically interesting to human beings. If this is so, we might be able to increase task interest by modifying various tasks in such a way as to include several intrinsically interesting components, perhaps to capitalize on our "curiosity drive" (Harlow, 1953). The work on "job enlargement" may, in fact, be a special case of this.

There are many approaches to this problem. Perhaps the only systematic experimental work in the area has been done by Irwin and his colleagues (1947), and they would be first to admit that they have barely scratched the surface. If we are to make training and its transfer to the job more efficient, however, we believe that extensive research must be done in the area of developing task interests.

[3] See Gebhard, M. E. (1948; 1949) on this point as well as the effect of the individual's level of aspiration on the change in task attractiveness. Also, see Irwin, F. W. (1947).

We can summarize this section as follows:

1. It is generally agreed that motivation will facilitate the learning of a task or an assignment. It is a *sine qua non* for the efficient performance of a task or an assignment.

2. Human motivation is not a simple one-to-one relationship between a goal and a response. The human being is subject to many competing goals both positive and negative, and the goal(s) which he will strive for are dependent on his perception of these goals and the relationship of his behavior to the attainment of the goals. Goals change in salience. Furthermore, the human being frequently is not aware of what goals he is seeking. Individuals responsible for industrial training must know these characteristics of goal-striving behavior, if they are to plan effectively and execute industrial training activities.

3. Adequate motivation of the learner in the industrial situation is dependent upon, first, proper reinforcement of behavior in terms of the perceptions of the trainee as to what is reinforcing. Second, the trainee must recognize the need for training and effect of the results of training on goal achievement. Finally, although extrinsic reinforcement, properly used, will facilitate performance (and perhaps learning), the most effective motivation comes from making the task or assignment intrinsically reinforcing.

Although motivation is a central problem in organizing and conducting industrial training, there are other factors which also affect the efficiency of learning and performance during and subsequent to learning. We now turn our attention to practice and conditions of practice in learning.

PRACTICE AND THE CONDITIONS OF PRACTICE

Practice

It is obvious to anyone who has tried to teach the simplest skill or to impart the most elementary information to another person that practice is of utmost importance. An individual learns that which he does. He will acquire and maintain, in practicing a motor skill, those kinds of behavior which he performs and which are reinforced. He learns through studying a new subject such as accounting. In studying, he is making implicit responses. Learning from lectures is more effective if the learner is able to rehearse covertly or overtly the points to be learned. It has been shown that a trainee learns a skill more efficiently while watching it on a training film if he also has the opportunity to practice the skill (Murnin, Hayes, and Harby, 1952). We can say, therefore, that for all practical purposes, practice is necessary for effective learning.

There is some evidence that "incidental" learning, or learning without intent to learn, may take place. The evidence, however, is not clear about the absence of practice in this kind of learning. Such learning which has a minimum of practice, however, is very inefficient. In fact, more carefully controlled experiments than those which now support the occurrence of incidental learning may show that incidental learning, if it really takes place, is characterized by a minimum of covert practice.

Practice is, of course, necessary for the maintenance of a skill or retention of knowledge. Forgetting takes place very rapidly unless practice is continued. In addition, there is some evidence that a thoroughly practiced skill will suffer less from interference of later activities than less thoroughly practiced skills. Unless opportunity for practice, overt or covert, depending upon what is to be learned is provided, learning will not be efficient; the desired behavior will not be acquired and maintained.

All practice is not equally effective in producing behavioral changes. There are many ways in which an individual can practice a skill or develop proficiency in a subject matter field. The way in which practice takes place will determine the speed with which a skill is learned and the level of skill developed. Acquisition of knowledge is a function of the way the individual practices in acquiring the knowledge. There is little experimental evidence on the relationship of practice or experience on the development and strength of attitudes. It is possible, however, that the nature of practice or experience has a profound effect on the way in which attitudes are developed and persist.

The effect of certain variations in the ways practice occurs and their relationship to learning have received intensive experimental investigation by persons who are specialists in the field of learning. Among the variations which have received the greatest attention are: massed vs. distributed practice, knowledge of results, reward and punishment, whole vs. part learning, meaningfulness of material to be learned, and guidance during learning. These investigations have established for certain of these variations clear evidence as to their effect on the acquisition and retention of skills and knowledge. The results are by no means as clearcut for certain other variations. In Chapter 6, we summarize the main conclusions now available concerning variations in practice and their effects on learning.

There are also certain limitations to these results when any attempt is made to generalize them to the industrial training situation. As we indicated earlier, studies of this kind, for the most part, were conducted in academic settings using nonindustrial tasks and subjects. The tasks used were relatively simple in comparison with many industrial tasks today. The motivation of the subjects was perhaps different from that of industrial employees.

A second, and possibly more serious limitation to these investigations from an industrial viewpoint, is that they are usually concerned with original learning of the skills and knowledge and not with their transfer to the job. In fact we know very little about relationship between variations in practice to the transfer of knowledge and skills learned in one situation to some other situation (Gagné and Bolles, 1958). This is of particular importance in industry since an employee more frequently than not utilizes skills and knowledge in different situations than the ones in which he originally learned them. The problem of transfer, as well as the effect of individual differences, and material to be learned on learning efficiency, are discussed in Chapter 6.

6 LEARNING AND INDUSTRIAL TRAINING: II

CONDITIONS OF PRACTICE

Massed vs. Spaced Practice

The usual work day in industry is eight hours; whether an individual is an experienced employee or a beginner he is expected to stay at work during these eight hours. If he is a learner, how should the practice of job skills be organized during the day to insure maximum learning and retention? Should he practice a given task in a continuous session until he becomes proficient or should practice on the task be spaced throughout the work day? In training designed for supervisors, is it more efficient to have ten 2-hour sessions spaced 3 days apart or to have five 4-hour sessions spaced at daily intervals? In essence this is the problem of managing practice from a temporal standpoint. Should it be massed or spaced to result in efficient learning and the maintenance of the behavior learned?

Frankly, we have no research evidence on the specific problems presented in the above paragraph. Logic would indicate that, if practice sessions are spaced too far apart, what the employee has learned in the first session may be forgotten by the time he gets to the second. On the other hand, if practice is too close together, or massed, the employee may not learn efficiently due to fatigue, boredom, or interference of various responses with each other. What then is the optimum arrangement of practice sessions over a period of time for efficient learning?

The evidence, at the present time, from the experiments conducted by learning theorists, suggests that spaced practice is more effective than massed. This is true if the skills and materials to be learned are to be retained over a long period of time (Hilgard, 1956, p. 487; Woodworth and Schlosberg, 1954, pp. 729–731 and 786–794). Results of experiments on massed vs. spaced practice in learning simple motor skills and memorizing verbal materials are fairly uniform in showing that spaced practice, with short rest periods, results in superior learning. It is entirely possible that the apparent superiority of spaced practice is due to the fact the rest periods or change in activity allow fatigue, boredom, and other inhibitions to dissipate. Under massed conditions, resistance from these sources may inhibit responses rather than actual learning. As we have indicated earlier, performance is not learning. Since we never observe learning directly, we infer it from performance. So it is possible that more learning takes place in massed practice than we infer from performance. Further, we may infer superior learning from spaced practice simply on the basis of performance unimpeded by fatigue, boredom, and other sources of repression.

There seem to be certain exceptions to the generalization that learning is more efficient under conditions of spaced as contrasted with massed practice. If the material to be learned is relatively short, perhaps a four-step list of instructions for starting a machine, it is often more efficient to mass trials (read the list over and over without pausing) than to space them. Moreover, other research has indicated that making a single trial longer, exposing the learner to the material to be learned for a longer period per trial, may be more efficient than spacing short trials (Underwood and Viterna, 1951).

Problem-solving situations are another possible exception to this generalization although insufficient research has been done to come up with more than a tentative statement about this. Where the learner must discover the correct solution from among a wide variety of possible responses, it is possible that forgetting of what responses have led to failure would occur under spaced conditions. Thus, exploration of the various alternatives all over again would be necessary on the subsequent trials. It is also possible that because of massing, a resistance to repeating the same response builds up. Massing would lead to a wider variety of responses, thereby increasing the likelihood of discovering the correct response. If the problem is too difficult, however, performance may become highly stereotyped. Thus, both massed and spaced trials may help in problem solving.

This discussion leaves unanswered another very important question, if spaced practice is generally superior to massed, what is the optimum interval between trials? To this question, we cannot give a definite answer. As Woodworth and Schlosberg (1954) have said:

> The optimum interval probably differs with the kind of task, as well as with the length of the work period. For the present, in the absence of universally applicable laws, each practical situation will require its own specific investigation to determine the optimal work and rest periods (p. 789).

We have been discussing the effects of distributed and massed practice on the acquisition of material thus far. What about the relative efficiency of these techniques on the transfer of the learning to a new situation, where the stimulus conditions are altered, motivation is different, and the frequency, the pattern, and mode of reinforcement differs? Because of the lack of adequate research, we can do little more than suggest that the effects of massing and spacing learning trials on transfer be studied intensively. It is probable that this research will have to be quite extensive and that even after several more years, we will be able to say little more than that the particular schedule for spacing practice will have to be determined experimentally for each learning situation.

Knowledge of Results

Most training experts would endorse the statement that telling a trainee how he is doing is essential for good training. It is difficult for the trainee to improve his performance unless he is given some knowledge of his performance. Is he performing correctly? If not, what is the nature of his errors? How can they be corrected?

Several reviews [1] of experimental literature dealing with knowledge of performance, or knowledge of results, indicate quite clearly that it is not enough to say, "Tell the trainee how well he is doing." First of all, let us recall the discussion in Chapter 5 in which we emphasized that trainees come into the training setting with diverse motives and differing perceptions of the situation. When confronted with the learning of a new task, operating a drill press or selling blankets to a department store buyer, he will have definite ideas as to what he is supposed to do and how he is supposed to do it.[2] These hypotheses as to how the job should be done will affect the way in which knowledge of results is received by the trainee, and whether this knowledge will facilitate learning. It is quite probable that any training situation will provide some knowledge of results. When a trainee pushes a lever or sorts a one-inch washer into a bin, what he has done has some effect on his environment. He can then judge the extent to which his performance coincides with his perception of an ideal performance. He, thereby, gains some knowledge of his performance. It should be emphasized that the standards the trainee sets up for himself and those of the trainer may *not* coincide. Even if the trainer carefully explains what the job cues are which will indicate success, the trainee may ignore these and attend only to those he considers in line with his hunches as to how the job should be done successfully.

An experience of one of the authors in training life insurance salesmen in how to get an interview is a clear illustration of this

[1] See, for example, Ammons, R. B. (1954), Gagné, R. M., and Bolles, R. C. (1958), or Wolfle (1951).

[2] This point and several others discussed in this section are brought out clearly by Ammons (1954). We have borrowed heavily from this paper in preparing this section. Ammons, however, should not be blamed for any interpretations which differ from his.

point. In this training, he was using a film showing a prospect. The trainee was to introduce himself to the prospect on the screen, describe the purpose of his visit, and then try to arrange an appointment. The time he had to do this was indicated by a white "time bar" at the bottom of the screen which got shorter as time ran out. When the time bar disappeared, the prospect would "talk" to the trainee and try to get rid of him. Then, another time bar would appear and the trainees would try again to set up an interview. Altogether, the trainee would have five or six chances to talk to the prospect, and the prospect would stall in various ways between every time bar. The trainer was careful to emphasize that the trainees did not have to take all the time available, but were to say what they had to say as well as they could briefly and concisely, and then wait for the prospect to "answer" them. The time bar, it was explained, was merely a device to give them an idea of how long they had before they would be "interrupted." In spite of this careful explanation and emphasis on what constituted good performance, some trainees spent most of their efforts in the early sessions trying to time their talks to coincide with the time allowed.

The author in question may have been narrow in his own perceptions, but it took a little time before he recognized that what the trainees were learning and what he had told them to learn were not the same. Some of the trainees became quite adept in finishing their talks just as the time bars disappeared. What they said while talking was unsatisfactory, yet these trainees seemed to be much more satisfied with their performance than the others and more enthusiastic as to the "effectiveness" of the films as a training device. These salesmen *were* learning, but not what they were supposed to learn. They were not stupid or stubborn, but were attending to cues which conformed with their ideas of the task to be learned. It took considerable effort to pull the attention of the trainees from the time bar to other cues such as the appropriate performance standards. Here again the trainer must be alert to the probability that the trainees' perceptions of the task to be learned will differ from his. If the trainees select irrelevant cues to use, they may concentrate on these and "end up responding only partially to the relevant cues, thereby learning nothing about the 'proper' task. . . ." Ammons (1954).

The trainer must look for developing consistencies in the trainees' behavior (timing their responses more and more closely to the disappearance of the time bars), which may be indicative of divergent perceptions. He then must devise ways to change these perceptions and draw attention to the appropriate standards of performance.

Perhaps the most common finding about the knowledge of results is that it affects motivation. Ammons (1954) cites over a dozen studies illustrating this point. Compared to trainees given no knowledge of results, those receiving some were less bored, reported for training on time more frequently, and had more favorable attitudes toward the training and/or experiment. Furthermore, as the specificity and amount of knowledge increase generally the motivation of the trainee will increase. This is true provided the trainee is not already performing so well that knowledge can have little effect on his behavior, or is performing so poorly that it may have a negative effect on motivation.

In addition, knowledge of performance administered properly will have a directive effect: "The more specific the knowledge of performance, the more rapid the improvement and the higher the level of performance" (Ammons, 1954, p. 7). Thus, telling a trainee that he is improving probably will not facilitate better performance as much as a careful spelling out of *what* was done which showed evidence of improvement. There is some evidence, however, that this generalization also is a limited one.

Burdening the trainee with too much information may be as bad as no information at all. The beginning trainee may be able to absorb only a small amount of information. Too much can be both confusing and, because of his probably inadequate performance, discouraging. The trainee not only has to learn the task, but also has to learn how to use the information he receives on the nature of his job performance. It appears, therefore, that the specificity of knowledge should be paced to the level of performance of the trainee. Although, as an example, voice quality —volume, tone, timing, enunciation, and pronunciation—may be important in making a convincing sales presentation, drawing attention to these factors might well be postponed until the trainee has demonstrated that he knows what to say and when to say it.

There is general agreement on another point. The longer we delay the administration of knowledge of results, the less effective it is likely to be. There is probably some optimal time interval (dependent upon the nature of the task) between the learner's response and the administration of such knowledge. It should not be so immediate that the trainee cannot use it in correcting his response. It should not be so delayed as to reward the trainee's behavior at too distant a time after he has made a correct response. The trainer, confronted with this generalization, may be in a dilemma. The skill he is developing may be such that he cannot tell if a response is correct until much later, perhaps after he examines the finished piece the trainee is producing. He then has at least two alternatives. He may try to get the trainee to reinstate symbolically the response to be rewarded, or he may build into his training equipment devices which will permit him to monitor the task as it proceeds. Suppose the trainer chooses the former alternative, but finds that the trainee cannot reinstate the response he made. In practicing a sales talk, the trainee may not remember specifically what he said on a particular trial. The trainer may then review what was said, rewarding as he goes the good things done and offering corrective advice where weaknesses occurred. Again, the degree of specificity used should be limited to that which the trainee can use at that time. The fact that the trainer can, however, review what was said may indicate interest in the trainee and thus have a motivating effect as long as the review is helpful and paced to the trainee's level of learning.

If the trainer chooses the latter alternative, it is important that he pay close attention to the next point concerning knowledge of results. Generally speaking, when knowledge of performance is removed, the trainees' level of performance will drop. It may not drop to the level it might have been if no knowledge of results had been given, but it probably will drop. At the present time, it is impossible to state what the factors are which account for this drop. Part of it is probably attributable to a drop in motivation. Part of it may also be due to the change in the stimulus conditions to which the learner is responding. Finally, part could be attributable (if knowledge of results is in part "reinforcing") to extinction. Despite our lack of information as to the specific reasons for the drop in performance, we can suggest that the trainer take the expected drop into consideration when planning his training program. If intrinsic cues supplying knowledge of results are too complex for the learner to grasp at the beginning of his training period, the instructor may supply artificial knowledge of results until the trainee has grasped the basic performance elements. Then, training on the intrinsic cues can begin as the artificial knowledge of results cues are gradually removed.

Finally, the trainer may want to pay careful attention to those trainees whose performance does *not* drop after such cues are removed. It is probable that these trainees have discovered cues which supply knowledge of results. If the trainees are aware of the nature of these cues (and they may not be), then these may be taught to other trainees. If the cues are not obvious to the trainee who is still performing at a high level, the trainer may have some difficult detective work to do. Even if successful, however, he may find the cues so subtle, complex, or maybe even spurious, that they will be of little help with other trainees.

The trainer, however, should keep one important point in mind. It is possible, or even probable, that trainees will begin to respond to other cues in the setting when obvious knowledge of results is removed. The trainer must attempt to determine what cues are available and disqualify those which will lead to undesired behavior. One way in which such cues can be discovered is to look for developing consistencies in the trainees' behavior and to relate these to cues then present in the training and/or transfer setting.

Knowledge of results can be a powerful factor in facilitating learning. Its control, timing, and specification are not completely understood; the trainer therefore must be aware of the intricacies described above and be ingenious in using this factor in training.

Reward and Punishment

The relative effectiveness of reward and punishment in changing human behavior has been a matter of discussion for many years. At times these discussions have become heated controversies. In spite of the attention given this problem, we still have no definitive answers. Part of the confusion concerning the effective use of reward and punishment on behavior has arisen because of lack of clear definition of the terms. For our purposes, we will call stimuli, which increase the probability of an "approach" response, rewarding. Those which give rise to an "avoidance" response, we will call punishing.

Most authors make statements such as Hilgard's with regard to reward and punishment: "Learning under the control of reward is usually preferable to learning under the control of punishment" (Hilgard, 1956, p. 486). When such statements are made, however, they do not imply that learning does not take place when the punishment is supplied as a consequence of a response. Punishment is generally used to eliminate an undesired response. If a worker continually damages a piece of stock, he may be punished in a number of ways—by the sight of the ruined stock, by his foreman's frown, negative comments or shouts, or by being fired. The question now arises as to what happens to the response which immediately precedes the sight of the ruined stock. Is it eliminated with repeated punishment, or is it merely temporarily suppressed? The evidence on this point is not clear; most of it does indicate that punishment suppresses the undesired response and that a discontinuance of the punishment would result in a reappearance of that response.

Whether the response is merely suppressed or totally eliminated, we still must look more closely at punishment to see how it is that punishment reduces the frequency of an undesired response. Dinsmoor (1954; 1955) maintains that the suppressive effect of punishment is due to the acquisition of avoidance responses which conflict with the undesired response. Thus, to put it simply, a worker eliminates the response of touching a hot steam line because he acquires new responses of pulling his hand away from the vicinity of the line when he is near it.

If an avoidance interpretation of punishment is appropriate, what does this tell us about the use of punishment in training? First, we can state that very severe punishment, although quite effective, may actually disrupt learning and/or result in "freezing." Punishing a worker severely for an incorrect act may both disrupt his total behavior and encourage complete avoidance of the punishing situation. A man who is severely reprimanded for seeking advice on a job procedure may avoid the reprimanding supervisor. Perhaps the supervisor may have thought that the man should not seek advice on such a trivial detail and wanted him to "use his head." He believes he can best impress this on the employee by a severe dressing down. His action may have the desired effect, and the man will not seek his advice on that procedural point again. But the employee may not seek his advice *at all* again. The worker has acquired a new response, of avoiding the source of punishment.

Mild punishment, on the other hand, may be quite effective, if administered immediately following the incorrect response, and if it is informative. Punishment should be administered immediately so that it will have its effect on the undesired response, not a later one. It should be specific to the incorrect response only and clearly differentiated from concurrent responses which are correct. It should be informative so that the proper avoidance response can be indicated. Simply put, punishment gives rise to the avoidance of the punishing situation. There are many ways to avoid the situation, some of which may be desirable, but others which may be even more undesirable than the response being punished. A combination of mild, informative punishment with reward for the correct avoidance response may constitute the most efficient use of punishment. If the correct avoidance response is reinforced, this should decrease the probability of the reappearance of the incorrect response when punishment is discontinued.

Whole vs. Part Learning

If a sales talk is to be memorized, is it more efficient to read the entire talk over and over again until it is memorized or should the learner master one paragraph, then the next paragraph, and then another until the entire talk is learned? In learning to piece up an end on a spinning frame, should the trainee practice the entire sequence of the task or should he learn each part of the operation separately? Numerous experimental studies (McGeoch and Irion, 1952, pp. 499–507) of the relative effectiveness of the whole vs. part approach to learning have been carried out in the past. The results of these studies are not clearcut. One or the other of these methods seems to be superior depending upon the characteristics of the learner, his customary methods of study and practice, and the nature and the length of the material to be learned.

Meaningful material is usually more easily learned. Since an entire sales talk would appear to be more meaningful than a paragraph, we should predict that the whole method would be more efficient. On the other hand, the complete talk might be quite lengthy, making mastery of it a very distant goal. Breaking the talk up into paragraphs would give the salesman a number of easily obtainable subgoals so that the mastery of a paragraph would be both rewarding and encouraging. On this basis, the part method would be superior.

The results of much research on this question supply us with little help in deciding how to lay out the salesman's learning task. Some experiments clearly indicate that the whole method is better. Others that the part method is superior. A combination of the two is frequently recommended, which is to learn one paragraph, then the second, and then learn these together; then learn paragraph three, put all three together, then paragraph four, etc. Whether this is, in fact, superior for a number of different learning tasks is unknown.

One thing is quite clear, the initial learning of single paragraphs is fairly simple. However, once each paragraph is learned separately, a major task still lies ahead of the learner. The trainee now has to relearn a number of things in order to put all the material together. In learning the first paragraph, the completion of the last sentence of that paragraph serves as a signal to return to the first sentence of the paragraph. In putting all the paragraphs together, the learner must overcome these responses and replace them with new ones. Briefly, the learner may find the part method more enjoyable at first, but will find it more difficult later on. The whole method will be difficult from the beginning and may discourage the learner because he fails to see any signs of progress. Perhaps the best advice is that of Woodworth and Schlosberg: "In a practical situation there is something to be said for the flexible plan of starting with the whole but watching for difficult spots that may call for special attention" (Woodworth and Schlosberg, 1954, p. 786).

Meaningfulness

In general, meaningful material is learned and remembered better than material which is not meaningful. It is difficult to state just what is meant by the term "meaningfulness," because no universal measure of this important concept has been developed. However, when we speak of meaningful materials, we are referring to those which are rich in associations and are easily understood. A paragraph as long as this one would be easier to memorize than a list of 100 adjectives. Similarly, new information in your own specialty is more easily learned than material in another specialty. In your own specialty, you are familiar with the meaning of many technical terms and have used these concepts in many situations; they are "your own." Delving into a new area requires the acquisition of new concepts and principles as well as the acquisition of the information being presented.

The implications of the rather consistent experimental findings (McGeoch and Irion, 1952, pp. 469–480) on meaningfulness both with respect to original learning and transfer to other situations is quite clear. In order to simplify the trainee's job, the material must be made as meaningful *to him* as possible. In reading through training courses or watching training films, the authors sometimes have wondered toward what audience the course or film was being aimed. Too frequently it appears that the training director is trying to write in terms which are most meaningful to himself or in terms which will impress his supperiors or peers. He seems to ignore the fact that the new trainee will not have the familiarity with terms, concepts, machines, and materials which will help him make sense out of what is being taught.

Therefore, the concept of meaningfulness has implications not only for the way in which material is presented to the trainee, but also for the preparation of the material which the trainer must carry to others. The trainer must try to think in the trainee's terms, to put his material across with examples and language which are familiar to the trainee.

At the same time, he must attempt to supply as many associations for new ideas and concepts as possible so that they become more meaningful. Thus, later learning and transfer which builds on such concepts becomes easier. A single example of "qualifying a prospect" may not be enough to give the life insurance trainee a grasp of the meaning of this term and an understanding of how he is to go about qualifying a prospect. One advantage of teaching machines (discussed in Chapter 7) may be that the numerous trials and examples used in teaching a concept supply a number of meaningful associations as compared to the usual single example or explanation given in class or in a text.

Meaningfulness of the material being taught, therefore, is a powerful aid to efficient learning. Care must be taken, however, to make sure that the material is meaningful to the trainee, not just to the trainer.

Guidance

The experimental evidence on the function of guidance in expediting learning is limited (McGeoch and Irion, 1952, pp. 287–290). It, however, has received considerable attention in nontechnical literature and in pep talks to foremen. Certainly, it is logical to assume that one of the major tasks of any instructor is guiding the learner in acquiring a new skill or knowledge. We, therefore, must examine the effects which guidance may have on promoting efficient learning.

The trainer can, first of all, offer effective guidance to a trainee by specifying the nature of the task to be learned and the standards of performance to be achieved. If a learner is given the initial concept of the task of hemming sheets as that of producing a given number of sheets per hour, with no guidance as to the quality required, this is what she will probably strive to achieve, number with complete disregard for quality. If a human relations course is presented as a method of manipulating employees rather than understanding them, the trainees will be oriented toward manipulation. Guidance given at the beginning of training will assist the learner in avoiding completely incorrect responses. In addition, it should give him immediate knowledge of results. Since this will direct his responses in the appropriate direction, the learner can escape much trial-and-error behavior in learning a task or acquiring information.

The trainee, however, must eventually learn to make correct responses without any assistance other than that which exists in the normal work setting. Therefore, to complete the learning of a task, guidance must be reduced and finally eliminated as the learning progresses. One efficient form of guidance then is to point out the cues in the setting which tell the trainee when and what responses are to be made. Continuing guidance for too long may encourage the trainee to rely solely on the cues supplied by trainer, rather than those in the normal work environment. If this occurs, the learning process will be retarded.

An important implication of the foregoing is that the nature of guidance should change as learning progresses. At first, a specification of the goals and the task to be learned might be most appropriate. As the learner attempts the task, the trainer focuses his attention on various parts of the task, first in terms of gross behavior and major environmental cues. As learning progresses, less and less guidance is employed, but when it is, it might well be of a different nature, a focusing of attention on the subtler aspects of both response and cue characteristics. The specific form of guidance will necessarily depend on the ability of the trainee and the point in learning at which the individual finds himself.

Smode, Beam, and Dunlap (1959) suggest several ways in which a skilled trainer can facilitate learning. We shall paraphrase them here. The skilled trainer can:

1. Focus the trainee's attention on relevant aspects of the task to be learned as learning progresses.

2. Estimate how difficult the task is for a particular trainee and adjust:

    a. the number of operations to be attempted at one time by this man

    b. the rate of practice

c. the range of error he will permit this trainee at this stage of learning

3. Detect incorrect patterns which are developing and correct them before they become established habits.

4. Determine areas where the trainee is weak and seems to lack confidence and provide extra practice.

5. Provide immediate knowledge of results for the trainee.

The skilled trainer can do all of these subtly and in such a way as to maintain the trainee's motivation. Essentially, his task is one of gradually molding the trainee's behavior, tolerating gross errors at first, but gradually raising his standards as the trainee masters the basic skills and knowledge. As he raises his standards, the points emphasized will change, too.

We have described the administration of guidance as a complex skill in itself. Earlier in this book, we have emphasized the need for training by line personnel. If these two points are placed in juxtaposition we are immediately reminded that "it is frequently easier to do something yourself than to ask (and show) someone else how to do it." This old saw is completely correct if the job to be done is complicated in the slightest, and also a job which must be done only once or twice. In training, however, we are more often concerned with tasks that must be done many times. As long as this is true, it is probably more efficient *not* "to do it yourself." When other pressures are great, many trainers may fall back on an abrupt seizure of the task to be learned in the name of guidance. Impatience on the part of the trainer which prompts such action can never be disguised as guidance. A skilled trainer neither shows the man "how to do it" once and then walks away, nor does he usurp the task entirely. The coach who calls all the signals during the scrimmage puts his quarterback under a severe handicap during the actual game.

INDIVIDUAL DIFFERENCES

Although learning is in part determined by the motivation of the trainee, and in part by the conditions under which the trainee practices, these are not the only factors which determine how well the trainee learns a skill or develops competence in an area of knowledge. Two trainees, practicing under identical conditions with equal motivation to learn, may acquire different behavioral responses in performing a task. One trainee may perform the task more effectively than would the other. The differential performance of these two hypothethical trainees could be a function of both native and acquired differences. The effect of individual differences on the results of an industrial training effort has been neglected frequently in both planning and evaluating the outcomes of a training effort. Aside from the obvious point that a low grade moron cannot acquire the skills necessary to become a plant manager, we must recognize there are important and sometimes subtle differences in the capacities of different individuals to absorb training.

A careful summary of the effect individual differences have on learning (Handbook of Human Engineering Data, 1952) indicates that learning can be affected by such variables as age, sex, motivational state, and capacities of the individual such as intelligence, motor abilities, etc. The same summary indicates also that these variables interact with the nature of the material to be learned in a significant way to produce the evidences of learning which are derived from the performance of learners. Of the various research approaches to the relationship between individual differences to learning, two seem of particular interest to the problem of industrial training.

First, the learning rates of individuals of high and low levels of intelligence have been compared. The evidence is not completely clear here, but does suggest that people of high intelligence learn simple tasks faster than those of low intelligence. There are, of course, many other abilities and their relationship with learning which could and should be studied: mechanical ability, verbal fluency, finger dexterity, etc. Studies relating learning rates on specific tasks to scores of relatively pure factor tests would give us considerable insight into this problem area.

Another general approach is a comparison of the later learning rates and levels of people who were initially low in learning scores with those who are initially high. In general, the few studies which have been done indicate that small differences in level after a standard number of practice sessions become large as practice progresses. The best learners continue to progress at a faster rate and reach a higher level. This generalization is tentative, however, and depends upon the level of skill at the beginning. If the best learner were near the peak of performance when practice started, little opportunity for gain exists. Differences in ability and experience must, therefore, be taken into account in applying this generalization. McGehee (1948) has carefully taken advantage of this generalization in his research showing that he can predict the final level of training performance based upon early training performance. Armed with such information, he has been able to eliminate early trainees who have a low probability of reaching standard performance.

A question frequently raised is whether differences in learning are correlated with differences in retention. For many years, psychologists have concluded that the correlation is rather substantial. Stroud and Schoer (1959), however, have questioned this assumption. They point out that most of the evidence supporting it is based on the analysis of learning and relearning scores; that is, by relating scores on the original learning to scores of relearning at a later time, a common method of measuring retention. They question this procedure because learning ability would probably be reflected in both sets of scores. Using recall as a measure of retention, they found the relationship with rate of original learning to be low. Relearning scores, on the other hand, were more highly correlated with original learning.

Where does this leave us? At the present time, the relationship between learning ability and retentive ability is in doubt. In fact, we might better talk about *abilities*, as there is probably considerable task specificity to consider. The issue will continue to remain in doubt as long as we must continue to rely on experiments which consist in learning simple tasks to a criterion of one perfect trial and retention over periods of days or weeks.

Unfortunately, the relationship of learning speed and individual differences has not received the intensive industrial research that is necessary to tell us much more about this important area. Until the question of grouping in schools was raised again in recent years, this area had received only sporadic attention from researchers. At this writing, this area is becoming more popular again, at least as far as educational research is concerned. There are few if any signs, however, of research on this important problem in industry, except as it is related to the selection problem.

It should be pointed out, however, that those who are responsible for industrial training should be alert to the implications of individual differences for the planning and carrying out of training programs. Management training programs, courses for supervisors, and even on-the-job training for operators will lose much of their effectiveness unless the fact of individual differences in trainees is given careful research and consideration in the development and execution of these programs.

THE NATURE OF THE MATERIALS TO BE LEARNED

The preceding section has indicated that there is an interaction between individual differences and the nature of materials to be learned in terms of the efficiency with which an individual learns. Although the evidence is not clearcut it appears that there is an inter-relationship between conditions of practice and material to be learned.

Problem Solving

The majority of the available experimental data deals with the problem of relatively simple learning of verbal and nonverbal tasks (McGeoch and Irion, 1952). There are little data available on learning involving complex mental processes implied by the concepts of thinking and problem solving and the factors which facilitate this kind of learning. However, a review of human problem solving (Duncan, 1959) tends to minimize the difference in performance in this type of activity and that in other classes of learning and performance. In summarizing the factors which affect this type of behavior, the author concludes that

> Problem solving performance varied most clearly as a function of simple sets, of a few kinds of complex sets, of changes in relationships

among the elements of a problem, of level of problem difficulty, of aids toward solution, and of certain characteristics of the subjects especially sex, age, and reasoning ability (p. 425).

Furthermore, limitations of our information arise from the fact that the tasks used in experiments on which these conclusions are based are dissimilar from the kinds of problems industrial employees are usually required to meet and solve. Can we assume that investigators of human problem solving are correct in their contention that

> . . . problem solving in human adults is a name for a diverse class of performances which differ, if it differs at all, only in the degree from other classes of learning and performance, the degree of difference depending upon the extent to which problem solving demands location and integration of previously learned responses (Duncan, 1959, p. 425)?

If so, we can use as our best guide for ordering training in this type of activity the principles set forth concerning other kinds of learning, such as rote, verbal, and psychomotor learning.

Attitudes

We have stressed from time to time in this text that industrial training is concerned not only with the acquisition of skills and knowledge but also with the development of attitudes. Again, we are faced with a paucity of research data on how attitudes are developed. Authorities are generally agreed that attitudes are acquired—an individual is not born with favorable or unfavorable attitudes toward his boss, his company, or socio-economic system of which he is a part. These attitudes come from experience. Allport (1935) states that attitudes are acquired by four methods:

1. integration of numerous specific responses of a similar type
2. individuation, differentiation, or segregation of response
3. dramatic experience or trauma
4. the adoption of ready-made attitudes of others

If Allport is correct in his description of the source of attitudes, he is saying more precisely that attitudes, as are other forms of behavior, are acquired as a function of experience; they are learned. This means that in attempting to develop or modify attitudes in an industrial situation we are confronted with the same type of problem we meet when we try to teach an employee a skill or impart knowledge. The effectiveness with which attitudes are developed in employees will depend upon the same factors of motivation, conditions of practice, and individual differences which influence any attempt to modify behavior by the process we call learning. Unfortunately, we have little specific information as to how these variables affect the development of attitudes. In this important area of human learning, we lack even the weak guides we have for directing learning in the acquiring of skills and knowledge.

Two general points can be made with respect to attitudes, however. First, the bulk of evidence indicates that newly acquired attitudes or those which do not have strong emotional components can be modified through training. Emotionally laden attitudes are much more difficult to change, and little is known about ways to modify them permanently. Certainly, the credibility of the person attempting to persuade the individual to change—his qualifications, knowledge, and fairness—help determine whether the attempt will be successful. Much interesting research is presently going on which should cast more light on this important area.[3]

Second, it may be that the difficulty in overcoming or modifying attitudes may be due to their being generalized to a much broader spectrum of stimuli than specific skills or knowledge. Skills may be quite specific to equipment or the environment. Attitudes, on the other hand, may be attached to many stimuli in a wide variety of situations. To the extent that this distinction is correct, we would expect that changing attitudes would be more difficult because of the wide variety of stimuli to which the new attitude would have to be attached in order to replace the old.

In our present stage of knowledge about the facilitation of learning in industrial training, there is little guidance which can be given to improve training procedures for teaching problem solving or for developing attitudes. Perhaps all that we can say

[3] See, for example, the work of Hovland, Janis, and Kelley (1953) on communication and persuasion.

is that learning in these areas may differ only in degree and not in kind from the learning involved in the acquisition of skills and knowledge.

THE LEARNING AND TRANSFER PROBLEM

Definitional or Real?

In industrial training we generally follow one or two procedures in teaching employees the skills and imparting the knowledge required for the performance of their jobs. Employees are either trained in the job environment in which they are expected to perform once their training is complete; or they are trained away from the job and are then expected to use the skills and knowledge thus acquired in the job setting. Even when trained on the job, the behavior required of an employee as a learner is not identical with that required of him as an experienced employee. Skills developed and knowledge acquired in vestibule schools and company classrooms must be utilized in a different setting from the one in which they were acquired. The problem of persistence of behavior in one environment, after development in another environment, is the classical learning problem of transfer of training.

A major problem confronting those responsible for training is one of transfer. The purpose of any training program is to further the goals of the organization. If we accept this thesis, it becomes apparent that we are not concerned simply with the acquisition of knowledge, skills, and attitudes. Our ultimate objective is to transfer that which is learned to the job setting. Despite the fact that this statement is an obvious truism, much of what has been written about training seems to ignore this basic point.

Learning theorists have contributed to the apparent schism between learning and transfer by focusing attention on one or the other of these two aspects of the training session to the exclusion of the other. More and more writers are beginning to question the reality of this schism. From a training standpoint we are concerned with the acquisition *and* maintenance of behavior which will contribute to organizational effectiveness. We want our trainees to acquire a skill, carry it to the job, and continue to perform this skill on the job for many months or years after training.

Are the principles which govern the original acquisition of a response different from those governing the transfer of this response to a new setting? If so, is it meaningful to talk about these two processes separately? If not, the artificial distinction may create tremendous problems of application.

We do not believe that this question can be answered satisfactorily at this time. We do not know enough yet. We suspect that even if we ultimately find that we are talking of two separate processes, these processes will not differ as much as we now appear to think they do. It is quite possible that additional research will reveal that the transfer problem is merely one of additional learning, that is, having acquired the response in one setting or with one trainer, we must now learn how to respond in the same way in a new setting or with the regular supervisor. This is not a new conception but is merely a way of talking about transfer without calling it that. But if we try to look at the problem of transfer in this way, we may see that our training problem is viewed differently. What are the implications? First, training cannot stop in the classroom, but must be continued to and modified for the job. This would place a good deal more emphasis on the inclusion in every training program of transitional material to assist the trainee in the application of newly acquired skills to the job. Second, in order to minimize the learning problem on the job, we will want to make the two learning situations as similar as possible. This might mean using the trainee's supervisor as his trainer, as well as using other means to maximize similarity of the two situations. It would also show why it is necessary to adopt similar modes of reinforcement in both training and transfer settings. Finally, it might require using the same reinforcement schedules on the job as used in training or vice versa.

Regardless of the eventual outcome of research on the learning-transfer problem, it is one to which we must pay serious attention. Too often we stop paying attention to the trainee once the job is "learned," whether this learning has taken place in the classroom or on the job. The transition from the "learning" to the "doing" may well be one of the most crucial and most neglected phases of the training problem.

When an individual must take a pattern of skills from one setting to another or must modify his responses to a familiar pattern of stimuli, he is confronted with the transfer problem. If what he has learned in training is appropriate to the new situation, we say that the transfer effects are positive. If the trainee is no better off than an untrained man, the effect is zero. If the trainee finds that his habit patterns interfere with the performance of the transfer task (as compared to an untrained man) the effects are negative. Skills and knowledge, when transferred from one setting to the next, can be helpful, have no effect, or actually be harmful. Transfer effects can be detected when a trainee moves from the training setting to the job, when the job or the equipment is changed, or in a number of similar situations.

A great deal of research has been done on original learning, and, in view of this, it is surprising how little has been done on the important area of transfer. Despite this limitation, we shall be able to state in a general way the conditions which make for positive, zero, and negative transfer effects.

Identical Elements

One principle that seems to stand up reasonably well is that of identical elements. If the responses and stimuli in one task have many elements identical to those in the transfer task, a person skilled in the former will become skillful in the latter more rapidly than the untrained individual. To maximize transfer from one task to another, the first task should resemble the second as much as possible. However, things are not quite as simple as this because we cannot make very good predictions about transfer effects unless we know how the stimuli and the responses of the two tasks resemble each other.

Most authorities would agree that if the trainee must make an old response to a new stimulus, positive transfer effects result. (Once you learn to stop at one red light, it is very easy to learn to stop at all red lights, despite the differences in hue, location, and surrounding environment.) In addition. as the similarity of the stimuli increases from one task to the next, positive transfer effects are greater, and the more likely is the trainee to make his habitual response to this new stimulus. Thus, a statistical clerk will find it easier to transfer from one model of a manufacturer's calculator to another than she will to transfer to that of another manufacturer. In the former example, the keys will probably be arranged similarly and the symbols on the keys will probably also be very similar.

The case for response similarity, however, is not so well established. This area is fraught with difficulties because we do not have good methods for defining what "new" and "old" responses are. We used to believe that maximum negative transfer would occur where we were required to make a new response to an old stimulus. If stimuli were identical, but a new response was required, we would expect maximum negative transfer effects in the form of interference of the old response with the new.

The situation is not this simple, however, as demonstrated by Gagné, Baker, and Foster (1950). They point out that maximum negative transfer occurs not when a completely new response is required by an old stimulus, but when the "new" response is an opposite one. (Instead of pushing the lever down when the red light goes on, we must pull it up.) To the extent that there is no reversal between the stimulus-response relationships from one task to the next, we would not expect negative transfer effects. (Instead of pushing down on the lever, we now push a button.)

It is extremely important that the points covering stimulus-response relationships be understood and applied not only to training but also to equipment design. The trainer must examine the stimulus-response relationships within various tasks and assist engineers in making the equipment usable. Smode, Beam, and Dunlap (1959, p. 3) cite a personal communication from Lund which emphasizes this point:

> On certain aircraft ordnance release switches and communications switches are mounted on opposite sides of the flight control yoke. This arrangement is mirror-imaged for pilot and copilot. It is not hard to imagine what can happen when a copilot of some experience finally advances to airplane commander. Ordnance can be released when all that was desired was to transmit a simple communication.

In industry, a "start button" on a new lathe placed where the "stop button" was on the old lathe could result in serious accidents. The trainer can simplify training and retraining and also contribute to safe practices by analyzing task stimulus-response relationships and conveying his findings to those responsible for the design or purchase of equipment.

Concepts

For many years, we have known that both the speed of original learning and the amount of transfer is enhanced when the trainee understands the concepts, rules, or principle involved in a given task. Judd (1908) showed that boys who were taught the principle of light refraction were superior in throwing darts at underwater targets than those who were not. In many of our training courses, especially those which include classroom lectures, we greatly emphasize concepts or rules. Too frequently we assume that a statement of a principle will result in its application at the appropriate time and place. Having taught a rule, we seem to feel we have done all that is necessary to maximize transfer. To do this is to misapply the principle. The trainees must not only understand the rule but must also learn to apply it under appropriate conditions. If they do not, the concept may remain an abstract bit of knowledge that is never applied to the job. Not only must they understand the principles, they must also learn the conditions under which it should and should not be applied. Practice in the latter area in realistic situations would probably be most beneficial.

Recent research on the principles of training has shed more light on the question of whether it is better to "give" the trainee the concept, or to let him "derive" it by solving a series of problems. Haselrud and Meyers (1958) gave students a number of coding tasks. For some of the tasks students were given the rules underlying the code; other students were not given these rules. For other tasks, the rules were given to the latter group of students and not the former. A week later, all were given new coding tasks using the same principles or rules. On the *original* tasks, many more problems were solved where the rules were given than where they were not. On the *transfer* tasks one week later, however, the students were definitely superior on those problems using rules which they had derived rather than those using rules which were given.

These results raise an important question of criterion. Are we concerned with performance in training or in the transfer setting? As trainers, the answer is obviously "both." But the more important long-range answer would be "in the transfer setting." If this is true, we should be aware of the dangers of accepting good classroom performance as a necessary predictor of good on-the-job performance or as a screen for admission to the on-the-job setting. In addition, we might wisely exercise more ingenuity in training so that the trainee can discover for himself the principles underlying the task. Perhaps the superiority of the derived principle is dependent upon the experience of the trainee in discovering it. He may learn that principles he knows do not apply, try others, find they do not, and then discover the correct one. This experience may be invaluable in applying the correct rule in the right place and, at the same time, may motivate the trainee to apply it. As yet, we do not understand the principle underlying *this* finding. Additional research is needed to clarify the situation.

Despite this lack of understanding, the evidence does indicate that transfer can be enhanced if concepts or principles, both their application and discovery, are emphasized in training.

Overlearning

Another principle which is important for both transfer and original learning is that of overlearning. This term is an arbitrary one, used by psychologists and others concerned with learning, to mean a thorough learning of the task. Frequently, it is applied to continued practice after the trainee has performed the task correctly once or twice. Continued practice until the specific stimulus-response relationships are well learned is extremely important in learning and transfer.

First, where several skills must be acquired and some of these conflict, maximal negative transfer effects will occur if the first task is only *partially* learned. Less negative effects will result if the first is fairly well established or overlearned. In training salesmen to master sales talks for several different products, for example, the trainer should require thorough mastery and use of one before going on to learning the next. If the talks are only partially learned, parts of one talk will intrude into another.

Second, overlearning will assist materially in transfer where the stimuli may vary somewhat from the original training setting. If training proceeds to the point where one response almost automatically follows the next, slight changes in the environment will interfere with transfer less. Each response becomes an important cue for the next. The trainee thus becomes less dependent on environmental cues. The point made here is especially important to the trainer running a vestibule school or to anyone conducting training off the job. Overlearning of task components will reduce interference between components in the original learning and assist in the transfer to the job.

In striving for overlearning, however, the trainer must be alert to the fact that he will tend to discontinue reinforcement as the trainee becomes more skilled. He will be tempted to assume that the trainee knows what he is supposed to do now so he needs no attention. If this occurs, motivation may drop, and the lack of reinforcement can lead to extinction. The decline in motivation may be offset in a number of ways, such as by an indication that less close supervision by the trainer is a sign of real progress on the trainee's part. Reinforcement cannot be eliminated completely, but must be reduced gradually and supplanted by intrinsic task reinforcement.

In summary, transfer of training is a vital and often neglected phase of the trainer's job. We include both transfer of training from the "learning to the doing" even though the learning is done on the job, as well as transfer from learning off the job to doing on the job. As we have seen here and will see more in Chapter 9, performance in training and on the job are not highly correlated. The low correlations typically found are probably due not only to the factors mentioned in Chapter 9 such as the unreliability and inappropriateness of the criteria employed, but also to repeated failure to recognize that the transfer of learning to the job may require additional training.

Transfer may be facilitated through the analysis of stimulus-response relationships required in training and on the job as well as by the teaching, discovery, and application of principles underlying the task to be learned. Finally, interference among task components in the original learning as well as in the transfer to the job may be minimized through overlearning.

THE NEED FOR SYSTEMATIC RESEARCH IN THE PSYCHOLOGY OF LEARNING IN INDUSTRIAL AND BUSINESS SITUATIONS

In the preceding sections of Chapters 5 and 6, we have summarized some of the principles and rules of thumb of managing the learning process derived primarily from nonindustrial research. We have stated that we must regard these "principles" as heuristic guides until they are validated in the industrial and business setting. Perhaps we can best justify this statement by pointing to some of the limitations which laboratory research has.

Difficulties arise immediately whenever we try to apply the results of laboratory research to the industrial setting. First, the subjects used are generally college students, rats, or monkeys. For the learning theorist concerned with testing a specific hypothesis, such subjects are quite appropriate. However, the abilities, motives, and reactions to the training situation differ in a number of unspecified ways for men and women undergoing industrial training.

Second, the criterion of learning employed is generally quite arbitrary and is considerably below that in industry. Very few experiments have required subjects to perform the learned task over months and years. If they did, would the principles be modified?

Third, the tasks to be learned are usually quite simple and easily acquired. Contrast the learning of a list of twenty nonsense syllables or a simple tracking task with learning to run a lathe or supervise a shift. To the extent that some principles are "task-bound" or to the extent that their application differs depending on the task, we are severely limited in applying them to the kinds of training tasks with which we are concerned.

Finally, much of what we have said has been based on studies of original learning. To the extent that different principles are involved in transferring training most efficiently, we are handicapped. The maintenance of behavior on the job may also require different or modified principles. We do not know. Until systematic research is done in business and industry, we will continue to operate in the dark.

One of the more crucial areas of research needed is that of application of learning principles to practice. We have enumerated a number of principles but we also are constantly confronted with the problem of applying them. If we are to train a new recruit to become a life insurance agent, what is the most efficient means of designing his training program? If we are to space his attempts to learn a sales talk, how long a time interval should we require between trials? How long should the talk be before we consider chopping it up into parts for memorization? At what point has he overlearned one talk so he can go on to the next? How do we find out if he has overlearned? If we use one schedule of reinforcement in training, how will this affect his reactions to that which he will receive from his prospects in the field? We have to motivate the trainee to learn. How? What motives are specifically relevant? What motives aren't specifically relevant?

Questions such as these are tough, realistic problems which confront all of us who are concerned with training in business and industry. Only through systematic research can we answer them. At the same time, research will help generate problems for the learning theorist who, in turn, will help to solve them. As we said before, we work with very different subjects, over very long periods of time, and under very different conditions. As we learn more about trainees' behavior, we will generate new problems for the theorist.

Sporadic research, however brilliant, will not give us answers to the many problems concerning learning which are required if we are to make training a useful management tool. What is required to answer these problems is systematic research. A systematic attack on a problem reduces the amount of work and research required to solve the problem. It enables whole areas to be explored at one time and eliminates those which are unfruitful. We can then concentrate on those areas which are more productive of results or show more promise. Systematic research will supply a more formalized and easily comprehensible basis for understanding the present principles of learning as well as the possible addition of new principles. The results of systematic research will simplify and improve the efforts required to train employees efficiently. It will make both the job of line manager and the training director easier. It also will result in training fulfilling more adequately its basic function in industry, assisting in the achievement of organizational goals.

A WAY OF THINKING ABOUT LEARNING AND INDUSTRIAL TRAINING

We have covered many points in discussing "Learning and Industrial Training." We would be remiss if we didn't try to summarize what we have said about learning, and indicate ways of thinking about it which we have found useful in industrial training. We, therefore, should list some focal points for all who are concerned with training people in industry, but we are very suspicious of lists. Unfortunately, they are often memorized through a mnemonic device in which the first letter of each item on the list is learned. The list is recited at appropriate moments, and used to cover up rather than reveal weak points in training programs. In the words of the sales trainer, "it gives the trainer a track to run on," or a handy-dandy check-off list that permits us to turn off all thought processes. We *P*repare the learner, *E*xplain the job, *S*how him how to do it, *O*bserve him do it, and then *S*upervise him or follow up on the training. Put them all together and they spell PESOS, or money in the sales trainee's pocket.

Such mnemonic devices can be extremely useful, if not used mechanically. The trainers who propose them hope they will not be used mechanically. Unfortunately, too many trainers feel that you can do all these (PESOS) as quickly as you can recite the word. In fact, with a check list there is quite a temptation not to: really look at the job; decide what motivation and preparation is most appropriate for the trainee; determine what explanation will be meaningful and what demonstrations most helpful; establish the frequency and length of practice periods, and the kinds and frequency of reinforcements; analyze the task in meaningful units with clearly obtainable goals and subgoals; or to provide for the maintenance and improvement of behavior on the job following training.

Yet, in spite of the inherent danger in a check list, a frame of reference for thinking about learning principles as applied to industrial training serves as a guide for organizing and directing training activities. Too often training is attempted in a haphazard manner with no basic concern for, and little knowledge of, what is known about the learning process. Each person responsible for training should use at least a quasi-scientific framework that recognizes some of the following (unlisted) points.

We are primarily concerned with acquisition and maintenance of desired behavior performed by individuals of varying perceptions, motives, and capacities. We must recognize that not all trainees have the capacity to acquire this behavior. As a corollary to this point, we must also recognize that some trainees will learn best under one training schedule and others will learn best under others. The background, motives, and perceptions of trainees as they come to training will require a flexible program to permit each to attach meaning to the task involved, achieve a desired end which is salient for him, and to learn to perform the task in a manner which is suitable for him. In some areas, such as selling, we may have to recognize that there are many paths to success and that the attempt to force everyone into one mold through training may be a foolish and wasteful endeavor. Briefly, whether our training is conducted in groups or with individuals, we must recognize that we are concerned with bringing *individuals* up to a certain standard of performance and must adjust our training programs and activities in training sessions to meet the training needs of the individual.

Since flexibility is required in training, we must state in more detail the ways in which a training program should be flexible. Individuals are multiply and differentially motivated. They will attempt to achieve some goal or goals in any training or work setting. To assume that trainees are motivated to learn just because they are there is naive. We must recognize the nature of these motives, reduce the strength of those which will conflict with learning, and supply or incite relevant motives by directing the learners attention to task-relevant goals and incentives. Where the task to be learned is complex, we must establish clearly attainable subgoals for the trainee. Once established, we must then reinforce appropriate behavior.

Perhaps most important, we must recognize that human beings are extremely sensitive to their environment, and that their behavior changes as a function of their effects on the environment which coincides with (but not necessarily results from) their behavior. Behavior which is reinforced is more likely to occur again, whether the reinforcement is intended by the trainer or not. However, behavior is shaped only gradually, especially when it conflicts with well-ingrained habitual modes of responding.

An intensive training session will be less likely to induce a permanent change in behavior, not only because of the limited practice available to the individual, but also because the trainee will see the training session as such and as something quite separate from the job. Trainees do seek meaning and will interpret their environment in ways which are meaningful to them. Because the human being is goal oriented, his perceptions are affected by his past experiences and motives, and because his behavior is shaped by the occurrence or nonoccurrence of reinforcement, we must shape our training program to consider these factors. If our training program permits the trainee to achieve desired goals he could not achieve before, then he will learn.

Once the task is learned, we must be concerned with maintaining this behavior in the desired form. Experience on the job, with other workers, or with customers, machines, and material will act to reinforce certain behavior and punish other behavior. The trainer, realizing this, must build his training program to take advantage of "good" influences in the environment and to combat or reduce the effectiveness of "bad" influences. We want the newly acquired behavior to be maintained, not modified. The implications are clear. In order to do an adequate job of training, we must first understand the learning process and the nature of variables which affect learning. Once this is understood, we must re-examine the job and job setting in the light of our new understanding. Unless we conduct this re-examination as "learning directors" rather than "trainers," we may very well fail to capitalize on inherent job characteristics which make learning easier; we may overlook barriers which make learning and behavior maintenance inefficient; and, we may continue to become enamored with each new gimmick or "revolutionary training device" as it comes on the market.

7 METHODS AND TECHNIQUES IN INDUSTRIAL TRAINING

METHODS AND TECHNIQUES

There is a plethora of methods and techniques used in industrial training. Some of them represent rather broad approaches to meeting training needs; others are narrower in scope and have been developed to meet a special training need or to improve on present techniques. We find production employees trained through broad methods such as on-the-job training, vestibule schools, and apprenticeship training. Similarly, in training executives, we find such methods as on-the-job coaching, apprenticeship training, and formal classroom procedures. Within the framework of these broad methods, many techniques are used to facilitate learning. In formal classroom training of supervisors, we find such techniques as role playing, case study, and lectures. In on-the-job training of production workers visual aids, demonstrations, and mock-ups of machinery are used.

In our discussion of training methods, we first discuss those methods of training which differ primarily in the amount of instruction received on and off the job. We then present data on certain selected techniques of teaching which are used either on or off the job.

Whether we are discussing methods or techniques, the reader should keep the questions of cost and profitability firmly in mind. Some techniques, like the lecture, may appear to be quite inexpensive because a single person can prepare his talks in a minimum of time and then present it to large trainee audiences. When we consider profitability, however, it becomes clear that we must add to our formulations that which is learned by each individual and whether or not that learning is transferred and maintained on the job. If the lecture results in no behavior changes or in undesired changes, it will be an extremely unprofitable training technique.

Only infrequently are these factors considered in the evaluation of a training technique so that we have little to guide us. Thus, we should be cautious not to overemphasize cost which is relatively easy to determine as opposed to a complete consideration of profitability which includes cost and also requires precise research to determine the contribution of the method or technique to the goals of the organization. This means that research on methods and techniques will have to include a much broader array of criteria to determine their relative profitabilities.

ON AND OFF-THE-JOB TRAINING

We have taken the position in Chapter 6 that some on-the-job learning must take place regardless of the nature and extent of training received off the job. If provision for transferring what has been learned during training to what must be done when training is terminated is not made, the training effort may be wasted. We have emphasized further that if behavior developed during the training period is to persist, once formal training is terminated, it must be reinforced when the employee takes over full responsibility for performing his job. We say, therefore, that all training should provide for learning activities and the maintenance of acquired behavior. We can, however, make distinctions between training methods in the degree to which the trainee is expected to acquire these skills, knowledge, and attitudes through experiences other than actual job performance. Essentially, we have a continuum, one end of which is on-the-job training and the other end is off-the-job training. Intermediate between these two extremes are the training methods called vestibule, apprenticeship, and similar procedures.

On-the-Job Training

Perhaps the most frequent method employed in the training of employees is on-the-job training. In this method, the learner, in acquiring job skills, knowledge, and attitudes, uses the machinery and materials which he will use once his formal training is completed. He learns in the physical environment in which he will eventually be required to perform his tasks. He will follow day-to-day operating procedures and will associate, during his learning, with his future superiors and peers. In practice, on-the-job training varies in formal organization from simply assigning the new employee to an experienced worker to be shown the job to a formal arrangement with trained instructors assigned to guide and evaluate the learning efforts of the trainee.

On-the-job training has much to recommend it to industry. The learner, at least in part, is paying his way by what he does in the process of learning the job. No special equipment is required for instructing him. From the point of view of learning principles, the method allows him to practice what he is expected to do once his training is completed. The problem of securing transfer of training, therefore, should be minimized.

Economy and maximization of transfer, however, are not inherent in an on-the-job training approach. The performance of trainees, using production equipment and materials, may be such that serious economic loss can arise from utilization of expensive equipment and materials to train the novices. Some tasks, because of their complexity or because of pacing or other pressures, may be more difficult to learn on the job than off the job. Other methods may result in lower training costs than on-the-job training. Finally, it is clear that the choice of trainer is too frequently made on bases other than those which would facilitate training.

In preceding chapters, we have pointed out the inherent weakness of production records as a valid and reliable index of an employee's performances. This certainly is true in the evaluation of trainee's progress in learning a job through on-the-job training. Factors beyond his control, such as machine maintenance, may make production measures inaccurate indicators of the trainee's progress. Generally, no diagnostic measures are available from on-the-job training. This means that, if adequate evaluation of a trainee's progress in on-the-job training is to be secured, provision will have to be made to secure valid and reliable measures.

The lack of diagnostic measures makes it extremely difficult for the trainer to supervise the trainee. Typical production records merely indicate the end product of the trainee's efforts. They do not show *how* he achieved that end product. Several trainees could be producing at 50% of standard but the reasons for this low production could be different in each case. It is imperative, therefore, to develop adequate diagnostic measures to supplement or replace typical production measures during training.

There are little or no data from carefully controlled experiments on the effectiveness of on-the-job training as contrasted with other methods of training. Merenda (1958), however, reports a study of the relative effectiveness of formal school training vs. on-the-job training of naval apprentices. Formal training was found superior. Unfortunately, the criteria used were written examinations for advancement in naval ratings. No evidence was presented that success on these examinations had any relationship to job proficiency.

Although it is theoretically possible to create on the job a maximum opportunity for trainees to learn, it is also very difficult. What mitigates against this is that, whether training takes place in a shop, on a production line, or in an office, the primary function of the shop, production line, or office is not *training*. It is production. Training on the job must take second place to the primary function. On-the-job training can be an effective training method but it requires hard work and careful planning by those responsible for training to make certain that the trainee has an optimum situation for learning.

Vestibule Training

Vestibule training in most ways is simply a variation of on-the-job training. The trainee uses the same equipment, materials, and machinery and follows the same procedures which he would use if he were learning the tasks in the actual work place. The training area is frequently removed from the actual work place and the usual production pressures are reduced. Ideally, a skilled trainer is in charge. The primary purpose of the vestibule method is training not production. In theory, this should result in a situation which is more conducive to learning than on-the-job training.

In spite of some seeming advantages to vestibule training as a method it has certain limitations from a practical standpoint. It may be uneconomical if only a small number of trainees are trained at any one time, if the equipment used is very expensive, or if equipment maintenance requires extremely high skills. It has definite limitations as to the types of jobs for which the method can be used. In practice, it has been used, primarily, to teach jobs involving the operation of one machine, or inspection and packing operations. It may be used for instructing trainees for less complex office tasks.

It is possible that vestibule training accentuates the problem of transfer of training from the learning situation to the actual work place. The absence of the pressures which make on-the-job training difficult, may make it more difficult for the trainee to maintain behavior learned once vestibule training is terminated. In addition, the trainee must adjust to another supervisor and other associates once he leaves the vestibule school. Certainly, careful planning of the activities of the trainee in the on-the-job situation are required if behavior learned in vestibule training is to be maintained.

One of the authors has used vestibule training in the training of workers for such textile jobs as fixers, weavers, and setters. Although the conditions in comparing the results of vestibule vs. on-the-job training were not completely controlled, there was some evidence that vestibule training did reduce training time and resulted in improved job performance on the part of the trainees. On the other hand, there is no evidence that effort spent in improving on-the-job training would not have produced the same results.

Integrated On and Off-the-Job Training

Integrated training, as the term is used here, is a method of training which requires the learner both to perform job tasks and to experience formal training in a classroom or laboratory in acquiring the skills and knowledge required to perform the job in an acceptable manner. Perhaps the most frequent form of integrated training is apprenticeship. It has been used, however, in presupervisory training where job assignments are closely integrated with formal class work. The method has been used also in the General Electric Company as one method of training manufacturing managers (Merrill and Marting, 1952, pp. 131–140). The primary purpose of the integrated job and formal training is to instruct and develop the trainees. Any production or services from the trainees is incidental to the method.

In general, integrated training has been used to train employees on jobs which require long learning periods and require skills and knowledge which cannot be taught effectively solely by on-the-job instruction. It allegedly has the advantage of giving the learner an opportunity to practice on the job the things learned in the class and to facilitate classroom training through the interchange of ideas gained in experiences with practical everyday problems. Heightened motivation as a consequence is also claimed.

Again, much that is claimed for the facilitation of learning by this method of instruction is not based on sound experimental evidence. Certainly, it is a common sense approach. Yet, careful curriculum construction and integration of class work with on-the-job experiences must take place if the method is to result in effective learning experiences for the trainee. Many formal apprenticeship arrangements call for a training period of four years with a given number of hours, frequently several thousand hours, to be spent in classroom or laboratory instruction. The amount of time and hours of classroom instruction may or may not be necessary to turn out a competent craftsman. Unfortunately, careful investigations of the relevance and degree of mastery of certain topics in relationship to efficient performance are rarely ascertained prior to setting up requirements for an apprenticeship program. Too often, tradition, the zealousness of subject matter specialists, and the need to fill up the classroom hours allocated to apprenticeship training govern what is the instructional content.

Since integrated training should help to maximize transfer of skills and knowledge from the classroom to the job, there is much to recommend this method. Yet the transfer is not automatic and must be planned, if it is to take place. Careful planning for transfer and precise determination of learning content in integrated training should do much to render this method an effective training approach.

Formal Off-the-Job Training

This differs from integrated training in that what the trainee does on the job and what he does in a classroom or a laboratory is not as closely related and is usually supplemental rather than central to learning to perform the job tasks. An apprentice undergoing integrated training will be taught mechanical drawing in the class in the morning, and in the afternoon will attempt to make working drawings in the machine shop. On the other hand, a supervisor may take part in a formal class in cost accounting and not make use of the knowledge acquired until weeks or months later.

Formal off-the-job training is used more frequently in training of supervisory, staff, and management personnel than with production employees. Yet, it may have definite value as a method with production workers when the purpose is to develop knowledge concerning processes or procedures, or to develop attitudes. With production employees, formal off-the-job training may not be able to substitute or replace actual job experience and practice. We have no research evidence on this point. All we have is one investigation which relies heavily on employee reactions. Employees in a power plant believed that formal classroom training was not as adequate as actual experience or cross training by other employees (Mann and Hoffman, 1960).

Formal off-the-job training may vary from a short course in improving reading speed to intensive instruction in an executive development course lasting for several weeks or months. The courses may be organized and taught by personnel on the company payroll; or, they may be organized and staffed by colleges, universities, professional and managerial associations, or by consulting organizations. Courses may be given at company locations, university campuses, or convenient resort areas. No one has ever made a precise estimate of the time spent by employees in formal off-the-job training or the costs of conducting such courses. Total costs must run in the millions.

The prevalence and frequency of formal off-the-job training cannot be taken as adequate measures of its value to the companies which sponsor or underwrite this training. Unfortunately, little effort is made to determine the effect training of this kind has on the efficiency of an industrial organization. Occasionally, research reports such as that of Fleishman, Harris, and Burtt (1955) have questioned seriously the value of formal off-the-job training of supervisors. Also, an occasional research study indicates that formal training at least modifies the behavior of executives even if there is no evidence that this modification had any effect on the attainment of organizational goals of their companies (Viteles, 1959).

Two points should be made with respect to formal, off-the-job training courses, one favorable and the other unfavorable. First, for many positions, organized training would be extremely difficult if the trainees were not pulled away from their jobs. The point is frequently made that day-to-day immersion in the details of a job, especially at higher levels, make it difficult to encourage broad changes in behavior such as long-range planning, understanding complex subject matter, and understanding of the relationship of broad principles to specific problems. In addition, a company may not be able to conduct such courses by itself. On the other hand, a major weakness of most programs of this kind is the failure to incorporate materials which will contribute to transfer of training. Only infrequently are provisions made for the application of principles learned to the job. Rarely is there any follow up to assist in transfer or insure its occurrence.

We can only make suggestions as to how to decide whether or not to use this method of training. First, referring to earlier chapters of this book, a careful determination of need before training can serve as a guide to see if formal off-the-job training is indicated. Certain skills, knowledge, and attitudes probably can be developed more effectively by this method than by others. Second, we can legitimately ask if the opportunity for transfer is provided. Third, an analysis of organizational climate will indicate whether the conditions are such that skills, knowledge, and attitudes developed in a classroom will receive reinforcement on the job. Unless the work situation is of a nature to provide reinforcement, the results of formal classroom training may be wasted and can result in frustrations for the individuals who went through the training experience.

Where possible, the decision should be made on the basis of research. In the study of several different training methods by Baxter, Taaffe, and Hughes (1953), referred to elsewhere, the training outcomes of the various methods varied so little that the final determination was made on the basis of cost.

SPECIFIC TRAINING TECHNIQUES

In our discussion of specific training techniques, we will make no attempt to discuss in detail all those in use in industrial training. We will indicate problems which occur frequently in selecting a technique or techniques to meet a training need. We are concerned more with the rationale of the technique rather than details of how to use it. Accordingly, we have devoted less space to well-known techniques and more to relatively new ones such as automated teaching or programmed learning, and business games.

After discussing some of the general considerations in the selection of a specific technique to accomplish a training task, we shall describe and comment first on those techniques in which there is human interaction: the lecture; conference; case study; role playing; and sensitivity training. Traditional methods are discussed first and are followed by more recently developed techniques. In the last part of this chapter, we discuss techniques using mechanical devices or the communication of an impersonal film or text with the trainee: television and films; training devices and simulators; programmed learning, automated teaching or teaching machines; and business games. Again, more commonly used techniques are discussed first. Although in business games and simulators frequently there is considerable human interaction, their common reliance on special equipment led to an arbitrary decision to treat them with the latter group of techniques.

General Approach to the Selection of Specific Techniques [1]

We need to establish a rationale for evaluating training techniques before we discuss each specific technique. Most techniques have vociferous advocates who become so emotionally involved with their technique that they see it as a panacea not only for industrial training but also for any problem of human behavior in industry. This is unfortunate since each technique has certain advantages, disadvantages, and limitations in a specific training situation. Even the frequently discredited lecture method may have real advantages for a specific training purpose whereas conference techniques may be unduly expensive and ineffective in the same training situation.

But logical analysis and conviction are not enough; nor are skill and deftness in using a wide variety of techniques tailored to the specific training problem. There is too little concrete evidence to guide those responsible for training in their selection of the best techniques or combination of techniques for each training situation. Role playing may be useful in training salesmen to tell their sales stories effectively. Are there other techniques which are superior? Is role playing an efficient method, considering training costs, time, number of students, and results? Do we understand what basic principles underlie this technique so that new techniques can be derived from it?

In brief, there is a definite need for carefully controlled research:

[1] See Smode and Yarnold (1960) for another approach to examining training techniques.

1. To examine the relative efficiencies of various training techniques under a wide variety of conditions, with a wide variety of trainees, and in a wide variety of industries. Only in this way can we begin the construction of a training technology which will permit the trainer to use the most efficient techniques for the problems at hand. Just as the engineer is able to consult a handbook in selecting materials to solve a stress problem, the training director needs an analogous source of information to use in solving his training problems.

2. To examine the "whys" of each technique. We need to know what it is about each technique which is effective. What are the learning principles incorporated into the role-playing techniques? What features conflict with established learning principles? If we knew the answers to these questions, we could improve the efficiency of the individual technique and derive new ones. We might even discover new learning principles in the process.

Both major research areas mentioned above are important. Of the two, the more difficult to research is the second. Design of experiments to uncover the underlying principles will be an arduous task. Each technique will demand numerous studies and many years to complete the job. The studies of mass communication techniques conducted at the Pennsylvania State University (Instructional Film Research Reports, 1956) give some idea of the magnitude of the task. This series of over fifty studies, primarily on training films, began the task of developing a technology and discovering the principles which underlie the effectiveness of certain film techniques. But even here, more must be done before basic principles are established. Even though "principles research" is the more difficult, it is research in this that will pay off in the long run. The results will not be immediate, but new techniques and new understanding will eventually aid the training profession in its coming of age.

We are not completely without data to substantiate claims for various training techniques. As we treat each technique, we cite some of the relevant research. But our primary description of training techniques is based on current usage and logical analysis. After indicating the general nature of each technique, we attempt to point to features of each which appear to conform with or conflict with the learning principles discussed in the previous chapters. This logical analysis, it should be emphasized, can best be considered the statement of a number of informal hypotheses which should be substantiated, clarified, or rejected by research in the industrial setting.

Selection of Techniques

The decision as to what technique to use in a particular training method should be made only after a careful analysis of the particular job, the information to be transmitted, the behavior to be mastered, the probable number of trainees, the job level, the abilities of the personnel to be trained, and the abilities of the trainers available.

Because of the many variables involved, it is extremely difficult and unwise to say that this technique is ideal for this level of supervision or that kind of job. We need, first, to complete the numerous analyses mentioned at the beginning of this section *before* deciding on the training technique to be employed. We shall assume, therefore, that we have made an operations analysis of the job for which we are planning training and are now considering what technique or techniques to use. In the absence of research data, what questions should we answer in evaluating a specific technique? Any guide which we obtain for determining the appropriateness of a specific training technique for a specific training purpose, in absence of research data, will be based on experience and logical analysis. A guide of this kind will be of greater service to us in a decision on a specific technique if we seek answers to questions covering the following aspects of the training situation and the training technique:

1. the kinds of behavior to be acquired (motor skills, concepts, verbal skills, attitudes, etc.)
2. the number of employees to be trained
3. the ability level of trainees
4. individual differences among trainees
5. cost in relation to various factors
6. the incorporation of alleged learning principles such as

motivation, opportunity for practice, reinforcement, knowledge of results, meaningfulness, and overlearning.

SPECIFIC TECHNIQUES—LECTURES, CONFERENCES, CASE STUDY, ROLE PLAYING, AND SENSITIVITY TRAINING

Lecture Method

The lecture method is the traditional method of transmitting information to others in formal classroom procedures. In industrial training, it has not been restricted to the formal classroom environment but is used whenever groups of employees are given instructions or explanations of procedures by a superior.

The lecture generally consists of an instructor verbally presenting information to a group of trainees. Characteristically, there is a minimum of overt activity on the part of the learners and little interaction between the students and the instructor. In some instances, the instructor's monologue may be broken by questions and class discussion. The very nature of the lecture procedure has rendered it a technique of limited value in industrial training.

First, there is the limitation of behavior to be acquired. Generally, it is useful only in the acquisition of conceptual knowledge although it may be used to set the stage for learning of motor and verbal skills. There is little experimental evidence that lectures can result in significant and permanent development or modifications of attitudes. The second limitation involves proper provision for learning on the part of the trainees. Generally, individual differences of trainees are ignored. Also, little opportunity is given for practice, reinforcement, knowledge of results, or overlearning. Ideally, the lecture should contain motivational material which makes clear the relations between the material to be learned and desired goals. The competent lecturer should be able to make the material meaningful to the learner. Whether motivation and meaningfulness of material actually occurs in most lectures is a moot question.

Planty, McCord, and Efferson (1948) contend that the lecture can be quite useful in training executives used to oral presentations as opposed to lower level employees. Perhaps this is true. One point seems evident, however. Unless careful grouping of trainees by ability and/or achievement level takes place, it may be difficult to achieve a level of instruction which moves everyone along at the appropriate rate. The lecture does not have as an integral characteristic the recognition of individual differences. Finally, there is a limitation as to the ability level of learners who can profit from a lecture. It is of limited usefulness in teaching employees who cannot grasp verbal presentations in an effective way.

The major seeming advantage of the lecture method is its economy. Depending on the skill of the lecturer and the facilities for seating learners, the lecture can be used to instruct a relatively large number of people at one time. When, typically, role playing and conference techniques can handle at the most 15 to 20 learners, the lecture may be used with 50, 100, or more. This economy, however, may be illusory since mere exposure to information does not guarantee behavior modifications. All the evidence available indicates that the nature of the lecture situation results in minimal behavior modifications. The lecture as usually employed, therefore, is of limited use in industrial training.

Conferences

In order to escape the limitations of the lecture technique, wide use has been made in industry of the conference technique. There is, however, considerable confusion as to what is meant by the term "conference." We agree with Planty (1948, p. 182) in his rejection under this heading of the "'free conference,' (as) a conversational boat ride on unchartered seas to an unknown port." Rather, we accept the concept of a conference as delineated by Busch (1949). This is a carefully planned meeting with a specific purpose and goals. The conference can be used for purposes other than training, but in training it can be used for: "executive training, supervisory training, job training in certain advanced fields, sales training, public relations training, safety education" (Busch, 1949, p. 41). In addition to the uses cited by Busch, the technique can be used in training designed to modify employees' attitudes toward quality, waste, discipline, and work loads.

Conference techniques are limited in training to the acquisition and understanding of conceptual data and to the development or modification of attitudes. It is of very limited use in the acquisition of motor skills, discriminations, and other perceptual motor activities. Its utility in the development or modification of attitudes is most apparent in the so-called decision-making conference. In conducting such a conference, the role of the leader is crucial. He attempts to define problem areas, obtain agreement as to the nature of the problem, and to direct attention of the group to its various aspects. He may also try to lead the group to a solution. He may serve as a resource person for information not available to the group. He usually must remain neutral, if a free play of emotions and attitudinal response is to take place during the conference. The task of preparing for and conducting a conference demands as much, if not more, effort than presenting a lecture.

In many training situations, where conference techniques are used, one of the problems is overcoming resistance to change, that is, to modify or change attitudes. Experimental evidence indicates that commitment to a position tends to strengthen the resistance to change in the face of counter arguments (Hovland, Campbell, and Brock, 1957). Basically, conference techniques are attempts to adopt "democratic" rather than "authoritarian" procedures to overcome resistance to changing behavior. As Maier points out:

> . . . some take the form of creating opportunities for expressing . . . fears so that they can be seen for what they are. Other techniques take the form of changing the person's perspective so that he can view his own situation differently and thereby see it without threats to his security. Still other techniques are designed to let the person discover the possible alternatives, and when he discovers them they contain no fear element (1952, p. 45).

The conference technique, therefore, may be used in an attempt to overcome resistance to changing behavior through insight into and reduction of those forces which lead to resistance and (because the group resolves the problem themselves) through capitalizing on the individual and group identification with that solution. There is some research which supports the claims for the conference approach in securing participation of employees in decision making. Coch and French (1948) report definite changes in attitudes and behavior of employees in a garment manufacturing company. This and similar research, however, has been severely critized by Viteles on the grounds that all relevant variables were not accounted for in the design and execution of the research. In some studies, participative groups may have received more training than the nonparticipative groups. In others, there were differences in the administration of knowledge of results which could account for the superiority of the participative groups (Viteles, 1953, pp. 163–169).

All conferences are not held for decision-making purposes or to promote attitudinal changes. In informational areas, the free discussion of various facts and points of view is said to lead to acceptance and a better grasp of new information. Support for this position is based upon the alleged benefits resulting from active participation of the trainee such as an opportunity for practice, heightened motivation, etc. These factors, on the other hand, must be weighed against increased costs and increased time consumption.

If the usefulness of the conference springs from participation of all trainees, it is obvious that the number of employees who can participate in a conference is severely limited because of the need for free expression. Large groups must frequently be broken down into smaller ones with a discussion leader for each subgroup. Often discussions get off the track and consume great amounts of time. Whether the technique is efficient or costly will depend on the personnel participating, the subject matter discussed, the need for discussion, the need for changing behavior or attitudes, the skill of the discussion leader, and similar factors. Where personal involvement with a decision (as yet unmade) is desirable, it may be more efficient to discuss it and come to a solution than to make the decision and hand it down to others.

Little is known about the ability level required for conferences, although many restrict it to first-line supervision levels and up. It is clear, however, that any conference must be held within the limits of responsibility of the participants and that these limits are clear to them.

We have said that conference techniques attempt to encourage expression of viewpoints for insightful effects and to gain identification with the outcome of the conference. In this sense, the conference probably incorporates motivational principles to a greater extent than a technique such as the lecture. In addition, the participants are more active, and, because of their own participation, the content is probably more meaningful.

What of knowledge of results and/or reinforcement? The leader is to play a neutral role and, if this is rigidly adhered to, he will neither praise nor reprove. However, he can and probably will guide the discussion in such a way as to give some reinforcement to the participation itself. If he goes beyond this and rewards or punishes certain kinds of behavior or expressions of opinion, he then loses his neutrality. The effects of reinforcement are quite powerful and can be used either by design or inadvertently to direct the group toward a particular conclusion. The purpose of any conference, therefore, must be clear in the mind of the leader so that he can lead the group to (his) desired ends or (openly) delegate the responsibility for whatever outcome is achieved to the group. It is the frequent failure to delineate purpose and responsibility which has laid the conference open to charges of subtle manipulation rather than forthright direction.

The group can also be a powerful source of reward and punishment, in some cases more powerful than the leader. The group can offer or withdraw its acceptance of a participant, can verbally punish or reward certain opinions, or can apply stronger sanctions on and off the job for deviant behavior. The discussion leader must recognize this and structure the situation in such a way as to minimize the effects of group reinforcement upon the quality of the participation and outcome for the group and individual participants.

The conference technique is not for the novice trainer. It requires skill, ingenuity, careful preparation, and a clear understanding of the role of the leader.

Case Study

The study of cases used in legal training is frequently used in training, especially in human relations training. Here, participants in a discussion group are given a case or problem. Through questions and discussion, they bring out principles and practices integral to the case. Rather than start with the principle and give illustrations of its application, the trainees are to study, discuss, and discover the underlying principles. Sometimes a solution must also be sought and achieved. A basic premise is that material so taught will be more meaningful and that the individual will learn and remember better those things which he discovers for himself. Flexibility of solutions to problems is encouraged and trainees soon learn that a given problem does not have *a* solution. The trainee feels that principles become less abstract; he is encouraged to actually get experience in looking beneath the surface of problems for underlying principles to use as guides to action.

Here again, we are concerned primarily with conceptual and attitudinal learning. Because of the nature of the discussions, groups must be small. The technique is most frequently used with supervisory personnel from the level of foreman and higher. The technique has the same inherent cost problems as exist in the various conference techniques, as well as the costs attendant upon case preparation and evaluation.

The heightened meaningfulness of a well-prepared case and the confrontation of the group with a realistic problem probably have definite motivational effects in addition to those of discussion under relatively free conditions. The opportunity for participation as well as practice on a realistic problem probably adds to the effectiveness of the training. The division of responsibility for reinforcement, however, exists again as it did for the conference method.

If we correctly understand the proponents of the case study technique, a major objective is the discovery of underlying principles. This is a worthwhile objective, but it is also here that we have seen many case discussions fail. Too often the strong pressures toward solution of a problem arise at the expense of a careful study of all facts, delving for more facts, and discovery of the principles prior to solution. Advocates of the technique are aware of this problem, and work hard to circumvent such pressures. Not all, however, are equally skilled in doing this. When the pressures are not overcome, a quick solution is achieved with consequent reinforcement of the inadequate methods used in achieving that solution. Again, this is a tricky procedure and requires considerable skill from the leader.

Role Playing

Maier defines role playing as the technique "of creating a life situation, usually one involving conflicts between people, and then having persons in a group play the parts of specific personalities" (1952, p. 87). Although originally developed for therapeutic purposes, it was quickly adapted to interviewer training, leadership training, supervisory training, sales training, and many similar situations where it was desired to develop skills in handling interpersonal situations. Even here, however, we must differentiate between the use of role playing as a means of presenting interpersonal problems as might be done in supervisory training as opposed to its use in simple drill and rehearsal of a skill such as might be done in mastering a sales talk.

The process of developing skills through role playing can take many forms depending upon the particular aspect of the situation emphasized. In leadership or supervisory training, the emphasis is frequently placed upon developing insight into the attitudes and feelings of others and the reactions of others to the trainee's behavior. In addition, the opportunity is frequently given, once insight has been achieved, to practice new kinds of behavior and to begin to develop skills in problem situations. Sometimes the emphasis is heavily on practice. A salesman may have been required to learn a talk and then is required to give it to his supervisor as the latter plays the role of a prospective client.

Because of the wide variation in use and emphasis, it is difficult to discuss this technique without making arbitrary distinctions or overemphasizing one use more than another. It seems, however, that in human relations training, the emphasis is heavily upon the development of insights, changing of attitudes toward others, and getting some (usually minimal) practice in developing skills.[2] In this sense, the technique becomes similar in use to that of case methods and, in fact, the two frequently blend together. Parts of cases are acted out by role playing to clarify points, develop insights, and change attitudes.

Conceptual and attitudinal material are again the focal point with some emphasis placed on the development of certain specific verbal skills. Although many trainees can observe role playing, relatively few can participate in crucial roles. Lawshe and Bolda (1958) offer suggestive evidence that role playing does have an effect upon verbal performance on training case tasks, but the effects of this technique on actual on-the-job behavior still needs adequate demonstration. The effects found, however, appear to vary with the role-playing case and the particular role played. The technique is also time consuming and expensive. Wide ranges of ability levels have been tapped, but again this technique is used most frequently at various supervisory levels or with employees who must deal with the public such as telephone service representatives.

Motivation is frequently heightened by the drama, although some individuals may become so enmeshed in getting rid of the problem presented by their role that they fail to learn much from playing it. Other learning features common to case methods are also inherent to the technique. Opportunity for practice is increased, but, as indicated previously, this is usually limited to a few persons.

Reinforcement is a problem here. To the extent that the trainee must interact with another trainee playing a role, the latter frequently controls the reinforcing elements in the situation. It is he who gives *immediate* reinforcement to what the first trainee says. To the extent that he deviates from the desired role, undesired behavior can be reinforced.

In sales training, role playing is frequently used to give the trainee practice in using a prepared talk he has learned. Here the emphasis is entirely on practice, although some role-playing supervisors also use the technique to demonstrate certain sales principles or permit trainees to play the prospective client hop-

[2] For a more complete discussion of role playing as used for human relations training, see Maier (1952).

ing that the trainee will develop insight into the reactions of the public to the sales talk. The emphasis is usually on the development of verbal skills. The trainee is given the opportunity to practice what he has learned, sometimes with another trainee and sometimes with his trainer. The latter sharply limits the number of trainees to one. The former permits the trainer to monitor several pairs of trainees but compels him to relinquish the control of reinforcement so vital to learning. As Weitz [3] has pointed out, too many sales trainees and their trainers "buy" when playing the client. The former may do this hoping that the favor will be returned when the roles are reversed. The latter does this to encourage the trainee or make him feel favorably disposed toward the trainer. Regardless of the motivation, such "buying" behavior too frequently reinforces poor performance. In addition, when the trainer "buys" most of the time, it establishes unrealistic expectations with respect to the frequency of reinforcement which the trainee will encounter with real customers. Such expectations that the job is easy might lead to rapid disillusionment, rejection of personal responsibility for failure, hostility toward the job, and subsequent resignation.

It is difficult and tiring, too, for the trainer to play a consistent role through repeated practice sessions. Variations in the role to relieve the trainer's boredom may make the task too difficult for the beginning trainee's level of achievement.

Despite these factors, role playing in such situations does supply motivation, especially if introduced properly, and the opportunity for practice is given. Unfortunately, such practice is limited to a few trials. The experience in role playing is highly meaningful, and adequate opportunity is present for knowledge of results and reinforcement, although they are not always appropriately supplied.

Sensitivity Training

Sensitivity training [4] under its various names (t-group training, d-group training, action research, and sensitivity training)

[3] Personal communication from Dr. Joseph Weitz.

[4] The theory underlying this technique and some of its applications have been described by Blansfield (1956), Bradford (1956, 1958), Weschler and Reisel (1958), Shepard (1960).

stems from the group dynamics movement begun by Kurt Lewin in the 1930's. It has had its ardent advocates and has been strenuously criticized (Whyte, 1953). Just what is sensitivity training? Originally, under Lewin's impetus, it was an effort to develop leaders who could secure and implement decisions for groups by democratic rather than autocratic methods. Although perhaps the purpose still remains, the focus has shifted to the development of persons who participate in the training laboratories. Individuals usually are taken away from their jobs or other activities for varying periods of time and live in intimate association with other members of their group. This laboratory training situation is designed to help individuals become more sensitive to dynamics of working groups. Proponents indicate that the participants learn to recognize covert factors which can either aid or hinder a group as it seeks to accomplish its tasks. The participants also are supposed to develop an awareness of how they influence others and the group as well as the ways in which they may be unconsciously hindering the work they and the group are trying to accomplish.

The technique does not rely upon instruction in the usual sense; it is suggested that the training consists in the trainees learning about group behavior through participating in it. They experience all the successes, misfortunes, and frustrations of the group as it attempts to solve problems or even to maintain itself as a group. The highly emotional nature of the group situation is claimed to be more effective in bringing about changes in behavior than is conceptual learning. Advocates state also that the group experience provides cathartic experiences for the individual members. Finally, the emphasis is not upon finding final solutions to problems assigned to the group. In fact, problems may not be assigned since the proponents believe the group will find enough problems in the dynamics of the group itself. They state that the major purpose of sensitivity training is to teach the dynamics of effective and ineffective group behavior. There is also the hope that what is learned will be used when the individual returns to his job.

What is the value of sensitivity training as a technique for use in industrial training? Sensitivity training, along with most other training techniques, has not been subjected to controlled experiments to evaluate its relative effectiveness in comparison with other training techniques. We examine it, therefore, from the point of view of the questions we have set up earlier as a guide for selecting training techniques.

It is obvious by the nature of sensitivity training that it is designed primarily for attitude modification though some social and verbal skills may result as a by-product. Generally, the number of people in sensitivity groups are small, thus making it an expensive procedure if a large number of people are to be trained. It would seem possible to use this technique with employees at most levels in the organization, but it has generally been restricted in industry to first-line supervisors and above. The costs of sensitivity training are high, but we examine this aspect somewhat more in detail later.

There is little doubt that the group situation can create a high degree of motivation but the motivation may be directed to the achievement of objectives other than those which are the main purpose of sensitivity training. Generally, reinforcement must come from the group as well as knowledge of results since the official group leader withdraws from the leadership role early in the training. There is, however, a definite question of how reinforcement will occur once the trainee leaves the sensitivity group and returns to his own environment. From descriptions of sensitivity training, there is little that can be concluded about provisions for meaningfulness and overlearning. Opportunity for practice is present but whether the opportunity is used will depend on the individual trainee.

As we have indicated, the costs of sensitivity training can be high as they include not only fees for personnel experienced in sensitivity learning, but also salaries and usual travel and living expenses for the participants. The crucial question, therefore, is whether this technique modifies the trainee's behavior in a manner which will allow him to contribute more effectively to the achievement of organizational goals. The testimony from participants in sensitivity training (and sometimes from their colleagues) indicates that the experience frequently results in both attitudinal and other behavioral changes. To a question from a participant in a conference on human relations training as to whether or not this technique had "any beneficial consequences back in the plant" Shepard (1960) replied:

> You mean, does all this help? I think that anybody in the refineries would say that it has had an important impact, although I am not sure that there would be general agreement on what the nature of the impact has been. We have seen some really remarkable problem solving in cases where the solutions mean differences in the way a unit is operated or in the way in which the relationships between two departments are worked out. However, it is too early to say what the long-run consequences will be. An action research approach means that the laboratory experience is only a part of a long-range program of organization development (p. 30).

This summarizes concisely the state of our knowledge about the long-range and "back home" effectiveness of action research, t-training, d-training, and sensitivity training.

SPECIAL TECHNIQUES—TELEVISION AND FILMS, TRAINING DEVICES AND SIMULATORS, AUTOMATED TEACHING, AND BUSINESS GAMES

Television and Films

Mass instructional devices such as television and films have many of the shortcomings of lectures since they depend on passive learning by the trainee. Compared with lectures, they do have certain advantages. Usually, the most skilled instructor available is used for all trainees. The subject matter presented can be more efficiently organized and generally is, thus maximizing meaningfulness for the learner. Close-ups of apparatus and equipment can be presented in a way not possible in a lecture. Finally, television and films can be used with thousands of trainees resulting in savings in instructional costs. The opportunity for trainer-trainee interaction, however, is less than is that of the lecture method unless mechanical devices are used for communicating with the television instructor or discussion leaders supplementing the telecast or films.

These advantages and disadvantages probably balance out in terms of how much is learned. Carpenter and Greenhill (1955) found no differences in achievement between groups of college students taught by lecture and groups taught by closed-circuit films and discussion leaders. They do, however, point to substantial savings in costs where large numbers of trainees must be exposed to films.

The research of Carpenter and Greenhill relies on comparisons of achievement on a final examination. Siegel, Adams, and Macomber (1960) have also tested retention of content in nine different courses one year or more after completion of the course and find no differences among large classes taught by television, large classes taught by an instructor, and small classes taught by graduate students.

As indicated previously, a technology of film instruction is developing mainly because of the research done by the Instructional Film Research Program at the Pennsylvania State University. Carefully conducted research on films indicates that learning from films may be enhanced by:

1. Using a slow rate of development of a limited amount of material in a film. Too many films try to put as much information as possible into each film to the detriment of learning.
2. Repeating the showing of the film. Research indicates that at least one reshowing enhances learning.
3. Writing and planning the film from the trainee's viewpoint—considering their present state of knowledge, ability, attitudes toward the subject to be presented, and the difficulties *they* encounter.
4. Encouraging audience participation by reminding trainees to look for important points and to try to remember them, and permitting discussion and questions during and between film showings.
5. Preparing the trainees to learn from the films. It is important to orient the trainees as to the subject matter to be covered, and the use to be made of the subject matter. Study guides used before or after films can be helpful.

Research also indicates that elaborate settings, color, dramatic effects, music, and various artistic effects add little, if anything, to the learning, even though adding to costs. One must remember, also, that what is learned from a film is quite specific, not general. A single film will convey limited information. To get even a limited generalization of content to broad areas, a whole battery of films may be necessary.[5]

Not all films necessarily develop passive learning, or learning through covert practice. As demonstrated by Murnin, Hayes, and Harby, even complex motor skills such as tumbling can be taught by repetitive loop films where trainees are given ample opportunity for practice under the guidance of minimally trained instructors. Films can also be used to bring about attitude changes, although the effects of these changes are generally not enduring.

Mass media instructional devices, therefore, can be effective in training. Many films and programs available today, however, still rely on artistic ingenuity in their production and ignore the advances in their production and utilization which have been developed through research. The weaknesses mentioned earlier are not all inherent in mass media techniques. They can be overcome, circumvented, or minimized through proper pacing, allowing opportunity for practice, enhancing meaningfulness, repetition, and other ways of applying principles of learning.

Training Devices and Simulators

Thus far, we have been primarily concerned with training in which concepts or verbal skills are acquired. Even when the techniques discussed have been used, with the hope of facilitating the acquisition of motor skills, the assumption seems to have been made that acquisition of vocabulary and verbal understanding of directions are transferable to motor performance. Many trainers realize, however, that opportunity for practice of motor skills is essential to the acquisition of these skills. Verbal techniques such as books, lecture, or discussion may precede actual practice, but the opportunity for manipulating the machinery or parts is also required.

Often it is inefficient, costly, or hazardous to train a man on the job. Commercial airlines and the military commonly use flight simulators to train men to operate aircraft or airborne

[5] For full details on additional factors of learning from films and the supporting research see: *Instructional Film Research Reports,* and May, M. A., and Lumsdaine, A. R. (1958).

equipment. An error committed while aloft may be fatal. Training aloft may also not permit the constant monitoring by a skilled trainer necessary for efficient learning. In industry, production line pacing, cost of materials actually processed, availability of machines, and lack of opportunity for training by skilled trainers may limit the use of on-the-job training as a means of producing skilled workers. Therefore, training devices which provide information displays such as dials and gauges as well as controls for actual practice may be provided. Simulators, which are devices which attempt to duplicate actual equipment and job conditions, are widely used.

The problems of constructing a training device and the wide range of factors which must be considered are indicated clearly by the work of Miller (1953). In 275 pages of text, he details these problems and factors. It is quite clear that the construction of a training device requires a great deal of planning. A review of the stages recommended by Miller, however, suggests that many of the same steps should be taken in preparation for any training task:

1. Prepare a task analysis of the job.
2. Select the tasks which are to be learned.
3. Decide on the level of skill expected of trainees.
4. Find out about the level of knowledge, abilities, and skills of probable trainees.
5. Find out about the level of knowledge, abilities, and skills of probable instructors.
6. Decide how the synthetic training will fit into on-the-job training.
7. Determine what controls, displays, and response-recording equipment will be necessary in the device for adequate training.
8. Integrate all information learned from steps 1–7 into a design recommendation.
9. Revise the design in terms of requirements of the trainer, trainee, and equipment.
10. Prepare instructions for use of the device in training (Miller, 1953, pp. 268–275).

Glaser and Glanzer (1958) point out that "part-task training devices" are frequently helpful where original or training equipment is complex or costly. Such devices provide opportunity for practice of parts of complex skills which are later integrated into the complete skill on a complete training device or on the actual equipment. According to these authors, the "advantages of part-task trainers are that they can use instructors who are specialists in one aspect; they have fewer malfunctions than more complex devices and are easily maintained; and they can be used often informally during spare time" (p. 28). They warn, however, of the dangers of oversimplification in the design of such equipment.

If motor skills are to be acquired, it seems very important that opportunity for practice be provided. Training devices and simulators provide for this in varying degrees. The problems of transfer are not completely understood, however, and considerable research is necessary before we will be able to design other than logical or psychological devices without testing the devices out themselves.

Most devices are limited to one trainee at a time. Some require constant monitoring by one or more trainers. To the extent that they do, they appear to be inefficient in terms of instructional costs. Automatic response-recording devices and programs which present the trainee with new problems depending upon his response reduce manpower needs, but at a substantial increase in equipment costs. The reduction of hazards and opportunity for continuous monitoring of the trainee's behavior, however, may more than pay for such costs.

The need for a training device or simulator will depend, of course, on the number of men to be trained and the period over which training will be conducted. On-the-job training may be cheaper, even though it temporarily disrupts production, if relatively few men have to be trained or training occurs infrequently.

It is difficult to discuss the learning principles incorporated into training devices because of the wide variety of devices in use. Some, because of their task similarity or "gadget appeal," supply fairly high motivation. All provide opportunity for practice, although the conditions of practice in poorly designed or poorly maintained equipment may actually be detrimental to the transfer of training to the job. Frequently, adequate maintenance is provided only for production equipment; in such cases, the trainee may devote considerable time acquiring responses necessary for adequate performance on the device but unneeded or actually undesirable on the job.

Reinforcement and knowledge of results may or may not be provided by the device. Where it is, and it is provided in the same way as it is on the job, this should enhance transfer. If supplemental knowledge of results is provided by the trainer or simulator during training, one should expect a drop in performance when the individual first transfers to the job.

Programmed Learning—Automated Teaching—Teaching Machines—Self-Instructional Texts

A rather recent development in the field of training is in the area of self-instructional materials, or programmed learning, automated teaching, or teaching machines. Since Skinner (1954; 1958) wrote his article on teaching machines, revitalizing and modifying the work of Pressey some thirty years earlier, the field of programmed learning has mushroomed. Although these two scientists advocate the use of teaching machines as a means of presenting programmed subject matter, considerable work has also been done using the same basic approaches in texts.

As Corrigan (1959, p. 24) has indicated, there are four basic features of programmed learning:

(1) the preparation and presentation of text materials in discrete program steps,
(2) the subdivision of course material into ordered progressive conceptual units,
(3) the active participation of the student during all discrete steps in the learning process, and
(4) the immediate knowledge of results for the student for each discrete item presented.

We have here an attempt to break textbook content down into highly organized, logical stages which demand active responding on the part of the trainee in such a way as to supply knowledge of results concerning *each* response immediately following the completion of the response. The construction of such material is known as "programming," and each individual step, requiring a response of the trainee, is known as a "frame." The programmed material may be presented by a machine which presents one frame at a time, or through a textbook arranged in special ways. Whether a machine or book is used is immaterial to our discussion at this point as an understanding of the programming is most important.

At the present time, there are two sharply contrasting approaches to programming—the approach of Crowder (1959) and that of Skinner and his followers. Crowder presents the individual with basic information and then requires him to select one of the several (usually four) responses. As he selects his response, he is directed to a frame which contains comments on his response. If the response is correct, he is praised, given supporting information for the response made, and then given new information and the opportunity to respond to a new question. If the response is wrong, the frame to which the trainee is directed contains information as to why the answer is wrong, adds additional, clarifying information, and directs the student to the original question to choose another response. (If the response indicates complete lack of understanding, the trainee may be sent through a subprogram or "branch" designed to give him intensive training before returning him to the main program.)

Crowder feels that such a program recognizes individual differences in knowledge. It permits the knowledgeable trainee to go through the material rapidly, reading only those portions which contain correct answers. A less knowledgeable trainee may have to read and respond to every frame in the program sequence. Crowder also assumes that learning takes place sometime during the reading of the explanatory materials and preceding the choosing of a response. The function of responding is to check on the communication process in the trainee's reading of the explanatory material. A Crowder-type or "intrinsic" program can be presented in a machine or in a scrambled book in which the pages to which the student is directed (depending on his responses) do not follow in the usual sequence. Instead, the first frame may be on page 16 and the four alternatives may direct the trainee to either page 5, 19, 8, or 23. Assuming the response accompanying page 8 is correct, the trainee might then be presented with a new series of response choices each accompanied by page 2, 21, 6, or 12.

Problem: Teaching the Use of Metric Measures of Length

(Note: In actual practice, the answer or answers would be presented following each frame, and would not be visible to the student while he is making his responses. To achieve the same effect in this sample, the column of answers should be covered and each answer exposed only after the question has been read and a response made.)

QUESTIONS	ANSWERS
1. When we measure the length of something we see how many inches long it is or how many feet long it is. A pencil, for example, is about six ______ long and a log might be about ten ______ long.	inches feet
2. Inches and feet are what we call units of measure. To describe the length of an object, we say it is so many units long, as nine inches or seven feet. Yards and miles are also ______ of length.	units
3. Sometimes different people use different ______ of measure, depending on what they want to say. One person may say a stick is two feet long while another says it is ______________ inches long.	units twenty-four
4. In the kind of units we have been talking about, twelve ________ are equal to one ________.	inches foot
5. Three feet or ____ inches equals one _____. There are 5280 feet in a _____.	36 yard mile

FIGURE 7.1 An example of programming (Klaus and Lumsdaine, 1959, pp. 4–5).

QUESTIONS	ANSWERS
6. Most scientists do not use inches, feet, yards, and miles as units of length. They use a unit called a meter which is 39.37 inches. Their unit, the _______ is a little longer than what we call a _______.	meter yard
7. A meter is 39.37 inches. To find the number of inches in two meters, we multiply _______ by 2, which gives us _______ inches. This is a little more than six and a half _______.	39.37 78.74 feet
8. A line one meter long is _______ inches long. One tenth of a meter is _______ inches long. One tenth of a meter is called a decimeter.	39.37 3.937
9. Since a meter is _______ inches, one tenth of a meter, or a _________ is about four inches.	39.37 decimeter
10. One hundredth of a meter is called a centimeter. There are one hundred _________ in a meter. There are ten _________ in a decimeter and ten _________ in a meter.	centimeters centimeters decimeters
11. One centimeter is about .4 inches. This is about the width of your finger. One decimeter is about _______ inches. One meter is exactly _______ inches.	4 or 3.937 39.37
12. There are ten millimeters in a centimeter. This means there must be one thousand _________ in a meter. Since a centimeter is about .4 inches, a millimeter equals about _______ inches.	millimeters .04

FIGURE 7.1 (*Continued*)

The approach of Skinner to programming can be characterized as an attempt to break the material down into very small steps. All trainees are assumed to know little or nothing about the material to be learned (unless a special program is being built), and the trainee is guided to a high level of responding by going through many small steps. Klaus and Lumsdaine offer this example of such a program (Figure 7.1).

The reader should note several features of this sample. As indicated by Klaus and Lumsdaine (1959, pp. 2–3), this program sequence requires:

1. active trainee response
2. feedback to the trainee following each response
3. prompt feedback
4. the use of small steps in the sequence (Note how slowly the various metric measures are introduced.)
5. careful sequencing of the steps (Again, note how the trainee is never required to supply an answer which has not been provided previously.)
6. ample practice for the trainee (The reader will notice the numerous opportunities for the trainee to use the numbers 3937 in various forms and at various times in the sequence. This provision for adequate practice should increase retention of the material.)

This approach to programming assumes that the learning takes place through the responses of the trainee and can be guaranteed only if he responds. Individual differences are handled in a variety of ways through branching or by building complete programs for groups of trainees with different levels of knowledge. Each frame is tried out on an appropriate group to make sure that it does the job of teaching and that it does not require responses lacking in the repertoire of the trainee. Crowder also follows this procedure in developing his programs.

Numerous small studies have been done on self-instructional materials in various forms.[6] Many have been studies of programming techniques. Coulson and Silberman (1960) found that although small steps take more training time they result

[6] Useful bibliographies of a number of studies are supplied by Corrigan (1959) and by Klaus and Lumsdaine (1959).

in higher achievement. Perhaps the only large scale study of the effectiveness of automated teaching has been conducted by Klaus and Lumsdaine (1960). In this study, about 450 high school students were exposed to the Harvey White televised physics series and regular lectures and homework. Some students were also given the opportunity to use specially prepared self-instructional textbooks. The group using the supplementary self-instructional texts performed better than those who did not have them available. This gain in performance is over and above the level achieved by daily TV lessons, classroom instruction, regular text assignments, and laboratory work. Of special significance is the fact that the special group of students were *not required* to use the self-instructional texts.

The same study, however, incorporated another interesting feature. Two schools did not use the televised physics lectures. Two classes in each school used the programmed material on the refraction of light in lieu of regular instruction, while three classes in each school used the program and had accompanying lectures. In each school, the differences in performance on an independently prepared examination were not statistically reliable. The evidence suggests that the programmed material alone did as well as the program *plus* lectures.

Based on this study, and a large number of smaller ones, it would appear that trainers are acquiring a new and valuable training technique. Interestingly enough, it is a new technique that has some well-conducted research behind it, and which incorporates a number of recognized learning principles. Despite this, it will probably go through the usual "fad" stage during which it will be acclaimed temporarily as a dramatic new development and then be de-emphasized in favor of another new technique. At the present time, book publishers are viewing self-instructional texts with both jaundiced and avaricious eyes. Numerous established firms are producing a variety of teaching machines, and new firms are cropping up to produce their own versions of machines.

Let us examine rather closely the present state of this new technique. First, it would appear that the only material programmed and researched thus far has been factual material or knowledge. Programs in English grammar, physics, mathematics, foreign language, electronic trouble-shooting, binary arithmetic, contract bridge, and other subjects have been developed. To our knowledge, programs involving attitudinal, motivational materials, motor skills, or the application of knowledge in the development of work habits either have not been developed or have not been tried out. Thus, only a segment of the vast array of topics of concern to training directors has been experimented with.

Second, the construction of a program is very costly. Experts in the field estimate that a single frame requires one-half hour to an hour to construct, edit, try out on appropriate trainees, and modify in terms of the trainees' responses. When one considers that 100 pages of text material may require 2000 or more frames, depending on the complexity of the material, the investment required in the time of a skilled programmer and adequate trials becomes apparent.

Third, the importance of a machine to present the program is as yet undetermined. Skinner and some of his followers contend that the machine is very important if for no other reason than to prevent cheating. Most machines are designed to prevent the trainee from looking ahead at the correct answer before responding. Whether or not this is important is unknown. It seems, however, that some machines may offer the advantage of easy movement from frame to frame (especially in a scrambled program), and the recording of the trainees responses for study by the trainer. The latter can also be achieved through a programmed text, but not with a guarantee against cheating. Besides, if time to respond is an important variable, time control cannot be provided through a text and many inexpensive machines. The machine, however, may limit the ease with which a course can be administered. A programmed text can be studied at home or in a hotel room. Many machines (although not all) would be available only in special training areas set aside for them. The importance of this factor will depend on the number of trainees and the facilities involved.

Although at first some felt that machines merely added unnecessary expense to programmed learning, a paper by Klaus and Lumsdaine (1960a) offers evidence that a printed programmed text may be more costly than putting the program on film and projecting in a teaching machine of some sort. In addition, the sheer size of programmed texts designed to cover complete courses would create storage problems. It is also possible that the presentation of the program by a machine will supply intrinsic motivation not available with a printed self-instructional text. The issues of the machine vs. text are not resolved as yet. We suspect that both will be used in various situations and that cost will most frequently determine the choice.

We have previously indicated that the intrinsic approach of Crowder was the first to recognize individual differences in knowledge or ability. The technique developed by Skinner is now incorporating means to provide for such differences. As far as individual differences following training is concerned, however, Glaser[7] makes an important point. In a number of small studies, he reports that the major effect of the type of program using the procedures of Skinner is to reduce the spread of scores among individuals trained with self-instructional materials compared to scores of those trained by conventional methods. Admittedly, poor trainees took longer, but level of achievement was higher. The major effect was a greater uniformity in scores of the former group. It seems that this is a very important point for those responsible for training and for the production of qualified trainees for various jobs. High level trainees would continue to do well or might do better whereas lower level trainees would do considerably better. The impact of such a situation on recruiting and selection practices might be immense. Perhaps some of the costs of program production would be recovered here.

The reader should be warned, however, that studies done thus far have used intraining or achievement test criteria as the primary measures of success of self-instructional techniques. We must still be concerned with the transfer of the material learned to the job. It may be that present programming techniques do not, in fact, facilitate transfer of knowledge to the job. It is even possible that they might interfere with such transfer.

Some of the learning principles incorporated in programming have been discussed. In closing this section, it might be worth-

[7] Personal communication from Dr. R. Glaser.

while to summarize them here. First, the requirement of a response on the part of the trainee may have a motivating effect. In addition, it seems to the authors that the approach of Crowder presents the trainee with more of a challenge as a game and might also have more interest because of the nature of the textual material. Both approaches supply opportunity for practice, although programs reviewed thus far would suggest that the small step approach of Skinner and his followers gives greater opportunity under more rigorously controlled conditions. Both supply knowledge of results and/or reinforcement quickly following each response. But the responses made by the trainee with a Skinnerian program have a high probability of being correct—much more so than is the case for the typical Crowderian program.

Evidence reported by Kaess and Zeaman (1960) would suggest that the opportunity to choose incorrect responses may be detrimental to learning. It should be added, however, that the study referred to did not use Crowder's technique of supplying supplemental information when an incorrect choice is made. Perhaps the addition of such supplemental material overcomes the adverse effects of making a wrong response. Both techniques try to heighten the meaningfulness of the subject matter to be learned. The approach of Skinner seems to give ample opportunity for practice under conditions of complete cueing, partial cueing, and no cueing of the desired response. In addition, a well-constructed program supplies opportunities to learn to discriminate each new concept learned from others. Crowder attempts to supply the same kinds of opportunities through textual rather than response-evoking material. Which approach is more efficient is undetermined.

It is probable that both approaches and modifications of them will be found to be very useful, depending on the material to be taught. The Crowderian approach may be more useful or interesting for teaching problem-solving materials. The Skinnerian techniques may show great strength in the acquisition of factual knowledge. The most important point, however, seems to be that self-instructional materials incorporate a number of learning principles and involve the trainee to an unusual and probably profitable degree.

Business Games

A business game has been defined:

> . . . as a set of rules corresponding to the economics of a business as realistically as possible with the limitations of a game structure. This type of gaming which can aptly be called "operational gaming" has no relation to "game theory" which is a theoretical approach to the solution of conflict situations. Operational gaming is essentially simulation and thus provides a framework for making trial-and-error decisions rather than developing optimum strategy (Andlinger, 1958; p. 115).

When business games were first introduced into management training by the American Management Association, the games used a high speed computer. Some of the better known business games are still centered around computer programs—those used by the American Management Association, University of California at Los Angeles, General Electric Company, and IBM. However, in 1958, McKinsey & Company developed a business game which could be played without computers (Andlinger, 1958). Greene and Sisson (1959) have described several games which do not require computers, and present directions for developing home-made business games for a specific company.

Greene and Sisson (1959) list some twelve advantages of business games in managerial training in contrast with on-the-job training and formal training by case study and formal training by case study and lecture:

1. The player should learn which key factors to observe in an actual on-the-job situation in order to understand the business' position. The game, therefore, should emphasize those factors or data that are thought to be most important in decision-making.
2. The game will illustrate what facts are important and may give some idea of the approximate quantities involved. For example, the student would learn in the Retailing Inventory Management Game that markups in retailing range from 20 to 60 per cent and not from 5 to 95 per cent.
3. A dynamic game should give the participant an opportunity to gain insight into the particular area of executive action abstracted in the game. Business problems are frequently too complex to permit intuition, years of experience, or even analytic tools to lead to an understanding of the overall situation. There is no guarantee that games *will* lead to insight, of course.

4. Playing a dynamic game forces the player's attention on establishing policies or strategies and on longer range planning. On-the-job experience tends to emphasize the "putting out fires" problem and the young manager very rarely gets a chance to participate in a long-range planning. A dynamic game gives him this opportunity.

5. The participant will gain practice in the use of decision assisting tools. Therefore, he will be able to make better use of break-even charts, financial statements, Gantt charts, and even such devices as linear programming and statistical inventory control. There is presently no other educational method which gives a student so much practice in decision-making as does a dynamic game.

6. A game can be used to illustrate the value of analytic techniques where they exist. In many business decision areas it is possible not only to develop a model of the situation but also to express this model mathematically and to solve the mathematics to give a specific rule for obtaining "optimum" decisions. Where such an analytic approach is possible, simple games may be used to illustrate its use and value. To do this, the game should be played through once before the student is instructed in the analytic procedure. The player will presumably make judgment decisions. After that, if the analysis and solution of the problem is taught and the game is replayed, using the optimizing method, its value is usually made quite evident.

7. Possibly games can be used as an aid in training people in operations research. The students could be permitted to play the game (as usual without knowing the game structure) and could be asked to develop the structure by using various analytic tools during the game.

8. There is no question that players become highly involved when participating in a business game. They tend to act as if the game represents a real business situation and that the objectives of the game are real-life objectives. As a result of the involvement, the participants should learn more than from the usual static case study in which the student tends to look on the solution as a one-time decision.

9. The type of game described in this book is dynamic. It has feedback which allows for actions taken in one period to affect future conditions and results. There is no other educational device that permits the dynamic nature of business to be illustrated as effectively to the student.

10. In game situations a large number of interacting variables must be simultaneously accounted for by the player. This is highly realistic and gives the player a better appreciation for the difficulty of making decisions in business.

11. Because time is compressed, the player can make as many decisions in a game in a few hours as he would make in an operating business in several years. There is no measure yet as to the direct value of this kind of experience but it should be considerable.

12. The game offers the functional specialist a vehicle for broadening his management horizons (Greene and Sisson, 1959, pp. 3–4).

These authors admit to certain limitations of business games. Rules for the games are usually designed so that novel approaches do not give the best results. In real business life, the novel approach does sometimes pay off. Playing and rendering a critique of a business game may be a time consuming affair of two to sixteen hours. This, plus computer time and time required to program a game, may make a business game a relatively expensive method of training.

Business games are so new in industrial training that we have only brief experience by which to judge their effectiveness in teaching. No research has been published on the relative effectiveness of business games in comparison with other possible techniques for training management personnel. As a matter of fact, this is true also of war games—the ancestor of business games—used for many years in the training of military personnel. Equally applicable to the use of business games in training is the statement of Greene and Sisson concerning their possible use in evaluating executive personnel: "The use of games for evaluating management personnel should not be attempted without extensive research to support the correlation between success in games and success in actual business" (1959, p. 4). For all we know, at this time, there may be a negative or zero relationship between the kinds of behavior developed by business game training and the kinds of behavior required to operate a business successfully.

SUMMARY

We have presented certain methods and techniques now used in industrial training or, at least, looming high in industrial training in the future. No attempt has been made to indicate "how" to use these techniques. Rather, we have attempted to give the reader some insight into each technique and the degree to which they employ or fail to employ basic learning principles. Certain criteria for selecting techniques are set forth. It is our earnest hope that research results will supplant these *a priori* criteria as training sophistication develops in industry and that these will cast more light on the profitability as well as the cost of the various methods and techniques.

We have made no mention of training programs as such: management training, supervisory training, production worker training, safety training, economic education, and the host of other training programs found in industry today. The effectiveness of a given program in terms of behavior changes in the learner will depend on the proper selection and execution of appropriate methods and techniques. The major test of a training program, however, is whether or not the behavior resulting from the program contributes to the attainment of organizational goals. This is ascertained in part by prior determination of training needs by methods suggested in Chapters 2–4 and by evaluating the results of the training programs, using research techniques presented in Chapter 9.

Authors' note: After this book was set into type, these references, one dealing with simulation and gaming and the other with teaching machines, came to the attention of the authors.

AMA Management Report No. 55. *Simulation and gaming; a symposium.* New York: American Management Association, 1961.

Lumsdaine, A. A., and Glaser, R. *Teaching machines and programmed learning—a source book.* Washington: National Education Association, 1960.

8 THE TRAINER

WHO TRAINS IN INDUSTRY?

Complete and accurate data as to who actually performs the tasks which constitute industrial training are not available. Surveys of the National Industrial Conference Board (Seybold, 1954) over a period of some twenty years have shown a trend toward centralizing the responsibility for training in a department usually called "The Training Department." These surveys, however, give little data as to whether or not members of this department or other individuals in the companies actually do the teaching of employees.

A study of personnel procedures in sixty-one large companies and governmental agencies in the United States indicates, with many exceptions, the following pattern of assigning training duties (American Institute for Research, 1952).

1. The training of production employees in job duties was the responsibility of first-line supervisors. They either performed the training or delegated it to some rank and file employee. The supervisors, in some instances, were assisted in the planning and organization of training by training department personnel. The

major exception to this pattern was found in the use of staff personnel to conduct training in apprentice programs or company technical schools.

2. The responsibility for planning and conducting training for managerial, supervisory, and staff personnel typically was assigned to training department personnel. The training department used both resources within the company, consultants outside the company, and agencies such as the American Management Association, colleges, and universities. This department usually was responsible for special training such as the orientation programs for new employees.

The authors of this report specifically deny any claim that this is a typical picture of the allocation of training responsibilities in industry. The companies surveyed were selected as organizations which had the reputation for being leaders in the area of personnel practices and procedures. Generally, they were the larger corporations in the United States. We suspect that as a company decreases in size or in emphasis on organized personnel functions, whatever formal training that exists is the responsibility of line personnel without any benefit of advice and assistance from training specialists. In some organizations, except for the minimum instructions as to where to hang his hat, the only training an employee receives is self-training.

The necessity for efficient use of training, if management is to receive any real value from this tool, was emphasized in Chapter 1. Also, what assistance in achieving organizational goals can be derived from properly executed training was indicated. In Chapters 5 and 6 certain concepts from the psychology of learning, which have direct bearing on whether or not a training effort is efficient, were discussed. The data indicate that there is definite, even if limited, knowledge concerning factors which facilitate or inhibit learning in the industrial situation. It also implies that individuals who are responsible for training or who carry on the training activities in a company should have more than a passing acquaintance with the field of knowledge known as learning.

The meager evidence available indicates that the responsibility for planning, organizing, and conducting training is assigned in a more or less haphazard manner. It seems that those who direct industrial enterprises pay little attention to the possibility that the individuals who are responsible for training will have an effect on training results. If training is to be effective, considerable attention and careful decision making must be devoted to the problem of who is to train. In this major problem are three closely related questions:

1. Who is to be held responsible for the planning, organizing, coordinating, and evaluating training?
2. Who is to be held responsible for seeing that approved training plans are properly executed?
3. Who is to do the actual training?

Generally, these problems have been treated as a single one, when considered at all. The answer usually given is that the supervisor is responsible for the training of his subordinates. This is a generality which requires careful examination. It has risen from fuzzy thinking generated by the poor question of "who shall train?" If, however, the question of responsibility for training is examined from the point of view of these three questions, we can secure a more adequate solution to the problem.

RESPONSIBILITY FOR TRAINING

We cannot quarrel with the general statement that the line manager in charge of a given unit is responsible for the training in the unit. In fact, he is responsible for scheduling, cost control, labor utilization, selection of personnel, and all phases of the operation of the unit. This does not mean that he personally collects the figures for the budgets, carries out the time studies, develops labor saving procedures, and personally performs the many other activities necessary to administer the unit. He has the responsibility for outcomes; he is responsible for delegating to competent individuals the duties of carrying on the many specialized activities found in modern industrial organizations. Yet many writers in the field of personnel and industrial training have taken the position that the line manager, personally, must perform the activities required to train his subordinates. Haire (1956) makes this point as follows:

> Training is the leader's job. He is peculiarly fitted for it by virtue of his control of the opportunities for need satisfaction on the job. The staff man is a consultant to help him but the leader is the man who must do the training (p. 122).

We can only partially agree with this statement. Training requires special skills and knowledge. It is an exceptional member of the line organization who has a ready command of these skills and knowledge. Certainly, there is nothing mysterious about them. A vice president, a works manager, and some assistant foreman could acquire them with adequate training, instruction, and study. Similarly, a vice president, a works manager, or an assistant foreman could become an expert industrial engineer, cost accountant, or research chemist. Yet, we place no special requirement on line personnel to become expert practitioners in all of the various technologies utilized in administering an enterprise or a unit of the enterprise. They are expected to be able to understand and utilize intelligently the data and services furnished by specialists. It is the responsibility of the line manager to accept or reject the services of the specialist; it is his responsibility also to see that operations based on the advice of the specialist are conducted in such a way that the outcomes which the advice anticipates have an optimum opportunity to occur. It is also the line manager's responsibility to evaluate the outcomes which result from the utilization of the advice and services of the staff specialist.

It is our contention that these statements concerning responsibilities describe the relationship which should exist between the line manager and the training specialist. Whether or not the line manager actually performs training activities will depend on circumstances which are discussed later. He is responsible for training to exactly the same extent that he is responsible for all activities which take place in the unit under his jurisdiction, as well as for the results of the activities. This line of reasoning can be made clearer if we seek answers to the three questions concerning responsibility for training asked on page 227.

Responsibility for Planning, Organizing, Coordinating, and Evaluating Training

It is our contention that the duties of planning, organizing, and coordinating training should be delegated by the line manager to the staff specialist. It then becomes the responsibility of this specialist to develop a training program which will assist the unit concerned in advancing its goals and making its proper contribution to organizational goals. The performance of the training specialist should be evaluated as to the adequacy of the training proposed as a means of securing the goals established for the unit. The average line manager should not attempt the actual operations necessary to develop specific training procedures and methods. He is not equipped for this activity because of inadequate skill and knowledge in the areas of learning and training; on the other hand, the line manager, using the advice and the assistance of the training staff specialist, should establish training policies and broad training procedures. He should review, approve, or disapprove training plans in terms of their possible contribution to goal achievement. The line manager, once a plan is accepted, has the responsibility for seeing that the plan has a maximum chance to succeed. Certainly, insofar as his general knowledge of training permits, he should participate with the training specialist in the development of training plans. Finally, he has the responsibility for letting his subordinates know that the training policies, procedures, and plans, by virtue of his approval, are his policies, procedures, and plans, and not simply those of the training specialist. The responsibility of the training specialist is that of developing, planning, and coordinating training activities which are needed by the organization. This is not the specific responsibility of the line manager. His responsibility is to approve or disapprove proposals for training which come from his training specialist.

The line manager is responsible for determining whether or not the training has achieved the goals established for this activity. The training specialist has the responsibility for evaluating how well the training plans are executed; he must evaluate the mechanics and procedures used in training. He further has the responsibility of reporting his evaluations to line management. This should be a responsibility which is understood clearly both by the training specialist and by all line personnel concerned.

Responsibility for Execution of Approved Training Plans

The training specialist has no authority over line personnel. If an assistant foreman disregards approved procedures in inducting a new employee, or if an instructor does not follow the prescribed methods in teaching a new employee, it is the responsibility of the line superior to see that he does. It is, however, the responsibility of training specialists to determine whether or not approved procedures for training are being followed. If approved procedures are not being followed, he must determine what is needed to correct the situation. Furthermore, it is his responsibility to call deviations from approved procedure to the attention of the proper line manager so that errors can be corrected. The training specialist's responsibility for this type of activity should be clear to all concerned with training. It is then the responsibility of line management to see that approved training procedures are carried out properly. Although training plans may have inherent faults which lead to inadequate results, we suspect that failure of a training effort is more frequently the result of faulty execution than of faulty planning.

This discussion may give the impression that a strictly formal relationship should exist between line management and the training specialist. Certainly, the ground rules of interaction should be drawn up as clearly as possible. The interaction, however, should not and cannot be as formal as we seem to imply. The training specialist will have much to learn from line personnel; in turn he should teach them much about the rationale of training. A cooperative, mutual give-and-take relationship must exist between the line manager and the training man if effective results are to come from any training effort.

Our statements about the responsibility of line managers and training specialists regarding planning, organizing, coordinating, executing, and evaluating training stem from a careful consideration of the functions of a "manager" in an industrial organization. We perhaps stretch the term "manager," but we place anyone in this category who has the responsibility for directing the efforts of others in achieving specific organizational goals and objectives. He also is an individual who must accept the responsibility of the failure of others to do what is necessary to achieve these outcomes. A manager is a first-line supervisor; he also is the president of a corporation. The function of a manager is fourfold: planning, decision making, implementing decisions, and evaluating results. He is not a "doer" in the sense that he performs the actual acts which are necessary for implementing a decision. When he starts performing the physical and mental activities required to implement the decision he ceases to be a manager.

The manager, therefore, functions in training as a manager. He does not perform "training." His planning and decision making determine, on the basis of data available to him, the training required in his unit and the goals of these training activities. His implementation of training is to delegate to competent personnel the planning and execution of the training activities required to meet the unit's needs. He evaluates training not as to its technical excellence but whether or not it achieves the determined goals. If the goal of a specific training activity is making available to the department by a certain date ten competent set-up men, his evaluation is whether or not this objective is met. If it is not met, then he has the responsibility of finding out why it is not met and seeing that corrective action is taken.

The Responsibility for Teaching

In industry, teaching takes place in many settings and is carried out in many ways. To maintain that all training must be conducted by the employee's superior ignores the fact of the diversity of teaching situations and methods found in industry. The actual teaching process should be carried out by the individual, either from within or from without the company, who can create a situation most conducive to learning by the employee. This individual does not necessarily have to be a top performer in the area in which he is instructing; he, however, must be competent in the skills or knowledge which the employee is required to acquire. Above all, he must be competent in the art of teaching.

So for different purposes, different persons in an organization may be assigned the responsibility for instructing. A new production employee will receive instruction concerning general company policies and procedures from a member of the personnel department; he will receive from the mill superintendent further instructions concerning specific procedures in the mill, and from his departmental foreman instruction on departmental procedures. His assistant foreman will give him specific information about work in his unit. The employee then will be assigned to a trained instructor, usually another production employee, who will teach him the specific skills and knowledge required to perform the tasks of his job. If later on a method of working is changed, he may receive instruction from a member of the industrial engineering department. If a major modification in equipment or machinery which he uses is made, an expert from the machinery manufacturer may be called in to teach him what these changes are and to assist him in modifying his behavior to meet the changed demands of the job. A similar sequence of receiving instruction can be experienced by a supervisor, a member of middle management, or the staff specialist.

In selecting persons as instructors from among company personnel, it is a waste of talent not to use the individual most competent in a given area, if he is capable of performing effectively as an instructor. The vice president for finance is the logical individual to instruct management trainees in financial management of the company, provided he meets the knowledge requirements and has the necessary instructional skills. Similarly, the master mechanic of a company is the logical instructor to teach certain aspects of machine shop work to apprentices. Not to utilize the knowledge and skill of such specialists just because they are not the immediate supervisor of the employees being taught is a foolish waste of manpower. Similarly, to expect a supervisor to be apt enough to instruct in every phase of behavior required of *all* his employees is, to say the least, unrealistic.

So the responsibility of teaching should be assigned to the

individual, within or without the company, who can assist the employee in modifying his behavior in the most effective manner in order to meet the demands placed on him by the requirements of his job. This may or may not be the immediate supervisor of the employee. The supervisor, however, must be cognizant of what the teacher is doing in instructing the employee. He should take the responsibility of evaluating the instructing process. He also must let the employee understand that whoever is actually doing the instructing is in reality an agent of the supervisor and that he is being taught methods or information which the superior expects to be carried over to the job. Once training is completed, it is then the supervisor's responsibility to reinforce the new behavior. It is here that the training of supervisors is too frequently deficient.

The Supervisor's Special Role in Maintaining Behavior

It should be made clear that the immediate supervisor of the trainee, by his actions, can negate the effect of competent instruction. The learner in a well-planned training program is taught specific methods of performing a given task. Certain attitudes toward waste and quality are developed. If the immediate supervisor indicates in any way that the methods taught and the attitudes desired are not prerequisites for satisfactory job performance, the learner will depart quickly and intelligently from the prescribed methods and attitudes. Since the superior is the source of rewards and punishments, the learner, generally, will try to behave in the way the superior considers adequate. This means that a superior must know the job methods being taught, the standards of performance required, and the work attitudes desired. He then will be in a position to reinforce the training procedures by his approval or disapproval of the learner in terms of the learner's conformance or nonconformance to training requirements.

As we have indicated, much learning in the industrial world takes place in a situation which is not identical with the situation in which the learned behavior must appear to produce goods or a service. A weaver learner is taught the manual skills of weaving in a vestibule school and then is expected to use these skills in the actual work situation of the weave room. An apprentice is taught the principles of mensuration in a classroom and is expected to use these in a machine shop. Supervisors are exposed, in conference rooms, to various training to develop skills, knowledge, and attitudes necessary to direct the behavior of subordinates. The situation in the day-to-day utilization on the job of skills and knowledge varies considerably from the training situation. If these skills, knowledge, and attitudes are to persist in the actual work situation, they must be reinforced in the work situation. The employee must become aware that the way he was taught to behave in training is the way he must behave on the actual job. In brief, the supervisor is responsible for reinforcing and maintaining the desired behavior, regardless of where or from whom it was learned.

If this is the supervisor's responsibility, what things should he know and do? Some jobs have intrinsic reinforcement built into them, and their execution gives immediate, correct knowledge of results; others do not. An employee can see that a hem in a towel is sewn correctly and that a given number of correctly hemmed towels are produced in a unit of time. But many industrial jobs do not offer immediate knowledge of results. Even in the case of towel hemming, the knowledge of results is not associated automatically with behavior taught the learner as the desired job behavior.

The reinforcement of correct behavior is, therefore, an important duty of the supervisor. He should provide in his day-to-day supervision of subordinates reinforcement of that behavior which has been taught the employee. He must look beyond the results and at the ways the results are achieved. This is especially important in those jobs where intrinsic reinforcement for *correct* behavior is not automatic. For example, a life insurance salesman may sell a policy to a prospect in spite of doing everything wrong in his sales approach. The prospect was simply ready to buy and waiting for a chance. The results, in this example, would reinforce the wrong kinds of behavior. On the other hand, a salesman may do an excellent selling job but with a prospect who would not buy insurance from anyone. This is the kind of situation in which a supervisor must provide the necessary correct reinforcement. If he does not, an inexperienced salesman will change his behavior in an undesirable way. The supervisor, by proper guidance of the employee, can reinforce the correct behavior even though the results, through no fault of the employee, are adverse.

This means that a supervisor must observe the employee as he performs his job duties both during and after initial training phases and until job behavior is established firmly. He thus will be able to establish schedules of reinforcement so that the employee will receive reinforcements in a proper time sequence and in an appropriate manner. It is true, of course, that where intrinsic reinforcement exists in the task, and this reinforcement is correct from the standpoint of the proper way to perform the task, the supervisor's role as a source of reinforcement can be minimized. If little intrinsic reinforcement exists in a task or the reinforcement which exists tends to perpetuate wrong responses, the supervisor must observe the employee's behavior carefully and adjust the reinforcement schedule appropriately.

If the supervisor is to control reinforcement, he must set up beforehand a number of standards of performance which will permit him to recognize the continuation of high level performance or the improvement in a given skill. Without such standards, reinforcement will be indiscriminate and will fail to contribute to the maintenance or improvement of job skills. Once such standards are set up, a good supervisor will then take the opportunity to use varied reinforcement—praise, notes of commendation, a raise, a dinner, inclusion on a routing list, a better machine or location, promotion, etc. Unless the standards are carefully established, however, the varied reinforcement will be ineffective in improving performance.

Although the immediate superior may not be the best equipped individual in the company to teach a subordinate a given skill or knowledge, he is in the best position to see that the skill or knowledge as taught is actually used in performing a task. To this extent, we will agree that the superior is the best individual to train a subordinate. He is in a strategic position to reinforce the behavior of a subordinate once it has been learned, and thereby maintain it.

TEACHING AND LEARNING

A general assumption both in industrial training and in education at large exists about the relationship between learning and teaching. In industry, it can be summarized by the bromide from Training Within Industry, "If the learner has not learned, the teacher has not taught." In general education, the relationship is expressed in less naive terminology but still installs the teacher as a central factor in the progress of the pupil. This general assumption about the centrality of the teacher in industrial training is summarized eloquently by Planty and his associates (1948):

> Teaching is the heart of the training program. It is to industrial training what direct labor is to production, and what the sales interview is to selling. Except for costly, unguided trial-and-error learning, it is the only activity that can result in desired new ability. Nothing else—neither course outlines, conferences, nor the physical arrangement of the classroom—is half so important. The value of a doctor to a sick man comes in his therapy, not in his pills and paraphernalia. The value of a training program lies in the teaching, not in synthetic formulas, texts, and training aids. The teaching act itself therefore deserves major attention. But in training departments all over the country the attention given to teaching itself is minor and inconsequential in relation to its importance (p. 41).

This assumption has been accepted with little or no research evidence concerning the relationship of the trainer to the efficiency of industrial training. Maier (1955, pp. 347–350) has shown that giving industrial trainers special training in "(1) techniques for establishing favorable social interrelations (2) methods for increasing motivation (3) procedures by which the trainer could guide and lead rather than push workers" materially affected the rate at which learners master the operations of a stitching machine.

A study from military training lends support to the assumption that an instructor has some effect on the learning process (Wattles, 1946). Three groups of trainees were instructed in voice-communication in the presence of simulated aircraft noise. The first group was given supervised practice by a trained instructor. A second comparable group practiced in the presence of an officer who performed no instructional functions. The third comparable group practiced without any supervision. Improvement for the three groups, in order, was substantial, a small amount, and no improvement. Controlled investigations of this type in industry are the exception rather than the rule. This is also true in the field of general education. Research on the relationship between the behavior of the teacher and pupil development constitutes a small minority of the numerous investigations of learning in elementary and secondary schools and colleges (Beecher, 1949; Domas and Tiedeman, 1950). The importance of the teacher or trainer is another of the many assumptions concerning industrial training which we must accept, at least in part, on faith. It is an area which requires research to demonstrate not only the relationship of the trainer's behavior to the learning of the trainee but also the relative importance of the trainer in comparison with other factors, in the training situation, which facilitate (or inhibit) learning.

We have something more than faith to go on in assigning to teaching and the teacher in the industrial world an important and perhaps central role in the outcomes of training efforts in industry. The evidence is indirect but convincing. First, consider the tasks which constitute the job of an instructor in an industrial situation. Miller, on the basis of an extensive analysis of the general problem of training, primarily in military situations, lists the following tasks of a trainer:

1. Motivating students
2. Explaining principles and relationships
3. Providing the student with a criterion of performance
4. Evaluating trainee performance
5. Communicating evaluations and directions to trainees
6. Adjusting degree of task difficulty
7. Adjusting to individual differences
8. Effecting transition of trainee from instructor-dependence to self-dependence
9. Operating training devices (Miller, 1953, pp. 37–49)

Ericksen (1958) lists the duties of an instructor as follows:

1. Giving information
2. Directing the learning process
3. Evaluating the trainee
4. Advising and counseling (pp. 3–8)

These statements of the tasks of an instructor are based primarily on military situations. Although industrial training is not identical with military training, there are many elements which are similar in both situations. Planty (1948), writing of the industrial situation, does not give a specific list of the tasks of a trainer in industry but in his discussion of the role of teaching he covers much of the same ground covered by Miller and Ericksen. Furthermore, the opinions of experts, based on a review of available published data, lead to the following statement about the tasks of an instructor:

> In general terms, the task of instruction has two aspects—it is both a "science and an art." As a science it consists in mastering the basic knowledges and skills in a specific area, in knowing the basic principles of learning and how it proceeds, in knowing the students, their ability level, background and interests. In addition to this basic information are the steps which precede instruction—analyzing the specific training task into its various steps and stages, considering the problems of each and planning efficient ways to meet them. As an art, teaching consists in getting the information to him in a clear and intelligible manner (Handbook of Human Engineering Data, 1952, Part IX, Chapter IV, Sec. 2, p. 1).

These, again, are the opinions of experts as to the tasks a trainer must perform. Little evidence is available as to what an instructor working in the industrial setting actually does. In fact, a careful operations analysis of the task of an instructor in industry is rarely performed.[1] This may grow out of the fact that instructing frequently is part of a task cluster in a job which exists for many reasons other than training employees.

Recent developments in automated teaching or programmed learning described in Chapter 7 raise some questions about the effectiveness of the instructor in training. Where the trainer is responsible for many activities and must train large groups, he cannot perform his job as trainer or learning director for each individual effectively. In addition, studies which evaluate instructor excellence in terms of trainee performance show that the reliability of instructor performance is low. The lack of reliability could, of course, be the result of a large number of mediocre trainers and very few good ones so that the range of

[1] Some efforts have been made at operations analysis of the instructor's tasks in military training. See, for example, Smith and Standoher (1955).

ability is too restricted to show reliability. On the other hand, results of such studies may justify the growing acceptance of self-instructional devices which automatically incorporate into their instruction sound learning principles with which many instructors do not or cannot teach. It may well be that the role and centrality of the trainer in industrial training will change.

Yet if we accept the judgment of experts about the tasks of an instructor in industry, we must agree that the way the instructor performs his tasks today will have specific, definite, and far reaching effects on the learning of the trainee. If optimum conditions for training exist in a company, these conditions can be negated by poor instructors. On the other hand, even with effective instructors, training efforts will not achieve maximum returns if many of the factors discussed earlier in this text are not present, and if the proper organizational climate for effective use of training is not established.

Another approach to assaying the importance of the instructor in industrial training is the assumption, by Haire (1956), among others, that training is one of the functions of leadership which should be performed by line management. Regardless of whether or not this is a leadership function of direct line supervision, the person in charge of instructing an employee is a representative of the management of the company. What he does and how he does it will have significant effect on the behavior of the trainee, not only in acquiring skills and knowledge, but also in developing attitudes toward work and the company. So not only in the tasks an instructor must perform in facilitating learning, but also in his position as a representative of management, can the instructor in industry be assumed to influence in a decisive manner the behavior of a learner. At least this is the safest assumption that can be made under existing training conditions and until experimental evidence produces more adequate evidence than we now have on the effect of the instructor's behavior on the learning of the trainee.

THE INSTRUCTOR IN INDUSTRY

The importance of the instructor is assumed not only in industrial training, but also in the broader field of public education. This leads to the question of what makes an effective instructor? Presumably, some industrial employees do a better job of instructing than others. In what way does the "good" instructor differ from the "poor" instructor?

Again, answers to this question, based on research, are not available. In the past, at least, there has been an assumption that the best performer is the most adequate instructor. Companies who have relied on this assumption in selecting instructors usually become disillusioned. High competence in performing a task is not a guarantee of competence in teaching others how to perform the task. Obviously, the ability to teach requires something more than task knowledge and skill. What is this "something more"?

An analysis of the few available research studies of the characteristics of efficient instructors suggest the following conclusion:

> Studies cited here point to a general knowledge factor—knowledge of teaching techniques, knowledge of subject, and general intellectual ability—as being most important, with personality factors less important. This ranking stands out strikingly when the criterion used is the actual gain which students make during a course of study and is further confirmed by mature student ratings (Handbook of Human Engineering Data, 1952, Part IX, Chapter II, Sec. II, p. 1).

The traits and abilities of a good instructor as evolved from an analysis of these studies are summarized in Table 8.1.

Although these conclusions may serve as a guide for selecting instructors for industrial training, their adequacy must be questioned on at least three points. Many of the studies are of the analysis of instructor behavior in the armed services. The others are based on the analysis of the work of instructors in public schools and colleges. It is possible that instructors in industry must possess the same characteristics of instructors in the armed forces or in general education if they are to perform their teaching assignments adequately. We rather suspect this is true. But reliable evidence must come from research on the problem and not from hopeful pronouncements of people writing a book.

The second problem is the acceptance as reliable for industry the data in Table 8.1 because of the restricted nature of the teaching situations in the studies analyzed. They primarily re-

Table 8.1

TRAITS AND ABILITIES OF A GOOD INSTRUCTOR

(From *Handbook of Human Engineering Data,* 1952, Part IX, Chapter II, Section II, Table 2.1)

a. Scholarship
   1. Has knowledge of subject
   2. Has good command of language
   3. Contributes to his field of knowledge; and keeps up-to-date
   4. Is interested in teaching

b. Academic Skills
   1. Organizes materials of the course clearly around definite objectives
   2. Is always prepared
   3. Arouses interest and stimulates curiosity
   4. Presents information skillfully with suitable illustrations
   5. Uses a variety of methods
   6. Adapts his methods to the level of his class and is alert to individual needs
   7. Analyzes errors and corrects specific difficulties
   8. Is fair and impartial in making tests and in grading
   9. Speaks clearly and does not use sarcasm or ridicule
   10. Is free from annoying mannerisms

c. Personality
   1. Is patient, sympathetic, and friendly with students
   2. Is at ease in social situations
   3. Has humor, tact, enthusiasm
   4. Is cooperative
   5. Is mature, self-reliant, and confident

port teaching in a formal class situation. Only one consists of what might be called "on-the-job training." Generally, in industry, training carried on in the formal classroom situation is minimal compared with training occurring at the place of work and in face-to-face contacts between persons or other situations much less formal than that found in the usual classroom environment. Again, it is possible that instruction in informal situations requires the same characteristics of successful instructors as that required of successful instructors in formal teaching. We simply do not know the answer to this problem, since we have no reliable data on which to base a conclusion.

Finally, lists such as these remind the authors of the lengthy lists of characteristics of good leaders. For many years, studies of leadership concentrated on the isolation or discovery of such traits. Most of such research can best be characterized as having a sterile outcome. More recent research has concentrated on the varied situations in which leadership occurs and on the numerous activities and behavior which might be characterized as leadership.

The area of instructor selection in industry is one of the many areas in industrial training which requires sound research if training is to make significant contributions to the achievement of organizational goals. Availability no longer is an adequate criterion for assigning an employee to duties of instruction. Yet as is true in many problems of human behavior, research here will not be easy. It must secure data not only on the behavior of the "good" instructor but also on behavior of effective teachers at different levels in the organization. It is entirely possible that the instructors who do an effective job of teaching production workers on the job may perform differently from instructors who are effective in apprentice training. A foreman who does a top notch job in the informal instruction of his assistant foreman in face-to-face contacts might not be able to conduct an adequate course in human relations in the training conference room of his company.

Research on instructors in industry should be directed first to identifying the various situations in which one employee acts as an instructor of another employee or group of employees. Once these various instructor assignments are identified the next step in research is an operations analysis of the specific instructor tasks.[2] This can lead not only to identifying what an instructor must do in instructing an employee in the duties of a specific job but will give clues also as to the knowledge, skills, and attitudes the instructor must possess if he performs his instructional assignment in an effective manner. It is possible that in the future some courageous company will dare to set up controlled experiments to determine the effect on the learning of employees

[2] See Chapter 3.

by instructors who differ in characteristics thought to be significant in differentiating between "good" and "poor" teachers.

Operations analysis of instructor duties may even lead to some suggestion of a division in instructional duties in training an employee. We referred earlier in this chapter to the fallacy current in training literature concerning the supervisor's duty as a teacher. We suspect that an operations analysis of the teaching of a relatively simple task like spinning may show that it can be done more effectively by two or more instructors rather than by a single instructor. The individual proficient in teaching the manual skills of this job may be totally inadequate in instructing in the patroling duties and quality requirements of the job. As we move up the industrial hierarchy, the necessity for multiple instructors would become even more apparent if the tasks of teaching these higher level jobs are subjected to a careful operations analysis. A plant manager can receive instruction from the vice president in charge of manufacturing in many areas of his duties and responsibilities. But there will be areas in which his superior will not be competent to instruct him; he then must receive instruction from someone else, learn it on his own without instruction, or remain ignorant. And the price of ignorance at this level in the company could be prohibitive.

We obviously have little reliable data to present on the characteristics of the "good" instructor in industry. This is a necessary area of research if industrial training is to make a significant contribution to the attainment of organizational objectives. Some areas of research have been suggested. Industry must face squarely the situation that training in industry will require carefully planned research not only in the area of instructors but also in all aspects of industrial training if significant progress is made in the utilization of this management tool.

TRAINING TRAINERS

We are probably presumptuous to attempt to outline the training requirements for industrial trainers. Since so little reliable data are available on the instructors' tasks, what we are suggesting consists primarily of hunches based on our observations of the task requirements of industrial trainers. These suggestions are tentative and unfortunately cannot be utilized in the cookbook fashion of JIT courses of the Training Within Industry program.

First, no universal training course for all who instruct in industry seems feasible or desirable. This seems true until research demonstrates that instructing in industry is a unitary task regardless of who is to be instructed in what. Certain common elements will probably exist in all training for instruction. The common elements, however, will receive different emphasis and be handled in more or less detail in terms of whom the instructor will teach and in terms of the knowledge, skills, and attitudes which are the purpose of instruction.

The training of trainers in industry should be tailored to meet the needs of the following major groups who are concerned with the training of others:

1. Supervisors who are responsible for the general overall training of the subordinates but who delegate the majority of training to others. The term "supervisor" is used broadly here to include all members of management, from the president of the corporation through first-line supervisors.

2. Supervisors who, although responsible for general overall training, also personally instruct employees. Usually, instruction of this sort is a face-to-face activity consisting of interviewing and counseling.

3. Employees, either staff or line, who are assigned the duties of on-the-job training of other employees over whom they have no line authority other than instruction.

4. Employees who conduct classes, courses, or conferences in the more or less formal classroom situation. These employees may conduct the training activities for all levels of employees from production workers through upper level managerial personnel.

Suggested Training for Supervisors Responsible for General Overall Training but Who Delegate the Majority of Training to Others

Since this group will be responsible for training in the units over which they have authority, it would seem that the following areas of industrial training require emphasis:

1. General nature, purpose, and function of training as a management tool.

2. Methods and procedures for analyzing training needs. It is possible that increased emphasis should be placed for some of this group on certain phases of analyzing training needs with less emphasis on the other phases for other members of the group. A plant manager perhaps should be more conversant with the methods and procedures for analyzing organizational needs than with procedures of operations analysis. A first-line supervisor in turn might need more intensive training in analyzing the job performance of his subordinates and less instruction in organizational analysis.

3. The psychology of learning and its applications to industrial training. Again differential treatment of this topic is indicated for different levels of the management hierarchy. The supervisor who must approve specific training plans or programs requires more intensive training in this area than the supervisor who is not required to perform this task. A plant manager, for example, might require more knowledge in this area to make decisions on plans for his unit than would be true of a vice president for production.

4. An understanding of the methods and techniques used in various kinds of training activities in industry. The knowledge should be intensive in those training procedures which are used or suggested for use in a specific unit.

5. An understanding and appreciation of how training research must be conducted in order to evaluate the outcomes of training together with an emphasis on the need for evaluation to determine whether or not training done in the organization is effective.

Suggested Training for Supervisors Who are Responsible for Overall Training and Who Personally Instruct Employees

It can be assumed that supervisors in this group will have been exposed to some of the training received by the supervisor in the previous group. Training for this group is the development of certain knowledge although specific skills also must be developed. Training for this group, therefore, is a matter of developing skills required in the man-to-man type of instruction which they must use. Training in the following aspects of instruction seem indicated:

1. Skill training in operations analysis usually will be necessary.
2. Skills in diagnostic analysis of the individual employee is an absolute requirement.
3. Skills in applying the principles of learning to the individual instruction situation are required. Particularly skills in appraisal interviewing and follow up seem to be a *sine qua non* (Maier, 1958; Lee, 1956).

Suggested Training for Employees Assigned Duties of On-the-Job Training of Other Employees over Whom They Have no Line Authority

For this group, instruction in training is acquiring both knowledge and skills, as well as developing certain attitudes toward the task of instructing. The following training seems desirable:

1. A general understanding of the function and importance of training in an industrial organization.
2. Development of specific skills in the diagnostic analysis of individual employees who are receiving instruction.
3. Some understanding of the general nature of the learning process and the applications of learning principles to the instruction required for teaching a specific task or task cluster.
4. Instruction and practice in organizing and conducting training on the job with particular emphasis on instructing an individual or a relatively small group of employees. This will require the development of some skill in the interviewing of employees in the instructional situation. At least as important is emphasis on factors contributing to transfer following training.
5. Some understanding of the nature of operations analysis as applied to the specific jobs in which they are instructing. Sometimes the instructor is required to make an operations analysis, and skill must be developed to perform this assignment. Other times, the skill required will be that of translating, or understanding the translation, of the operations analysis into an instructional procedure.

Suggested Training for Employees Who Instruct in More-or-Less Formal Classroom Situations

This group of industrial instructors will have tasks more similar to those of instructors in public education than is true of the other groups considered here. Yet their task is somewhat different. Generally, they are dealing with adults who have some degree of expertness in or at least some experience with the subject matter of the training. They may be attending training sessions under duress from company pressure, or to please their boss. The sessions are usually secondary to their main industrial purpose of running their jobs satisfactorily. Furthermore, their ego is usually involved, not so much as to success or failure in the training *per se*, but rather in the effect of their performance in training on an important aspect of their lives—their jobs. As a whole, teaching a group of employees in a formal classroom situation can require instruction of the highest order, if the aims for which the training is given are attained. The following training is suggested for this group of industrial instructors.

1. A general knowledge of the purpose of training as a management tool.
2. Instruction in the analysis of the individual employee's progress in learning the subject matter, skills, and attitudes which are the purpose of the training sessions. This also includes instruction in how to construct measuring instruments to evaluate classroom performance.
3. An understanding of the nature of the learning process and the principles of learning as applied to instructing groups in a formal classroom situation. This requires specific training in the procedures and methods used in organizing and presenting the subject matter of the training course.
4. Emphasis on factors contributing to transfer of training to the job. This should include numerous exercises to demonstrate how such principles as identical elements, concepts, and overlearning can be applied to specific training situations.
5. If special techniques are used, training which will lead to successful use of these techniques. Role playing, the incident technique, and conference leadership requires special knowledge and skills which the usual well meaning amateur industrial

instructor must learn, if he is to use any of these methods adequately. Even the use of visual aids and simulators require the acquisition of skills which usually are not in the repertoire of the average industrial employee who is drafted for classroom instruction. Training, therefore, is required in the techniques of teaching.

We have assumed that instructors in our groups 2, 3, and 4 are competent subject matter specialists. We shall, however, make this explicit. An individual must have a reasonable degree of competence in knowledge and skills if he is to instruct another person in tasks requiring these skills and knowledge. He does not have to be a star, but he must at least be capable of playing on the team if he is going to act as coach in an industrial training program.

We have stated that training instructors in industry should be tailored to the requirements of the tasks which are required in the training duties of different classes of instructors. Furthermore, we have given broad suggestions as to the areas which should be covered in training for classes of industrial employees who have duties including industrial training. As an example of how these general suggestions can be made more specific we will outline a course designed to train first and second line supervisors. Generally, they are supervisors who have responsibility for overall training in their department or section but also who from time to time personally instruct an employee or a group of employees.

The methods of instruction in this course are a combination of lecture-class discussion, demonstrations and experiments, and individual project assignment. Lecture is held to a minimum although unevenness in the background of the trainees may require some lecture sessions to assist in establishing a common ground for instruction. Actual classroom attendance is scheduled for 32 hours, and project work will take from 20 to 30 hours. Generally, each class session is two hours long, with a break between the first and second hour. Each participant is furnished a notebook in which he can insert mimeographed resumes of the main points covered in each session as well as other material, including project assignments.

The following is an outline of the sixteen sessions of the course and the assignments required of the trainees.

COURSE OUTLINE FOR INSTRUCTOR TRAINING

Session I. The Place of Training in Industry

1. Pretest on contents of course.
2. This is a discussion session to set the stage for the subsequent sessions. The instructor attempts to get agreement among the groups as to the following:
   (*a*) What is training trying to accomplish in an industrial organization.
   (*b*) What training can contribute to achievement of organizational objectives. The limitations of training.
   (*c*) What deterrents to effective training exist in the company.
   (*d*) Where the responsibility for training lies in a company.
   (*e*) What are the steps necessary to securing effective training.
   Certain examples of results of efficient and inefficient training both within the company and outside the company are presented and discussed.

Assignment: Each member of the class constructs a policy statement concerning the function of training and the responsibility for training in the company.

Session II. Operations Analysis—1

1. Policy statements of the various members of the class are read and discussed. A policy statement which receives the approval of the class is developed as a guide for action in further class sessions.
2. Demonstration. A relatively simple manual task is performed in two ways. One way of performing the task is more efficient than the other way. The difference in performance is not obvious. The class is assigned the task of determining which of the two ways of performing the task is the more efficient and why. Discussion subsequent to the demonstration centers on the implications of the demonstration for training and the necessity for careful operational analysis as a basis of sound training.
3. Lecture. This emphasizes the need for careful operations analy-

sis as a basis for planning training and the various possible methods used in operations analysis. Finally a method of operations analysis which the supervisor can use on many of his jobs is described in detail.

Assignment: Study of the method of operations analysis presented as useful for supervisors from material prepared for the group. The class is informed that they will be asked to use this material at the meeting of the class to analyze certain tasks which will be performed in class.

Session III. Operations Analysis—2

1. Review and questions concerning the method of operations analysis prescribed for their use.
2. Performance of an operations analysis of task presented by the means of a motion picture. The task is relatively simple but not familiar to the observers.
3. Presentation by individual members of their operations analysis, discussion of these analyses, and construction of a master one by entire class.

Assignment: Perform an operations analysis of a specific job which each member of the class supervises. It is to be prepared to present at the next class meeting. Review material on operations analysis.

Session IV. Operations Analysis—3

1. Presentation by individual class members of the operations analysis made per the assignment. Discussion and criticism of the analyses.
2. Demonstration showing how to translate operations analysis into an instructor's guide sheet for teaching a task using task in Session III.
3. Practice on converting an operations analysis into an instructor's guide sheet for teaching a task.

Assignment: On the basis of operations analysis made of the job in their department, individual class members should prepare an instructor's guide for a task in the job analyzed.

Session V. Learning Principles and Industrial Training

1. Presentation by individual class members of their instructor guides. Discussion and criticism.

2. A demonstration experiment to illustrate the nature of learning in a simple motor and a simple verbal task.
3. Lecture setting the stage for examination of certain learning principles applicable to the acquisition and retention of skills and knowledge.

Assignment: Continue preparation of the instructor's guide for the job analyzed. Complete assignment for Session VII.

Session VI. Learning Principles—Motivation

1. Demonstration experiment on learning under conditions of high and low motivation.
2. Classroom discussion of the implications of this demonstration and the factors of motivation of learning among industrial employees.

Assignment: Continue work on instructor's guide for job. Read and study summary of materials presented in Sessions V and VI.

Session VII. Learning Principles—Conditions of Practice

1. Demonstration experiment on meaningfulness in learning a motor task and a verbal task. Discussion of implications of experiment for organizing practice.
2. Class discussion on factors which are conducive to effective use of practice, that is, reinforcement, meaningfulness, transfer effects, etc. Presentation of experimental results in this area.

Assignment: A learning experiment on conditions of practice to be performed before the next session of the class. Read and study summary of material presented in Session VII.

Session VIII. Learning Principles—Guidance of Learning

1. Demonstration experiment on the effect of knowledge of results in learning a motor task.
2. Class discussion of ways and means of properly guiding trainees in learning. Presentation of experimental results in this area.
3. Summary of class work on instructor guides turned in at previous session.

Assignment: Review materials presented in Sessions V–VIII with the view to utilizing in planning the mechanics of a training program for a specific industrial job.

Session IX. Organizing a Training Plan—1

1. Class reviews operations analysis and instructor guide for job analyzed in class in Session III with the view to developing a training plan for this job utilizing the principles of learning from Sessions V–VIII.
2. Class is divided into work groups of three to four individuals to draw up a training plan for this job.
3. Training plans are presented, discussed, and criticized in class.

Assignment: Work out a training plan for the job which each class member has analyzed and construct an instructor's guide. Read and study materials summarizing methods of preparing a training plan.

Session X. Organizing a Training Plan—2

1. Presentation by individual class members of training plans for their specific jobs. Discussion and criticism of plans.
2. Lecture. Summarizing contents of course to date.

Assignment: Review all materials presented to date. Be prepared to ask for clarification of any points at next class meeting.

Session XI. Man Analysis—1

1. Brief session to clear up any class questions.
2. Demonstration to illustrate problems of securing valid, reliable, and pertinent data on the job performance of an employee.
3. Lecture on the use of measures derived from job performance of employees to analyze the degree of skill and knowledge the employee possesses.

Assignment: Analyze the objective job performance measures for a period of one month of a group of employees performing the same job. Rank the employees in terms of this analysis. Read and study materials covering this session.

Session XII. Man Analysis—2

1. Review analysis of job performance measures made by class members and discuss their implications from a training standpoint.
2. Demonstration on the use of a diagnostic rating procedure in

analyzing the job performance of an employee. Use a previously prepared film.

3. Lecture on the use and abuse of rating procedures.

Assignment: Develop a rating form to be used in analyzing the job performance of a specific job in the class member's department. Use this form to rate four or five employees. Read and study materials covering this session.

Session XIII. Man Analysis—3

1. Presentation of rating forms and results of use by class members. Discussion of implications for training of the results of the diagnostic ratings of employees.
2. Lecture-discussion on the use of work samples and performance tests in analyzing job performance from a training standpoint.
3. Develop with class suggestions, a performance test for the job for which an operations analysis was made in class in Session III.

Assignment: Develop a performance test for the job analyzed by the individual class member. Read and study materials covered in this session.

Session XIV. Guiding the Industrial Trainee

1. Review and discuss performance tests developed by individual class members.
2. Lecture—summarizing methods of diagnostic man analysis.
3. Demonstration-discussion of correcting an employee's errors in performing a task. A simulated learning situation is used in which the learner makes deliberate mistakes in performing a task. Class members role play the instructor's assignment in detecting and correcting the errors of the learner.

Assignment: Read material covering techniques useful in correcting the mistakes of learners.

Session XV. Organization Analysis

1. Review and discussion of techniques used in guiding the individual trainee.
2. Presentation to class of data on personnel in a hypothetical department in terms of job performance, age, turnover data, etc., as a basis of discussing the general training needs in this department.

3. Lecture-demonstration on the steps necessary to perform an organization analysis for training purposes.

Assignment: Each class member performs an organizational analysis in his own department concentrating on one or two major job classifications. Use material covered in Session XV as a guide. Two-week interval between this and next class meeting but individual meetings with class members to assist in their organization analysis.

Session XVI.

1. Presentation of organization analyses by individual members of class and discussion of these analyses.
2. Post-test.

We are not suggesting that the course as outlined will be a panacea for training problems in industry. In fact, it is now in a developmental stage and will certainly be modified as a result of experience with it in an industrial situation. Its major claim is that it is the result of a careful analysis of what first- and second-line supervisors need to know about training if they are to use, effectively, this management tool. It is our firm conviction that their understanding of training must go deeper than that provided by the popular JIT program. This course should provide this firmer understanding.

WHO WILL TRAIN?

This chapter has considered the problem of who will train in industry. The careful reader has realized that a simple, concise answer to this question has not been supplied. The failure to answer this question comes from the fact that there are little or no reliable data on which to base an answer. Research on the problem of who should train in an industrial situation is practically nonexistent. Until such research is conducted, we will have no reliable answers not only to this question but also to many important questions in industrial training.

Accordingly, we have presented our opinions based on extensive experience in training and on the available research data. We have questioned the accuracy of the recurring contention that only a superior can teach effectively his subordinates. A line of reasoning concerning the responsibility for training and for teaching has been presented.

We have presented what are practically *ex cathedra* statements about the effect of the instructor on the learning of the trainee. Similar statements have been made concerning the tasks of an instructor and the characteristics of "good" vs. "poor" instructors. We have urged strongly the necessity of research in determining what tasks should be assigned to instructors, how instructors should be selected, and how industrial personnel should be trained to execute training assignments.

9 EVALUATION OF TRAINING

THE STATUS OF THE EVALUATION OF TRAINING

Evaluation of training in industry is in much the same category Mark Twain placed the weather. There are frequent references, both oral and written, to the necessity for evaluating training, but little evidence of any serious efforts in this direction. As Wallace and Twichell (1953) indicate: "Everyone agrees that it is important to give workers good training. Unfortunately, it is a long step from agreement that training is a 'good thing' to the discovery of what training is good and how it can be made better" (p. 25). The same authors conclude that little experimental evidence is available on the relative merits of different training procedures or "that training as it is being carried out in specific situations produces any improvement in workers' performance at all" (p. 25).

The absence of evaluation from the industrial training scene is even more surprising when we consider the dollars spent each year, either directly or indirectly, on training by American industry. It is entirely possible, as Wallace and Twichell (1953) believe, that this lack of evaluation of training "lies in management's reluctance to 'waste time' in testing something it has convinced itself is good. Training programs are uniformally excellent—by expert opinion and proclamation" (p. 25). It seems to us that this reluctance may have deeper roots and lies in management's general attitude and belief toward the training (as shown in Chapter 1). Training has been considered as an activity which requires no special skills or knowledge and has no special background of information, technology, or theory. It is one of the necessary evils of running a business but not one that requires a skilled practitioner to reduce its malevolent effects. On the other hand, when management accepts training as one of the necessary tools for efficient operation of the business, the question of evaluation must then be given serious attention and action. For it is from careful and critical evaluation that management will be able to get the answers to the following questions:

1. Are the dollars being spent on training producing the results needed by the organization?
2. What improvements can be made in training procedures which will result in greater returns on the dollars invested in training?
3. Is training necessary in this area or this situation to improve organizational effectiveness or should the money spent on training be used in some other activity which will contribute more effectively to the attainment of organizational goals?

Admittedly, the evaluation of training is not a simple problem, since we are dealing with measuring human behavior or the results of human behavior. The techniques for securing these measures and the measures themselves are primitive in comparison with measures and techniques in the physical sciences. There have been, however, within the last two decades rapid advances in both methods and measures for studying human behavior. There exist, also, in improved accounting systems, mechanization of records, and electronic computing devices found in most industries, methods which can be adapted to the intricate problems of training evaluation. When management views training as a management tool and asks how well this tool is being used, research ingenuity can utilize these two areas both to improve and to utilize training in securing organizational goals.

This chapter deals with the problems of evaluating training and the procedures necessary if the evaluations are to serve management's ends of proper utilization of training as a tool of management.

THE GENERAL PROBLEM

The evaluation of training is not a simple process. We are trying to determine what changes, if any, in the skills, knowledge, and attitudes of employees take place as a result of being subjected to certain experiences which are called "training." We also are trying to determine how these skills, knowledge, and attitudes contribute to the attainment of organizational objectives. It is entirely possible for a training activity to develop skills, inculcate knowledge, or modify attitudes in such a manner that the resulting behavior of employees not only does not contribute to the achievement of organizational goals but actually retards this achievement. The problems of evaluating training are therefore:

1. Determining whether or not the training procedures under consideration actually result in the modifications of the behavior of the employees concerned.
2. Determining whether or not the outcome of the training procedures have any demonstrable relationship to the achievement of organizational goals.

Let us illustrate these problems. A plan to train new employees in the skills, knowledge, and attitudes required to operate a power sewing machine has been developed and put into operation. The initial level of these characteristics of the employees who are being trained are known. Records are kept on their daily progress both in quantity and quality of production. The number of hours required for each operator to reach a level of production at which the amount of production equals the amount paid the operator has been determined. Also, the number of hours of training required for each operator to reach a level of production 10% beyond this breakeven point is known. It is a reasonable assumption that the experiences to which we have exposed these operators have resulted in the level of performance they show at a given time in their training. On the other hand, if these employees practiced the task or received instructions other than provided in the training program we have no assurance as to the effectiveness of the training. Nor is there any information as to the relative effectiveness of the training procedures used as compared with other possible training procedures or the absence of any formal training.

It is in the latter area that the major problem of the relationship of the training given to the attainment of organizational goals is found. If the objective of training power machine operators is that they can produce a unit of goods at a given price with X number of dollars used in training, we can then make a judgment on the basis of our records as to how well this has been achieved. (This is true only if we show that the training procedures alone produce the results which are in our records.) It is possible, however, that by modifying or improving the training of power sewing machine operators the time required for training can be reduced and the costs of producing each unit of goods will be reduced. Evaluation of training then becomes a problem of comparing the results of one method of training versus another method. It requires establishing relationships among the experiences called training, the behavior modifications called skills, knowledge, and attitudes, and the measures of achievement of organizational goals which we accept as evidence of the degree to which these goals are reached.

Evaluation of training, therefore, generally has two major aspects. First is that of assessing whether or not the training results in behavior which furthers the achievement of organizational goals. The second is that of comparing various possible means or techniques of training to determine if any one or combination of techniques are superior for the purpose of achieving the desired results.

Evaluation, however, should not be confused with what we prefer to call a "diagnostic" approach to the investigation of training. The diagnostic approach concentrates on the individual trainee: what individuals should learn to perform a specific task or job; whether or not and how well they are learning these required items; and what can be done to facilitate acquisition and retention of the skills, knowledge, and attitudes required to perform the job. The purpose of diagnosis is to correct training procedures, to facilitate learner progress, or to correct the learner's efforts to acquire the necessary behavior. Many of the procedures necessary for a diagnostic study of training have been described in earlier parts of this book. We do not describe them again except to say that they go hand in hand with evaluation as we use the concept, that is, a determination through careful research of whether or not and to what extent training contributes to the attainment of organizational goals and the effectiveness of various forms of training.

We have indicated that organizational goals may be broad and long range; they may also be circumscribed in scope and relatively short range. They may even take on the nature of subgoals. Examples of each type of goal will come readily to the reader. Whatever the nature of these goals, the evaluation of training requires establishing causal relationship between training and achievement of organizational goals, and the problems are basically the same as in establishing a causal relationship between any two classes of phenomena, whether physical or social. First we must secure measures, representing the phenomena concerned, which have certain characteristics. Second, these measures must be secured in such a way and under such circumstances that valid inferences can be made in regard to causal relations. We consider first the characteristics of measures and second how these measures must be obtained.

THE CHARACTERISTICS OF MEASURES

Measures used in evaluating the results of training have been classified in various ways (Thorndike, 1949; Lindborn and Osterberg, 1954; Goodacre, 1957; MacKinney, 1957). Since depth and accuracy in evaluating training varies considerably with the type of measures used, we propose to describe these possible measures under certain broad headings. Actually, the different categories are not mutually exclusive.

Although we hold no particular brief for our system of classifying measures over those used by others in this field (and in reality we are indebted to many others but particularly to Thorndike [1949]), we have found it useful to think of these measures as falling into four broad categories: (1) objective-subjective, (2) direct-indirect, (3) intermediate-ultimate, (4) specific-summary.

Objective-subjective. The major distinction between an objective and a subjective measure is its source. A measure is objective if it is derived from overt behavior and does not require the expression of a belief, opinion, or judgment. If the measure represents an opinion, a belief, or a judgment, it is subjective. The following examples illustrate the difference between these measures.

The number of relays assembled by an operator in a given period of time is an objective measure of one aspect of his job performance. His supervisor's opinion as to his level of skill is a subjective measure of the operator's job performance. Similarly, the amount of absenteeism in a department might be an objective measure of the morale of the employees in the department whereas the answers given by employees on a morale audit would be classified as a subjective measure of morale. As a general rule, we are on safer grounds using objective rather than subjective measures in establishing causal relationships. This, however, is not always true. In some situations, carefully devised subjective measures are the more adequate measures of the results of training. In other situations, the only available measures are subjective. The subjectivity-objectivity of a measure is not necessarily an index of its worth in training evaluation. Its value depends, rather, on other characteristics which are discussed later in this chapter.

Direct-indirect. A measure is classified as direct if it measures the behavior of the individual or the results of his behavior. An indirect measure assesses the action of an individual whose behavior can be measured only by its influence on the actions of others. An example clarifies this distinction. A group of operators are trained in waste reduction and the results measured, using an established waste index. Any change in the waste index, everything else being equal, is a direct measure of the behavior of operators trained. In contrast, a group of supervisors are given training in the prevention of waste in a specific operation. Generally, the only way these supervisors can reduce waste is by influencing the behavior of their subordinates. In this instance, any change in the waste index in the departments of the supervisors is an indirect measure of the effectiveness of training. In fact, evaluation of supervisory and management training would be impossible in many instances without the use of indirect measures since much of the work performed by people in these positions involves influencing the actions of others. It is, however, more difficult to make causal inferences from indirect measures, and extreme care is required in securing these measures if the causal inferences are to have any validity.

Intermediate-ultimate. Each job or position in an organization has a definite purpose or it should not exist in the organization (Thorndike, 1949). Training designed to prepare an individual to perform his specific function in an organization should be evaluated in terms of how well he contributes, through his job, to organizational goal attainment. Since this contribution is a temporal affair, we rarely, if ever, are able to secure a measure or measures of his ultimate value to an organization. Consequently, measures must be used which are available at various times in his work in the company. These have been called "intermediate" as contrasted to "ultimate" measures. Examples of intermediate measures are found frequently in reported evaluation of training activities. A grade made on an achievement or trade test belongs in the intermediate category; the amount of time required to learn a task, that is, to solo a plane, is another example. Attitude measures toward specific company practices, turnover, absenteeism, and safety statistics may fall also into the group of measures known as intermediate. These are perfectly legitimate measures for use in evaluating training provided their limitations are understood and their relationship to ultimate measures are positive. McGehee (1948) has shown that intermediate measures secured early in training are indicative of ultimate level of performance in a complex industrial job. More recently, Ryan and Smith (1954) have reviewed this and other similar studies and have concluded for factory jobs that "probably a safe estimate is that one fourth or one third of the learning period will be sufficient to predict later success in most jobs" (p. 441).

The problem of using intermediate rather than ultimate measures requires the establishment of a definite relationship between the two. What a mechanic in training is able to score on an achievement test of mechanical understanding may be related positively, zero, or negatively to how well he can handle a drill press or interpret a blueprint in everyday job performance. An illustration of the dangers which exist in using intermediate measures whose relationships to ultimate measures is unknown comes from the work of Severin (1952). He made a survey of much of the training literature and summarized the relationships found between grades assigned in training and on-the-job performance measures. The relationships were not very far from zero. When grades on tests, whose relationships with on-the-job performance are unknown, are used as the only measurers of training effectiveness, we gain little information and run a serious risk of deluding ourselves by accepting good grades as proof of the training's utility. The evaluation of training using such a measure is accurate only in established relationships between ultimate measures and the intermediate measures. Intermediate measures may be the only measures available within a meaningful time space. Yet unless these intermediate measures have real meaning in relationship to ultimate job performance measures, they are of relatively little value in determining the success or failure of a training effort.

Specific-summary. Somewhat related to the problem of intermediate and ultimate measures of training outcomes is the problem of measures which are used as an index of successful performance of a specific phase of a job or as an index of the degree of performance of the total job against its potential contribution to organizational goals. The former type of measures are called "specific" or in the words of Thorndike are "Specific criteria of performance in a limited behavior unit" [1] (p. 133). Examples of this type of measure might be found in a training program to improve the manner in which secretaries answer their telephones or to teach supervisors how to use reports in a standard cost system. In contrast, a "summary" measure would

[1] Thorndike (1949) has discussed at length the problems of using specific and summary measures. The serious student should read this as well as Thorndike's treatment of the entire problem of measurement.

be an index of how well an individual performs all the critical aspects of his job. This type of measure might be needed in an attempt to evaluate the results of sending management personnel to an advanced management program at a university. Both types of measures have a definite use in evaluating training but should not be confused. Furthermore, specific measures usually can be collected under conditions which allow for more sanitary use in drawing causal inferences than is true of summary evaluations. It is much more difficult to secure summary evaluations which meet the strict requirements of a measure to be used in the evaluation of a training activity.

These four categories of measures are not mutually exclusive. A rating scale could be a subjective, intermediate, direct, and specific measure. It also could be a subjective, direct, ultimate, and summary measure. We simply find these categories useful in thinking about measures. Regardless of their type, measures must have certain characteristics, if they are to be used for causal inference in studying training outcomes. These characteristics deal with the quality and quantity of the measures and usually are called relevance, reliability, and freedom from bias. Furthermore, in an industrial situation these measures also must be practical.

Relevance. Perhaps the best way to examine this concept is to look at an investigation which was designed to evaluate the results of a training program in human relations (Katzell, 1948).

A group of supervisors were given a course in human relations. Near the beginning of the course the enrollees were given a questionnaire containing items on supervisory practices, company policies affecting personnel, and on human factors in industry (File and Remmers, 1943). Near the end of the training program another form of the same questionnaire was administered to the supervisors. Six months after the conclusion of the course a form to rate the training program was sent to the participants. Although the results of these questionnaires or ratings are immaterial for our purpose, we can indicate that the author concluded the course was a success. What we are concerned with are the measures used and the concept of "relevance."

Presumably the reason for this course was to bring about

changes in the behavior of the supervisors so that they would perform their jobs in a more effective manner particularly in dealing with their subordinates. Neither of the measures used to evaluate training was shown by the author to have any relationship to the on-the-job behavior of the supervisors or the effect of their behavior on their subordinates or the goal attainment of the organization. There is no clear evidence that an improvement in the knowledge of principles of human behavior has a high positive relationship to effective performance in the area of human relations. It is even doubtful that the principles contained in the questionnaire would be accepted by the majority of experts in the field. There also is some evidence that the questionnaire used has a reasonably close relationship to so-called tests of intelligence (Millard, 1952).

There is perhaps a little more, but very little more, justification for the rating used. After all, the respondents were asked to indicate how useful the course was in connection with their work. Just how it was used or the results achieved from use of the course was not explored. There is a tendency, however, among supervisors to look favorably upon most training sponsored by the company. Whether this is a factor here would be hard to determine. Certainly, it is legitimate to inquire how well received a training program is by those who take it. But the value of a course in changing behavior and accomplishing its purpose is not a matter of a popularity contest. In justice to the author of this paper, he is well aware of the limitations of these two measures. He points out that data on productivity, accidents, absenteeism, turnover, grievances, and suggestions would have been more desirable measures *if available.*

The measures used in this study are not relevant unless the purpose was to change opinions or to obtain from the supervisors acceptance of the course as a "good" thing. If the purpose of the course was to change supervisory behavior in such a way as to improve the job performance of their subordinates, the measures were not relevant.

This points up the fact that the question of the relevance of a measure for evaluating training immediately raises the question of "to what?" It is our contention that the measures used in evaluating training must be relevant to one or both of the following:

1. the major performance requirements of the job for which the training is being offered
2. the attainment of organizational goals which are served by the behavior of the individuals who are receiving training.

An evaluation of three methods of training insurance salesmen illustrates clearly the use of measures with varying degree of relevance (Baxter, Taaffe, and Hughes, 1953). The measures were (1) a test of knowledge, (2) a job satisfaction check list administered at the end of 6 and 12 months, (3) number of terminations, (4) the costs of the three different training methods, (5) ratings by supervisors of the agent's actual job performance, and (6) total new business sold by agents at the end of 6 and 12 months. Of these six measures, one is directly related to a major job requirement: knowledge. Two are related to organizational goals: termination and costs of training. Two are related both to organizational goals and job requirements: production and supervisory rating. It is hard to place the job satisfaction measure in either of these categories unless we can assume that job satisfaction is related to production positively and to termination negatively. If this is true, it is related to both categories. The measure of knowledge also is questionable from the standpoint of relevance unless it is shown to be related positively to job performance or can be assumed to be a prerequisite for undertaking the job at all. It should be emphasized that the measures chosen seem to have the characteristics of relevance to a much higher degree than those used in the report (Katzell, 1948) described earlier in this chapter.

The relevance of a measure is a matter of judgment. This judgment should be made by the individuals responsible for the training activity. Generally, this should be line managers since they are the ultimate consumers of the results of training. The training specialist can be of assistance, however, in objectifying these judgments and indicating sources of irrelevance in various possible measures of the outcomes of training. It is especially important that when intermediate measures are used in training evaluation their relevance to ultimate measures be carefully determined. It is conceivable that an intermediate measure might be negatively related to the ultimate function of a position or job in an industrial organization. For example, in naval aviation, it might be possible for grades on a course in navigation to be negatively related to a pilot's effectiveness in combat.

Wherry (1957), in commenting on the rational or judgmental approach to the evaluation of a measure, believes "As of today there is real hope that these methods will become judgmental only in the sense that all measurement is essentially judgmental, that they will become empirically based and empirically checked in the best sense of mathematical theory building" (p. 4). Real advances are being made in this field of research but Wherry's forecast of techniques yielding empirical rather than rational solution to these problems is still only a hope. The relevance of measures still remains in the realm of judgment. Our best efforts toward establishing relevant measures of training outcomes must be directed for the present toward securing proper judgments of relevance by individuals qualified to judge the measures and utilize them in directing training activities.

One way, perhaps, of improving the relevance of training measures (and eliminate unnecessary training efforts) is to demand that the purpose of a training activity be clearly stated and relevant measures of its outcomes be established before the training is undertaken. Any training activity for which relevant measures cannot be obtained is certainly open to question as an activity deserving managerial support.

Reliability. Reliability is the second desirable characteristic of measures used to evaluate training. It is, perhaps, not as important as relevance; however, measures which appear to be relevant but which lack reliability have no value in assessing the outcome of training.

A measure is reliable to the extent that repeated use of the measure with the same individuals yields consistent results. Generally, in training evaluation, we are concerned with what Thorndike calls relative consistency (Thorndike, 1949). Training should result in behavior changes. Measures used to describe these changes should change in amount during training. They should, however, be the type of measure which retains the individual in the same or nearly the same relative rank if no training takes place between the initial or later measurement. A measure that fluctuates from time to time and from competent user to competent user under such conditions would contain so many factors contributing to error as to give very little information as to the actual performance of the individuals undergoing training.

In the evaluation of training, it may be appropriate to use production records as measures of training effectiveness: the number of units produced per day, the amount of waste resulting from the operation, or the number of first quality units fabricated. We are concerned, however, only with the effect of training on these measures. If other factors such as machine servicing, quality of raw materials, and even the humidity affect these measures to a considerable extent, the measures on an individual may vary radically from time to time due to these factors rather than to training procedures. The measures are inconsistent and do not give an accurate picture of changes in behavior which result from training. The same effect in reverse can come from machine-paced jobs or from restriction of output on the part of the operators. Production records may be high in measured consistency and totally unreliable because the consistency is an artifact.

Thorndike distinguishes between the source of low reliability from extrinsic causes, as suggested above in the production records example, and low reliability arising from inconsistency of the performance of individuals from time to time due to intrinsic causes such as health, energy mobilization, and motivation (Thorndike, 1949). Intrinsic unreliability can be decreased by increasing the behavior samples used. This, in a limited way, may also decrease extrinsic reliability if extending the number of observations increases variations from external causes. If this increases variablility in the measures, the alternate for reducing low extrinsic reliabity is the control of these external factors. For example, securing consistent machine servicing or consistent raw materials might improve reliability in production records which were unreliable due to these factors.

It is well to remember in selecting and evaluating measures that production records should be suspect automatically in both relevance and reliability. These records are kept for a different purpose than the evaluation of training. They may serve their primary purpose quite well and be useless as training criteria. Ready-made relevant and reliable measures are hard to find for training evaluation.

Reliability of a measure is determined by statistical procedures. These procedures have been described in detail by Thorndike (1949), among others. The training director and others who attempt to evaluate training should become familiar with these procedures.

Freedom from bias. Measures can be low in relevance or reliability or both because of contamination. Contamination can also cause spuriously high reliability. Apparently relevant and statistically acceptable, reliable measures may be of little or no use in evaluating training because these measures are biased. Measures become biased or contaminated in a number of ways. Essentially they become contaminated when they are not gathered under conditions completely independent of other variables.

Suppose a training course is established in a department. Half the men in the department go through training whereas the other half do not. Instead, the latter group continues on the job. Sometime after completion of the course, the supervisor is asked to rate the efficiency of all the men in his department. The trained group, in terms of the supervisor's ratings, is significantly superior to the untrained.

Bias enters in this situation because the supervisor knew which men were trained and which were not. If he thinks that the course is worthwhile or he has become sensitized to look for evidence of improvement in the trained men, it is no surprise that this group receives superior ratings. On the other hand, the results could have been reversed if the supervisor's biases had operated in the opposite direction. The supervisor may be trying to be fair, but as long as he knows which men were trained and which were not, his judgments will be contaminated. Even if they were not, there is no method for determining they were not and so these judgments are, for evaluation purposes, worthless.

A second example of bias which affects relevance and perhaps reliability was found when an effort was made to evaluate the effect of a training program designed to teach novices to weave. Weavers are generally paid on the basis of the rate of the production of the looms which they operate. This amount of cloth expressed in terms of "picks" serves as a basis of pay. It seemed that this should serve as one measure for evaluating weaver training. Statistically the measures had high reliability. Supervisors in part judged weavers' performance by amount produced. This seemed like an ideal measure until it was found that the production of a weaver was affected not only by his efforts, but also by the services he received from loom fixers and battery hands. His production was affected also by the condition in which his loom set was left by the weaver, fixer, and battery hand on the preceding shift. A weaver with an efficient crew of auxiliary helpers following an efficient weaver and crew could outproduce with less effort other less fortunate weavers.

Hemphill and Sechrest (1952) report an interesting instance of contamination of measures used in the study of the performance of B-29 air crews. One measure, bombing data, had no reliability. Another measure, superiors' ratings of air crew performance, had relatively high reliability. These authors found a statistically significant relationship between the unreliable bombing data and the reliable superiors' ratings. This paradox was explained by the fact that the superiors who did the ratings had access to the bombing data and were influenced appreciably in these ratings by these data. If only the superiors' ratings had been used as measures of air crew performance, they would have been accepted as a reliable measure even though the reliability was the result of contamination from an unreliable measure.

Other examples of bias in measures could be given. Bias arises either from the fact that measures are not collected independently or from operating conditions related to and affecting the measures. Although the difficulties of freeing measures from the latter source of contamination are fairly evident, the problem of obtaining measures which are independent and unaffected by knowledge of training conditions are too frequently overlooked. In addition, the research requirements for keeping some data confidential in order to avoid dependence in measurement are frequently misunderstood by management or operational personnel. Careful evaluation of training requires analysis of measures to guard against bias affecting relevance and reliability.

Practicality. Since training is a tool, a means to an end, its evaluation must be done with consideration to economy and convenience of operating personnel. Occasionally, excellent measures can be developed by modification of an existing operation. In the example of biased weaver production figures, we could have controlled the effects of extraneous factors by systematic rotation of weavers from crew to crew and from shift to shift. This was not done, however, because it would have caused administrative difficulties as well as resentment from the personnel involved. It was not *practical* to secure measures of training effectiveness using weaver rotation.

Since training should be the responsibility of line management, it is important to remember that the acceptance of this responsibility will not be enhanced by evaluation procedures which create problems in the production of goods or services—the primary objective of their departments. Any wide departure from routine practices for evaluation purposes requires careful presentation to operating management. After all, training is only one of the numerous responsibilities of a foreman or plant superintendent. The training specialist should strive to put in the hands of operating management measures of effectiveness which, in addition to being relevant, reliable, and free from bias, can be used routinely by supervisors in determining the effectiveness of routine, on-the-job, training procedures. Training is a day-to-day affair in a well-managed department and should not take on the character of a special and temporary project. Measures, therefore, must be practical.

Single and multiple measures. Although we have used the words *measure and measures* almost interchangeably in the preceding section, it is entirely possible that we have given the impression that we are seeking a single measure or index of the outcome of training. Although it may be true in certain instances that one act or behavior sequence is the primary outcome we are seeking through training, this is true for only a small number of jobs. Industrial training is used to modify or develop skills, knowledge, and attitudes. In many jobs, equal attention has to be given to development in each of these areas. A millwright not only must know what he should do but he must also be able to do what is required. He must have certain attitudes toward quality of workmanship and responsibility to his employer, to his supervisor, and co-workers if he is to perform his job in a satisfactory manner. It is possible that some single measure can be used to characterize the performance which is an end result of his having acquired certain kinds of knowledge, skill, and attitudes. The performance of a sewing machine operator or a typist might be characterized by the number of units produced in a given time. The relative success of an inspector could be measured in terms of percentage of correct classifications.

Frequently, however, several measures, some of which are different from others, may be necessary to describe adequately the degree of success in performing a job. In this connection, Rush (1953) has pointed out that research in developing adequate selection techniques frequently is based on the assumption that success is unitary. There is only one kind of success in sales. Good salesmen do similar things in order to succeed. In an extensive statistical study for the Burroughs Adding Machine Company, he examined the interrelationships of thirteen success measures and found that these could be combined into, not one, but four relatively independent success factors. In addition, the variables which could be used best to predict these factors were different from each other. The factor, "Objective (Sales) Achievement," was predicted best by the number of accounting courses taken and by previous selling experience. The factor, "Learning Aptitude" (dealing with technical knowledge and training grades), was predicted best by a business arithmetic test and grades received in college.

Although Rush's findings are probably not universal to all sales situations, the point he makes is quite clear. It is probably a mistake to assume that there is only one avenue to success. Training courses, even in a specific area such as supervision, are broad in scope. The need for trying out a number of measures and studying their interrelationships to see what they have in common is an important avenue to advancing the frontiers of training evaluation.

Research similar to Rush's is not available on jobs such as those of foreman; however, investigations such as that done by Walker, Guest, and Turner (1956) indicate that the supervisor's job is by no means a unitary task. The authors list the following activities in which the foreman engages and the approximate amount of time spent in each activity (p. 84).

Topic	Total Minutes spent	Percentage of Total Time
Foreman's performance of an operation	94	19.5
Quality	88	18.2
Personnel administration (assignment, procurement, etc.)	79	16.5
Materials	66	13.8
Equipment, tools, jobs, and fixtures	47	9.8
Work progress	34	7.0
Employee job performance	24	4.9
Personal relations with other non-job related topics	20	4.1
Production schedule	2	.4
Safety	1	.2
Housekeeping	1	.2
Work standards	0	0
Grievances	0	0
Injury or illness	0	0
Meeting	0	0
Miscellaneous	2	.3
Topic unknown	25	5.1
Total	485	100.0

One measure alone could not be expected to characterize the degree of success achieved by an individual performing so many diverse functions. We are of the opinion that in a broad training program such as foremanship training we are confronted not with the problem of securing one relevant, reliable, bias-free, practical measure, but rather of securing several measures with these characteristics.

We must not overlook the fact that multiple measures will frequently increase our understanding of what has happened during training and specific factors which did or did not contribute toward its overall effectiveness. A research program designed to evaluate the effectiveness of a training film could rely on a single criterion—sales. If we realize that the trainee must first learn the information presented, next learn how to present it orally, and later learn how to adapt what he has learned to a given sales situation, we might want to use a partial criterion such as a test of knowledge to see, first, if the information presented was acquired. If it was not, we begin to get insight concerning the lack of impact of the film on the ultimate criterion of sales. Even if we measure at every point in training, however, from the learning of the information to the demonstration of the ability of the trainee to use this information and adapt it to a variety of simulated sales situations, we will gain more understanding if we measure what happens outside the classroom. Activity measures, such as the number of customers seen, might serve as a valuable intermediate criterion to facilitate understanding of the film's effectiveness. There are limits, of course, to the number of measures which can be used without bringing about the collapse of the research program. But judicious choice of partial and intermediate criteria can be most useful.

In instances where the various components of the course are to be evaluated, these components can be compared with their appropriate measures. Many times, however, some single, overall measure of success of the training course is required. We then are confronted with the proper combination of these measures to give the most accurate description of the degree of success achieved in performing the job. Suppose the following measures are available on the job performances of a group of foremen: labor costs under his control, seconds produced in his department, waste, success in training new employees, number of complaints and grievances, number of suggestions for process improvement from his department, amount of preventable turnover and absenteeism, degree to which he maintained production schedules, and development which has taken place among his assistant foremen. The problem now becomes one of combining these eleven criteria in an optimum way so that they in com-

bination are related as nearly as possible to the ultimate measure of successful foremanship.

Ghiselli and Brown (1955, pp. 82–85) have listed six of the methods available for combining several criteria:

1. equal weighting
2. weighting according to the judgments of experts
3. weighting according to the reliability of the criterion measures
4. weighting according to an assumed underlying variable of job success
5. multiple cutoffs
6. the "Dollar Criterion."

The assignment of equal weights contributes little to the solution of the problem. In the list of possible foreman performance measures, consider equal weight to all variables. If some of these are highly interrelated, for example, giving equal weight to each will overload the composite measure with several measures of a single success factor. Serious objections might also be raised to giving equal weight to "meeting production schedules" and "number of suggestions for process improvement."

Weighting according to the judgments of experts is fairly simple, but the experts may be unable to agree on the importance of the success measures. Ghiselli and Brown (1955) present evidence showing only moderate agreement between experienced job analysts.

Weighting according to reliability can lead to very awkward results. It does seem logical to give maximal weight to the most reliable measure. However, the highly reliable measure may cover only a single (and possibly insignificant) facet of success.

The assumption of an underlying variable of job success frequently is not met. Rush's (1953) data show some success measures to intercorrelate quite low. When several important measures fail to correlate with each other, it is difficult to make such an assumption and weight according to the correlation of each variable with this "underlying factor."

Where each success measure is considered critical to success on the job, the multiple cutoff method may be used. Here, a worker is an overall success only if he is successful in every phase of his job. We suspect that only a minority of jobs would logically fit such a scheme. In most, a deficiency in one area can be offset by superiority in another. A high-producing life insurance salesman may be forgiven for a lapse rate that is above average, or a foreman who has his labor costs under control may cause only moderate concern if his absentee rate is higher than normal. If such forgiveness is not possible, however, and the training being evaluated is broad in scope, such a technique might serve to identify trainees who are "complete successes."

Finally, the "dollar criterion," which takes a cost accounting approach to this problem, seems very logical. Here the man's success is evaluated by the costs and productive returns attributable to him in dollars and cents. Even this approach has its difficulties. The procedures are costly, and allocation of expenditures to many jobs is extremely difficult. In some cases, the assignment of losses or gains to staff personnel would be practically impossible and would require guesswork.

Each of the techniques discussed, therefore, has its weaknesses. An awareness of the variety of techniques available for combining measures is extremely valuable to the training specialist. Often he may desire the assistance of another specialist—a measurement specialist—to assist him in evaluating the components and helping him in the combination of these into a single, composite measure.

The proper and useful evaluation of training depends upon securing measures which meet certain requirements. It has been our experience that these measures are not found ready made in most industrial situations. Generally, measures available have been collected for purposes other than training evaluation. Although they may serve these purposes adequately, they permit no causal inferences between training and the results of training. Some of the problems in obtaining relevant and reliable measures have been sketched in this section. A few suggestions for solving these problems have been made. It is our hope, however, that both the training specialist and managers will learn to demand that the relevance and reliability of measures be established before they are used to evaluate training. It is perhaps too Utopian to expect, however, that relevant and reliable measures either be in existence or available before training is actually undertaken.

SECURING MEASURES

If we are to establish causal relationships between training and the results of training, we need relevant and reliable measures. Measures, however, can be both relevant and reliable and useless for evaluating training if they are secured under certain conditions. The basic procedures for securing measures which allow causal inferences are the well-established procedures for the investigation of the relationship between phenomena in both physical and social sciences. Stated without elaboration, they consist in showing that condition X is the direct result of condition y and not of conditions a, b, c to n. In training, this means that what occurs as a result of training is attributable to training and not to the chance or systematic changes in the circumstances under which the training takes place. The problems in collecting measures under these conditions have been described by various writers (Jahoda, et al., 1951; Festinger and Katz, 1953; Underwood, 1957). We shall try to make these approaches clear by specific examples from the literature which reports efforts to evaluate training.

The procedures used for securing measures of the outcomes of training are numerous. They can be classified into certain broad categories by when the measures are secured and by whether or not a control group or groups are used. By control groups, we mean employees who did not receive the training or received training different from that received by the group for whom we are trying to determine the results of training. These procedures, using this system of classification, fall into the following types:

1. measures after training without a control group
2. measures before and after training without a control group
3. measures after training with a control group
4. measures before and after training with a control group.

After training, no control group. This method of collecting measures is the most frequently reported procedure for evaluating training It is also the most naive, the least defensible, and the most difficult from which to draw any causal inferences. An example will illustrate the inadequacy of this approach in evaluating training. Claims are made that a picture-book manual reduced training costs by 50% in teaching employees to operate a control board in an oil refinery (Mustillo, 1957). The author modestly admits this is an estimate. He is frank enough, also, to admit that prior to the use of this manual two other manuals had been used and presumably some training in addition to the use of manuals took place. There is also the possibility of supervisory pressure on the operators to learn the controls. Yet the entire credit for improved job performance is given by the author to the picture-book manual. It is entirely possible that the author is correct in his claims for the picture-book manual. However, he has left uncontrolled the factors of prior training, exposure to other manuals, and possible pressure from other sources on the operators. Furthermore, he presents no evidence as to the use of the picture-book manual. To substantiate his claims he would have to produce evidence that the picture-book manual was the only factor which results in the outcomes which he reports.

Before and after training without a control group. Much of the results claimed by Training Within Industry (1945) programs during World War II fall into this category. For example, one claim for training programs under the auspices of the TWI was that production increased from 10 to 50%. No evidence was given that other factors such as improved equipment, better scheduling, better materials, improved supervision, or patriotic fervor were not factors in the claimed increase in production. This method of evaluating training consists simply in getting a prior measure, conducting training, securing post measures, and assuming nothing but the training resulted in the improvement on the post measures. Anyone who knows anything about a business or industrial situation immediately recognizes the fallacy in this assumption. TWI may have resulted in the industrial improvements claimed but there is no evidence of causal relationship between training and claimed training outcomes.

McGehee and Livingstone (1952) also are guilty of using the before and after method without control groups in a reported study of waste reduction in a textile mill. Although their approach is inadequate in establishing causal relationships, they do recognize that variables other than the training used could have caused the changes observed. They investigated the factors which produced waste and found that these factors were reasonably constant in the periods before, during, and after training. Their causal inferences concerning the relationship of training are slightly more defensible than is true of evaluations using this technique which fail to hold constant or to allow statistically for conditions which might bring about the outcomes attributed to training.

The before and after method without a control group in collecting measures for training evaluation is rarely defensible. This is particularly true when the outcomes of training can be measured only after a considerable time lapse. It can produce no accurate data as to the relative effectiveness of different training approaches to the same problem. It can give no answer as to whether or not training in a given situation is absolutely necessary. Only when the other variables which might affect the outcomes of training are held constant can causal relationships be inferred legitimately from measures secured by this procedure. It is extremely rare that this situation exists in industry or business.

After training with control groups. This method of securing measures for the evaluation of training is well illustrated in a reported study of gunnery training in the air force (Ewart, 1950). It is particularly appropriate to industry and business since it compared methods of instructions used frequently in industry: oral instruction with visual aids, illustrated manuals, and motion pictures. Three groups of air force personnel were trained by each of these different techniques; a fourth group received no training. Knowledge of the subject matter of gunnery was tested by an examination immediately after training and two months after training. Scores on these tests showed a definite superiority for the motion picture instructional technique. Can we then conclude that the film was the causative factor in the differences in the performance of this group as compared with the other groups? The answer, of course, is no. No evidence is available to indicate that the four groups used in the study were comparable in ability to learn gunnery or that they were comparable in knowledge of, and experience in, this subject prior to the investigation. As a matter of fact, subsequent analysis of the amount of learning of superior and inferior trainees (superior and inferior in terms of the post-tests) indicated a differential effect in favor of the film for the inferior learners. The weakness of the after only method with controls is the necessity of making certain in any evaluation of training using two or more groups that these groups are comparable on all factors which would have any influence on the outcomes of training. Since it is extremely difficult to match groups adequately on these factors in industrial training, causal inferences drawn from evaluations using the after only method with control groups are of questionable validity.

It is possible, however, to draw legitimate causal inferences from training evaluations using after only measures with control groups. An investigation reported by Adams (1957) gives an excellent example of this type of training research. In his investigation of the relative effectiveness of manual and electric typewriters in teaching typing, he followed a procedure which minimized the effect of prior experience and aptitudes for learning typing. His two groups were selected initially by means of a typing pretest. He then placed the eighty students in two categories of previous and no previous typing experience and divided these groups randomly into two groups. One group was taught using manual typewriters and the other using electric. He then checked on the effectiveness of his randomization by comparison of the two groups by age, years of education, general ability and aptitude for code learning. The comparisons of the groups along with other procedures used "to control unnecessary between-groups variation in instructional procedures, content, and other factors affecting learning so that differences in proficiency between the groups would be due to differences in training devices and/or necessarily confounded procedures" (p. 228) allowed him to draw legitimate inferences concerning training and the outcome of training.

Careful attention must be paid to the composition of the groups used as experimental and as control groups. Normally, these groups should be made up of employees who are selected and assigned to one group or the other in a random fashion. This random assignment gives a good chance of equalizing any factors associated with the employee which might give him a better chance of doing well in training than others. If previous research data are available, certain factors may be identified which contribute to success either in training or subsequently on the job. Such factors might be length of experience, education, intelligence, special aptitudes, previous training, and many others. When such factors are known, greater precision in evaluation can be obtained by matching employees with similar characteristics and randomly assigning one member of each pair to the control group and the other to the experimental group. The problem of securing comparable groups for comparison of training procedures is a complex one. Even where extreme care is exercised, overlooking a critical factor can bias any conclusions from such a study. The precautions and procedures necessary for matching groups has been described in a thorough manner by Underwood (1957). We strongly recommend that anyone attempting to evaluate training by matched group technique become familiar with this reference. This is particularly essential if measures after training are the only measures which will be used.

Before and after training with control groups. This procedure for securing measures in training evaluation avoids the majority of the pitfalls inherent in the other procedures described. An illustration of this method is found in an evaluation of a human relations program reported by Canter (1951). Canter[2] divided two groups of supervisors so that they were relatively comparable in the factors of age, years of education, and experience. One group he sent through a 20-hour course in human relations. The other group did not receive this training. He tested both groups with a battery of six tests and questionnaires both prior and subsequent to the training given the one group. Changes favoring the trained group were found on certain of the tests but not on others. Canter concluded that these changes were a function of the training received. Except for a few weaknesses in his research, it seems to us that Canter is justified in making causal inferences about the results of training. Unfortunately, the group of supervisors who received the human relations training were all from one department whereas those who were not trained came from another department. Such a procedure creates sizable statistical problems. What the effect

[2] Although Canter's experimental design is excellent, the relevance of his measures is questionable.

on having different superiors and working in a different psychological as well as physical environment on the before and after behavior of both the trained and untrained group cannot be determined.

Certain administrative objections also may arise in industry to the use of control and experimental groups. This is particularly true if the control group is simply pre- and post-tested and given no training at all. An attitude may develop among employees that the "trained" group is receiving special attention and are "fair-haired" boys. McGehee and Gardner (1955) report the use of an experimental design which reduces this objection to control and experimental groups for the evaluation of training. Prior to training, measures were secured on all employees who were eligible for the training program. A group was selected for training, and the rest of the employees were informed that they would receive the same training at a later date. At the end of training for the first group the same measures were again secured on both the trained group and the untrained (the control) group. The untrained group was then trained and measured subsequent to the training:

	Measures before Training	Measures after Training		Measures after Training	
Group	Either Group	Action	Group I	Action	Group II
I. Experimental	53.4	Training	75.9		
II. Control	55.7	No training	60.7	Training	69.3

This procedure has the added advantage in that the results from training Group II substantiates the results obtained in training Group I. It is true there is no control group for Group II. But the fact that securing measures before training of Group II shows no effect and now after training a statistically significant difference is shown reinforces the belief that training was effective as shown by the original comparison of the control and experimental groups.

Attention from management or evidence of interest from management in some phase of employee activity may induce changes in employee behavior aside from the effect of any program instituted to induce change. This effect was dramatically demonstrated in the Hawthorne studies (Roethlisberger and Dickson, 1939). The experimental group, although not grasping the formal training, may feel the "Hawthorne effect," and the final measure may be influenced by that effect.

How can this effect be avoided? Suppose, for example, a program for training supervisors in time study is developed and experimental and control groups are used to evaluate the training. Prior and post measures are secured on both groups but only the experimental group is trained. Both groups show the same sort of change in behavior in handling time study problems. Can we conclude that the training has no effect on supervisory behavior? By no means. The mere fact that management has shown an interest in time study may have stimulated the control group to improved efforts in handling time study problems.

Solomon (1949) has suggested a method of using both three and four groups to control this effect. In the three-group method there are one experimental group and two control groups; in the four-group method there are one experimental and three control groups. In the three-group method, the experimental group is measured, trained, and remeasured; the first control group is measured, not trained, and remeasured; the second control group is not measured initially, is not trained, but is measured at the time the experimental group and the first control group are remeasured. In this way, the "Hawthorne effect" can be estimated in evaluating the results of a training activity. It will be reflected, in this case, in the final differences between control Group I and control Group II. The four-group method is carried out much the same way as the three-group method with control Group II and III not being initially measured but measured at the time the experimental group and control Group I are remeasured. Control II is then trained and control Group III is not trained. Both of these groups are then remeasured. This is in effect a replica of the before and after procedure with control groups and gives a firmer basis for any conclusions drawn as to the effect of training. It might be argued that this procedure is impractical in an industrial organization. It should be remembered, however, that all employees usually cannot be trained simultaneously in a given knowledge, skill, or attitude area. With a little ingenuity the Solomon procedures can be followed in most industrial training where it is suspected the "Hawthorne effect" might obscure the results of training.

MEASURES AND STATISTICS

Up to this point we have omitted any reference to the techniques of comparing measures secured in evaluating training. If this were done, we would have to summarize in a brief space the contents of technical books in the area of statistics. We are not certain we are competent to do this nor that it would add appreciably to this section of the book. The reader should be aware that handling quantitative data requires specialized knowledge and skills. Frequently, this knowledge and skill is not part of the repertoire of those who manage training in industry. It is our suggestion that, in the evaluation of training, the evaluator, if he is not statistically sophisticated, obtain the advice and assistance of individuals competent in this specialty. Such consultation should take place in the early planning phase of the evaluation so that the final research design will provide for measures which are suitable to statistical treatment. Frequently, the statistician is called in only after the study is completed. If the data are not gathered properly the only assistance he may be able to offer would be to explain how the study should have been done.

SUMMARY

This chapter has outlined the problems and approaches to evaluating training. It has suggested why so little real effort has been made to evaluate training procedures. It has further outlined why training must be evaluated if it is to be used successfully as a tool by management in achieving organizational goals. It is our sincere belief that principles and problems of training evaluation should be understood in broad details by line management. And we believe and sincerely hope that the training specialist of the future will spend less time in flannel board perambulations and more time in training evaluation. We are confident he will if management accepts training as a management tool and asks loudly what training has contributed to the achievement of organizational goals.

BIBLIOGRAPHY

Adams, H. L. The comparative effectiveness of electric and manual typewriters in the acquisition of typing skills in a navy radioman school. *Journal of Applied Psychology*, 1957, **41**, 227–230.

Adkins, D. *Construction and analysis of achievement tests.* Washington: U. S. Government Printing Office, 1949.

Allport, G. W. Attitudes. In Murchison, C. (Ed.), *A handbook of social psychology.* Worcester, Mass.: Clark University Press, 1935.

American Institute for Research. *Collection and evaluation of information on personnel and training research activities for government, business, and industrial organizations.* (Mimeograph) Pittsburgh: American Institute for Research, 1952.

Ammons, R. B. *Knowledge of performance, survey of literature, some possible applications and suggested experimentation.* WADC Technical Report 54-14, Wright Air Development Center, 1954.

Andlinger, G. R. Business games–play one! *Harvard Business Review*, 1958, **36**, 115–125.

Aprecella, J. C., and Thompson, G. C. The changing labor force. *The Conference Board Business Record*, 1957, **14**, 505–509.

Argyris, C. Techniques of "member-centered" training. *Personnel*, 1951, **28**, 236–246.

Argyris, C. The individual and organizational structure. *AMA Personnel Series No. 168.* New York: American Management Association, 1956.

Argyris, C. *Personality and organization.* New York: Harper & Bros., 1957.

Argyris, C. The organization: what makes it healthy? *Harvard Business Review*, 1958, **36**, 107–116.

Asch, S. E. *Social psychology.* New York: Prentice-Hall, 1952.

Baker, R. A., Scott, S., MacCaslin, E. F. *Development of proficiency tests for basic combat and light infantry training, HUMRRO Technical Report 19–55.* Washington: The George Washington University Human Resources Research Office, 1955.

Barnes, R. M. *Work sampling.* New York: John Wiley & Sons, 1957.

Baxter, B., Taaffe, A. A., and Hughes, J. F. Training evaluation study. *Personnel Psychology,* 1953, **6,** 403–416.

Beecher, D. E. *The evaluation of teaching.* Syracuse, N. Y.: Syracuse University Press, 1949.

Blankenship, A. B. Methods of measuring industrial morale. In Hartman, G. W., and Newcomb, T. (Eds.), *Industrial conflict: a psychological interpretation.* New York: The Cordon Co., 1939.

Blansfield, M. G. Executive development: a group training approach. *Personnel,* 1956, **32,** 441–448.

Bradford, L. P. (Ed.), *Theory of t-group training.* Washington, D. C.: National Training Laboratory in Group Development. (*In preparation.*)

Bradford, L. P., Lippett, G. L., and Gibb, J. R. Workshop: human relations training in three days. *Adult Leadership,* 1956, **4,** 11–26.

Brayfield, A. H., and Crockett, W. H. Employee attitudes and employee performance. *Psychological Bulletin,* 1955, **52,** 396–424.

Bright, J. R. Does automation raise skill requirements? *Harvard Business Review,* 1958, **36,** 85–98.

Brogden, H. E., and Taylor, E. K. The dollar criterion—applying the cost accounting concept to criterion construction. *Personnel Psychology,* 1950, **3,** 133–154.

Busch, H. M. *Conference methods in industry.* New York: Harper & Bros., 1949.

Campbell, D. T. The indirect assessment of social attitudes. *Psychological Bulletin,* 1950, **47,** 15–38.

Canter, R. R., Jr. A human relations training program. *Journal of Applied Psychology,* 1951, **35,** 38–47.

Carpenter, C. R., and Greenhill, L. P. *An investigation of closed-circuit television for teaching university courses. Report No. 1. Instructional Film Research Program.* University Park, Pa.: Pennsylvania State University, 1955.

Carpenter, C. R., and Greenhill, L. P. *An investigation of closed-circuit television for teaching university courses. Report No. 2. Instructional Film Research Program.* University Park, Pa.: Pennsylvania State University, 1955.

Charters, W. W., and Whitley, J. B. *Analysis of secretarial duties.* New York: Williams and Wilkins, 1924.

Coakley, J. D. Human operators and automatic machines. *Personnel Psychology,* 1950, **3,** 401–412.

Coch, L., and French, J. R. P., Jr. Overcoming resistance to change. *Human Relations,* 1948, **1,** 512–532.

Cook, D. W. Psychology challenges industry. *Personnel Series No. 107.* New York: American Management Association, 1947.

Cordiner, R. J. *New frontiers for professional managers.* New York: McGraw-Hill Book Company, 1956.

Corrigan, R. E. Automated teaching methods. *Automated Teaching Bulletin,* 1959, **1,** 23–30.

Coulson, J. E., and Silberman, H. F. Effect of three variables in a teaching machine. *Journal of Educational Psychology,* 1960, **51,** 135–143.

Cronbach, L. J. *Essentials of psychological testing.* New York: Harper & Bros., 1949.

Crowder, N. A. Automatic tutoring by means of intrinsic programing. In E. Galanter (Ed.), *Automated teaching: the state of the art.* New York: John Wiley & Sons, 1959.

Dale, E. *Planning and developing the company organization structure.* New York: American Management Association, 1952.

Davis, E. L., and Cantor, R. R., Jr. Job design. *Journal of industrial engineering,* 1955, **6,** 6–24.

Dinsmoor, J. A. Punishment: I. The avoidance hypothesis. *Psychological Review,* 1954, **61,** 34–46.

Dinsmoor, J. A. Punishment: II. An interpretation of empirical findings. *Psychological Review,* 1955, **62,** 96–105.

Divesta, F. J., Roach, J. H. L., and Beasley, W. Rating conference participation in human relations training. *Journal of Applied Psychology,* 1951, **35,** 386–391.

Domas, S. J., and Tiedeman, D. V. Teacher competence: an annotated bibliography. *Journal of Experimental Education,* 1950, **19,** 101–128.

Drucker, P. F. *The practice of management.* New York: Harper & Bros., 1954.

DuBois, P. H. (Ed.) The classification program. *AAF aviation psychology progress research report No. 7.* Washington: Government Printing Office, 1947.

Duncan, C. P. Recent research on human problem solving. *Psychological Bulletin,* 1959, **46,** 397–429.

Eisner, S., and Rohde, K. Note taking during or after the lecture. *Journal of Educational Psychology,* 1960, **50,** 301–304.

Ericksen, S. C. *The special instructional problems of teaching aviation in the class room.* Nashville, Tenn.: Vanderbilt University, 1958.

Estes, W. K. et al. *Modern learning theory.* New York: Appleton-Century-Crofts, 1954.

Ewart, E. D. *Evaluation of instructional techniques described as effective by flight instructors.* Civilian Aeronautics Administration Division, Research Report No. 63, 1950.

Festinger, L. *A theory of cognitive dissonance.* Evanston, Ill.: Row, Peterson & Co., 1957.

Festinger, L., and Katz, D. (Eds.) *Research methods in the behavioral sciences.* New York: The Dryden Press, 1953.

File, Q. W., and Remmers, H. H. *How supervise?* New York: The Psychological Corporation, 1943.

Flanagan, J. C. Critical requirements: a new approach to employee evaluation. *Personnel Psychology,* 1949, **2,** 419–425.

Flanagan, J. C. The critical incident technique. *Psychological Bulletin,* 1954, **51,** 327–358.

Flanagan, J. C., and Burns, R. K. The employee performance record: a new appraisal and development tool. *Harvard Business Review,* 1955, **33,** 95–102.

Fleishman, E. A. *Leadership climate and supervisory behavior: a study of the leadership role of the foreman in an industrial situation.* Columbus, Ohio: Personnel Research Board, The Ohio State University, 1951.

Fleishman, E. A., Harris, E. F., and Burtt, H. E. *Leadership in industry—an evaluation of a supervisory training program.* Columbus, Ohio: The Ohio State University Bureau of Educational Research Monograph, No. 33, 1955.

Fleishman, E. A., and Hempel, W. E. Factorial analysis of complex psychomotor performance and related skills. *Journal of Applied Psychology,* 1956, **40,** 90–104.

Foundation for Research on Human Behavior. *Assessing managerial potential (report of a seminar).* Ann Arbor, Mich.: Foundation for Research on Human Behavior, 1958.

Gagné, R. M. *Methods of forecasting job requirements.* (Paper presented at a symposium on electronics maintenance, Washington, August, 1955.)

Gagné, R. M., Baker, K., and Foster, H. On the relation between similarity and transfer of training in the learning of discriminative motor tasks. *Psychological Review,* 1950, **57,** 67–79.

Gagné, R. M., and Bolles, R. C. *A review of factors in learning efficiency.* ASTIA Document No. AD 162275, November, 1958.

Gebhard, M. E. The effect of success and failure upon the attractiveness of activities as a function of experience, expectation and need. *Journal of Experimental Psychology,* 1948, **38,** 371–378.

Gebhard, M. E. Changes in the attractiveness of activities: the effect of expectation preceding performance. *Journal of Experimental Psychology,* 1949, **39,** 404–413.

General Electric Company. *The effective manufacturing foreman.* New York: General Electric Company, 1957.

Ghiselli, E. E., and Brown, C. W. *Personnel and industrial psychology.* (2nd ed.) New York: McGraw-Hill Book Company, 1955.

Glaser, R., and Glanzer, M. *Training and training research.* Pittsburgh: American Institute for Research, 1958.

Goodacre, D. M. The experimental evaluation of management training, principles and practices. *Personnel,* 1957, **33,** 534–538.

Greene, J. R., and Sisson, R. L. *Dynamic management decision games.* New York: John Wiley & Sons, Inc., 1959.

Greenly, R. J. Job training. *NAM labor relations bulletin No. 35.* New York: National Association of Manufacturers, 1941.

Haire, M. *Psychology in management.* New York: McGraw-Hill Book Company, 1956.

Handbook of Human Engineering Data. Medford, Mass.: Tufts College Institute of Applied Experimental Psychology, 1952.

Harlow, H. F. Motivation as a factor in new responses. In *Current theory and research in motivation: a symposium.* Lincoln: University of Nebraska Press, 1953.

Haselrud, G. M., and Meyers, S. The transfer value of given and individually derived principles. *Journal of Educational Psychology,* 1958, **49,** 293–298.

Hemphill, J. K., and Sechrest, L. B. A comparison of three criteria of aircrew effectiveness in combat over Korea. *Journal of Applied Psychology,* 1952, **36,** 323–327.

Herzberg, F., Mausner, B., Peterson, R., and Capwell, D. *Job attitudes: review of research and opinion.* Pittsburgh: Psychological Services of Pittsburgh, 1957.

Herzberg, F., Mausner, B., and Synderman, B. B. *The motivation to work,* New York: John Wiley & Sons, 1959.

Highland, R. W., and Berkshire, J. R. *A methodological study of forced-choice performance rating. Research bulletin 51-9.* Lackland Air Force Base, Texas: Air Training Command Human Resources Center, 1951.

Hilgard, E. R. *Theories of learning* (2nd ed.) New York: Appleton-Century-Crofts, Inc., 1956.

Horst, P. *The prediction of personal adjustment.* New York: Social Science Research Council, 1941.

Hovland, C. I., Campbell, E. H., and Brock, T. The effect of "commitment" on opinion change following communication. In Hovland, C. I. (Ed.) *The order of presentation in persuasion.* New Haven: Yale University Press, 1957.

Hovland, C. I., Janis, I. L., and Kelley, N. N. *Communication and Persuasion.* New Haven: Yale University Press, 1953.

Instructional Film Research Reports Vols. I and II. (NAVEXOS P-1220 and P-1543) Port Washington, L. I., N. Y.: U. S. Naval Training Device Center, 1956.

Irwin, F. W. Some situational effects upon performances. In Churchman, C. W., Ackoff, R. L., and Wax, M. (Eds.), *Measurement of Consumer Interest.* Philadelphia: University of Pennsylvania Press, 1947.

Jahoda, M., Deutsch, M., and Cook, S. W. *Research methods in social relations.* Part I. New York: The Dryden Press, 1951.

Jenkins, J. G. Nominating techniques as a method of evaluating air groups. *Journal of Aviation Medicine,* 1948, **19,** 12–19.

Judd, C. H. The relation of special training to general intelligence. *Educational Review,* 1908, **36,** 28–42.

Kaess, W., and Zeamen, D. Positive and negative knowledge of results on a Pressey-type punchboard. *Journal of Experimental Psychology,* 1960, **60,** 12–17.

Kahn, R. L., and Cannell, C. F. *The dynamics of interviewing.* New York: John Wiley & Sons, 1957.

Kahn, R. L., and Katz, D. Leadership practice in relationship to productivity and morale. In Cartwright, D., and Zander, A. (Eds.), *Group dynamics.* Evanston, Ill., Row, Peterson, and Co., 1953.

Katzell, R. A. Testing a training program in human relations. *Personnel Psychology,* 1948, **1,** 319–330.

Katzell, R. A. Industrial psychology. In Farnsworth, P. R. and McNemar, Q. (Eds.), *Annual Reviews of Psychology.* Palo Alto, Calif., Annual Reviews, Inc., 1957, **8,** 237–268.

Kendler, H. H. Learning. In Farnsworth, P. R., and McNemar, Q. (Eds.), *Annual Reviews of Psychology.* Palo Alto, California: Annual Reviews, Inc., 1959.

Kennedy, John L. Gaming theory and its relations to industrial psychology. (A paper presented at 1959 meeting of the American Psychological Association in Cincinnati, Ohio.)

Kershner, A. M. *A report on job analysis.* Washington: ONR Report ACR5. Office of Naval Research, Dept. of the Navy, 1955.

Klaus, D. J., and Lumsdaine, A. A. *Self-instructional supplements for a televised physics course.* Pittsburgh: American Institute for Research, 1959.

Klaus, D. J., and Lumsdaine, A. A. *An experimental field test of the value of self-instructional materials in high school physics.* Pittsburgh: American Institute for Research, 1960.

Klaus, D. J., and Lumsdaine, A. A. Some economic realities of teaching machine instruction. (Paper presented at the meetings of the American Psychological Association, Chicago, Illinois, September 3, 1960.)

Kretch, D., and Crutchfield, R. S. *Theory and problems of social psychology.* New York: McGraw-Hill Book Company, 1948.

Lawshe, C. H. The training of operative personnel. *Journal of Consulting Psychology,* 1944, **8,** 154–159.

Lawshe, C. H., and Bolda, R. A. *Role playing as an industrial leadership training technique.* (Mimeo.) Lafayette, Ind.: Occupational Research Center, Purdue University, 1958.

Lee, I. J., and Lee, L. *Handling barriers to communications.* New York: Harper & Bros., 1956.

Lindahl, L. G. Movement analysis as an industrial training method. *Journal of Applied Psychology,* 1945, **29,** 420–436.

Lindborn, T. R., and Osterberg, W. Evaluating the results of supervisory training. *Personnel,* 1954, **31,** 224–227.

Life Insurance Agency Management Association. *The "fulltime" agent.* Hartford, Conn., 1953.

Life Insurance Agency Management Association. *An experimental evalua-*

tion of the sales method index—continuous record. Hartford, Conn., 1955.

Life Insurance Agency Management Association. *Ordinary agent sales method index: trainer's manual.* Hartford, Conn., 1957.

Life Insurance Agency Management Association. *The public looks at life insurance.* Hartford, Conn., 1958.

Life Insurance Agency Management Association. *Life insurance goals: a psychological model.* Hartford, Conn., 1959.

Machie, R. R., Wilson, C. L., and Buckner, D. N. *Practical performance tests for electrician mates and radiomen.* Los Angeles: Management and Marketing Research Corporation, 1953.

MacKinney, A. C. Progressive levels in evaluating training programs? *Personnel,* 1957, **33,** 72–77.

Maher, H. Studies of transparency in forced-choice scales, I. Evidence of transparency. *Journal of Applied Psychology,* 1959, **43,** 275–278.

Mahler, W. R. *Twenty years of merit rating.* New York: The Psychological Corporation, 1947.

Mahler, W. R., and Monroe, W. H. *How industry determines the need for and effectiveness of training.* New York: The Psychological Corporation, 1952.

Maier, N. R. F. *Principles of human relations.* New York: John Wiley & Sons, Inc., 1952.

Maier, N. R. F. *Psychology in industry.* (2nd ed.) New York: Houghton Mifflin Co., 1955.

Maier, N. R. F. *The appraisal interview.* New York: John Wiley & Sons, 1958.

Mann, F. C. and Dent, J. W. The supervisor—member of two organizational families. *Harvard Business Review,* 1954, **32,** 103–112.

Mann, F. C., and Hoffman, L. R. *Automation and the worker.* New York: Henry Holt & Co., 1960.

Marks, R. An evaluation of alternate job designs in relationship to employee morale and organizational goals. (A paper presented at the 1958 meeting of the American Psychological Association in New York City.)

Mathewson, S. B. *Restriction of output among unorganized workers.* New York: The Viking Press, 1931.

May, M. and Lumsdaine, A. A. *Learning from films.* New Haven: Yale University Press, 1958.

McGehee, W. Cutting training waste. *Personnel Psychology,* 1948, **1,** 331–340.

McGehee, W. Persistent problems in training. In Dennis, W. (Ed.), *Current trends in industrial psychology.* Pittsburgh: University of Pittsburgh Press, 1949.

McGehee, W. Are we using what we know about training? Learning theory and training. *Personnel Psychology,* 1958, **11,** 1–12.

McGehee, W., and Gardner, J. E. Supervisory training and attitude change. *Personnel Psychology,* 1955, **8,** 449–460.

McGehee, W., and Livingstone, D. H. Training reduces material waste. *Personnel Psychology,* 1952, **5,** 115–123.

McGehee, W., and Livingstone, D. H. Persistence of the effects of training employees to reduce waste. *Personnel Psychology,* 1954, **7,** 33–39.

McGeoch, J. A., and Irion, A. L. *The psychology of human learning.* New York: Longmans, Green & Co., 1952.

McGregor, D. An uneasy look at performance appraisals. *Harvard Business Review,* 1957, **35,** 89–94.

Merenda, P. F. The relative effectiveness of formal school and on-the-job methods of training apprentices in Naval occupations. *Personnel Psychology,* 1958, **11,** 379–382.

Merrihue, W. V., and Katzell, R. A. ERI—Yardstick of employee relations. *Harvard Business Review,* 1955, **33,** 91–99.

Merrill, H. F., and Marting, E. *Developing executive skills.* New York: American Management Association, 1952.

Millard, K. A. Is 'How Supervise' an intelligence test? *Journal of Applied Psychology,* 1952, **36,** 221–224.

Miller, N. E. Experimental studies in conflict. In Hunt, J. McV. (Ed.), *Personality and the behavior disorders.* Vol. 1. New York: Ronald Press, 1944.

Miller, R. B. *Handbook of training and training equipment design.* Pittsburgh: The American Institute for Research, 1953.

Miller, R. B. *A method for man-machine task analysis.* Wright Patterson Air Force Base: WADC Technical Report, 53-137, 1955.

Murnin, J. A., Hayes, W., and Harby, S. F. *Daylight projection of film loops as the teaching medium in perceptual-motor skill training.* Human Engineering Report 269-7-26, Special Devices Center, Port Washington, L. I., N. Y., 1952.

Mustillo, A. D. Picture book speeds training. *Factory,* 1957, **115,** 83–84.

National Training Laboratory in Group Development. *Explorations in human relations training: an assessment of experience. 1947–1953.* Washington: National Education Association, 1953.

Nation's Business. How to raise productivity 20%. August, 1959, **47,** No. 8. Pp. 30 ff.

Nuckols, R. C. Levels of aspiration as a factor in consumer buying intentions. (Paper read at 1959 meeting of American Psychological Association, Cincinnati, Ohio.)

Payne, S. L. *The art of asking questions.* Princeton, N. J.: Princeton University Press, 1951.

Peterson, D. A., and Wallace, S. R., Jr. *Manual for career analysis procedure.* Hartford, Conn.: Life Insurance Agency Management Association, 1955.

Planty, E. G., McCord, W. S., and Efferson, C. A. *Training employees and managers.* New York: The Ronald Press Co., 1948.

Regans, D. and Frederiksen, N. Performance tests of educational achievement. In Lindquist (Ed.), *Educational Measurements.* Washington: American Council on Education, 1951.

Richardson, M. Forced-choice performance reports: a modern rating method. *Personnel,* 1949, **26,** 205–210.

Roach, D. E. *Supervisory qualifications and training needs analysis.* Columbus, Ohio: Nationwide Insurance Company, 1958. (An unpublished technical memorandum.)

Rood, J. E. How foremen trainees learn by doing. *Personnel,* 1956, **32,** 409–422.

Roethlisberger, F. J. Training supervisors in human relations. *Harvard Business Review,* 1951, **29,** 47–57.

Roethlisberger, F. J., and Dickson, W. J. *Management and the worker.* Cambridge: Harvard University Press, 1939.

Rupe, J. E., *Research into basic methods and techniques of air force job analysis I.* San Antonio: Human Resources Research Center, Air Training Command, 1952.

Rupe, J. E., and Western, R. S. *Research into basic methods and techniques of air force job analysis, II.* San Antonio: Air Force Personnel and Training Research Center, 1955.

Rupe, J. E., and Western, R. S. *Research into basic methods and techniques of air force job analysis, III.* San Antonio: Human Resources Research Center, Air Training Command, 1955.

Rupe, J. E., and Western, R. S. *Research into basic methods and techniques of air force job analysis, IV.* San Antonio: Air Force Personnel and Training Research Center, 1956.

Ryan, T. A. *Work and effort.* New York: The Ronald Press Company, 1947.

Ryan, T. A., and Smith, P. C. *Principles of industrial psychology.* New York: The Ronald Press Company, 1954.

Rush, C. H., Jr. A factorial study of sales criteria. *Personnel Psychology,* 1953, **6,** 9–24.

Seashore, H. G., and Bennett, G. K. *The Seashore-Bennett proficiency tests.* New York: The Psychological Corporation, 1946.

Severin, D. The predictability of various kinds of criteria. *Personnel Psychology,* 1952, **5,** 93–105.

Seybold, G. *Personnel practices in factory and office; Studies in personnel policy No. 145.* New York: The National Industrial Conference Board, 1954.

Shepard, H. An action research approach to organizational development. *The Management Record,* 1960, **22,** 26–30.

Siegel, A., and Courtney, D. *Development of practical performance measures.* Philadelphia: Institute for Research in Human Relations, 1953.

Siegel, L., Adams, J. F., and Macomber, F. G. Retention of subject matter as a function of large group instructional procedures. *Journal of Educational Psychology,* 1960, **51,** 9–13.

Simon, H. A. *Administrative behavior.* (2nd ed.) New York: The Macmillan Company, 1958.

Skinner, B. F. The science of learning and the art of teaching. *Harvard Educational Review,* 1954, **24,** 86–97.

Skinner, B. F. Teaching machines, *Science,* 1958, 128, No. 3330.

Smith, M. Social situations, social behavior, and social groups. *Psychological Review,* 1945, **52,** 224–229.

Smith, R. J., Jr., and Standoher, F. T. *Critical requirements of basic training tactical instructors.* San Antonio: Air Force Personnel and Training Research Center, 1955.

Smode, A. F., Beam, J. C., and Dunlap, J. W. *Motor habit interference.* Stamford, Conn.: Dunlap and Associates, 1959.

Smode, A. F., and Yarnold, K. W. *Recent innovations in methodology for training and training research.* Stamford, Conn.: Dunlap and Associates, 1960.

Solomon, R. L. Extension of control group design. *Psychological Bulletin,* 1949, **46,** 137–150.

Staff, A. G. O. Personnel Research Section. The forced-choice technique and rating scales. *American Psychologist,* 1946, **1,** 267.

Stagner, R. Dual allegiances: a problem in modern society. *Personnel Psychology,* 1954, **7,** 41–47.

Stagner, R. *The psychology of industrial conflict.* New York: John Wiley & Sons, 1956.

Stead, W. H., et al., *Occupational counseling techniques.* New York: American Book Co., 1940.

Stodgill, R. M. Leadership, membership and organization structure. *Psychological Bulletin,* 1950, **47,** 1–14.

Stone, C. H., and Kendall, W. E. *Effective personnel procedures.* Englewood Cliffs, N. J.: Prentice-Hall, Inc., 1956.

Stroud, J. B., and Schoer, L. Individual differences in memory. *Journal of Educational Psychology,* 1959, **50,** 285–292.

Stuit, D. *Personnel research and test development.* Princeton: Princeton University Press, 1947.

Suttell, B. J. Evaluating potential officer effectiveness in a training situation. *Journal of Applied Psychology,* 1955, **39,** 338–342.

Taylor, C. W. Pre-testing saves training costs. *Personnel Psychology,* 1952, **5,** 213–239.

Thayer, P. W., Antoinetti, J. A., and Guest, T. A. Product knowledge and performance—a study of life insurance agents. *Personnel Psychology,* 1958, **11,** 411–418.

The training within industry report, 1940–1945. Washington: U. S. Govment Printing Office, 1945.

Thorndike, R. L. *Personnel selection.* New York: John Wiley & Sons, 1949.

Tiffin, J. *Industrial psychology.* (3rd ed.) Englewood Cliffs, N. J.: Prentice-Hall, Inc., 1952.

Tiffin, J., and Greenly, R. J. Experiments in the operation of a punch press. *Journal of Applied Psychology,* 1939, **23,** 430–460.

Tiffin, J., and McCormick, E. J. *Industrial psychology.* (4th ed.) Englewood Cliffs, N. J.: Prentice-Hall, Inc., 1958.

Underwood, B. J. *Psychological research.* New York: Appleton-Century-Crofts, Inc., 1957.

Underwood, B. J., and Viterna, R. O. Studies of distributed practice. IV. The effect of similarity and rate of presentation in verbal-discrimination learning. *Journal of Experimental Psychology,* 1951, **42**, 296–299.

U. S. Employment Service. *Training and reference manual for job analysis.* Washington: U. S. Employment Service, 1946.

Viteles, M. S. *Motivation and morale in industry.* New York: W. W. Norton, 1953.

Viteles, M. S. 'Human relations' and 'humanities' in the education of business leaders: evaluation of a program of humanistic studies for executives. *Personnel Psychology,* 1959, **12**, 1–28.

Walker, C. R., Guest, R. H., and Turner, A. N. *The foreman on the assembly line.* Cambridge: Harvard University Press, 1956.

Wallace, S. R., Jr., and Twichell, C. M. An evaluation of a training course for life insurance agents. *Personnel Psychology,* 1953, **6**, 25–43.

Wallace, W. L., and Gallagher, J. R. *Activities and behaviors of production supervisors: PRS report No. 946.* New York: The Psychological Corporation, 1952.

Wattles, T. L. *How to teach gunnery.* (Rev. ed.) Washington: U. S. Department of Commerce, 1946.

Weschler, I. R., and Reisel, J. *Inside a sensitivity training group.* Los Angeles: Human Relations Research Group, Institute of Industrial Relations and Graduate School of Business Administration, University of California, 1958.

Wherry, R. J. The past and future of criterion evaluation. *Personnel Psychology,* 1957, **10**, 1–6.

Wherry, R. J. An evaluative and diagnostic forced-choice rating scale for servicemen. *Personnel Psychology,* 1959, **12**, 227–236.

Whyte, W. F. *Leadership and group participation.* (Bulletin No. 24 New State School of Industrial and Labor Relations.) Ithaca, N. Y.: Cornell University, 1953.

Whyte, W. F. *Money and motivation.* New York: Harper & Bros., 1955.

Wirdenius, H. *Supervisors at work: a description of supervisory behavior.* Stockholm: The Swedish Council for Personnel Administration, 1958.

Wolfle, D. Training. In Stevens, S. S. (Ed.), *Handbook of experimental psychology.* New York: John Wiley & Sons, 1951.

Woodworth, R. S., and Schlosberg, H. *Experimental psychology.* (Rev. ed.) New York: Henry Holt, 1954.

Yoder, D., and Nelson, R. Salaries and staffing ratios. *Personnel,* 1957. **34**, 16–22.

Zaleznik, A. *Work satisfaction and development.* Boston: Harvard University Graduate School of Business Administration, 1956.

INDEX